A Brick Wall

A Brick Wall

How a Boy with No Words Spoke to the World

Bobbie J. Gallagher, BCBA

ISBN: 1533252920
ISBN 13: 9781533252920
Library of Congress Control Number: 2016908313
CreateSpace Independent Publishing Platform
North Charleston, South Carolina

Dedication

You are the answer I give to everyone when they ask me, "How do you do it?" or "How did you get through it?" I adore you Billy Gallagher, I cannot imagine going through life without you.

To my three children, Chelsea, Alanna, and Austin without you, I am not me. You are my reasons for everything I do.

Contents

Foreword

"THIS MOM THING is hard," writes Bobbie Gallagher in this highly personal, extraordinarily moving account of an amazing journey raising a family that includes Austin and Alanna—two now-grown children with autism—and a third child, Chelsea, who she describes as the "best big sister two siblings could ever have."

I marked every page of this book with a BIC yellow highlighter and was amazed, even awed, by Bobbie's persistence, wisdom, resilience, and above all her love for her family. She heaps praise on her beloved husband Billy—her rock, the strong one. Together, they are an inspiration to all parents of children with autism.

Doctors told the Gallaghers not to worry when telltale early warning signs of autism first manifested in both Austin and Alanna. Alanna couldn't possibly have autism, one doctor said; she only needed "a good swift kick in the ass. "With that, the Gallaghers began a lifelong search for credible answers and effective, durable, scientifically proven interventions such as Applied Behavior Analysis.

Inspired by the needs of her own children and all families who struggle with autism, today Bobbie Gallagher is a Board Certified Behavior Analyst. Over the course of over two decades, the Gallagher family's quest for solutions coupled with tenacious advocacy not only benefitted their own children but made enactment of landmark legislation a reality.

As prime author of key federal autism laws, I can state categorically that the sweeping changes in public policy and research funding all started with the Gallaghers. Their demand for a comprehensive federal investigation of a significantly elevated prevalence of autism in Brick Township, New Jersey, was the catalyst for new laws that authorized huge funding increases for the National Institutes of Health, the Centers for Disease Control and Prevention, and the Health Resources and Services Administration, and created the Interagency Autism Coordinating Committee.

A Brick Wall takes us behind the scenes and offers an intimate look into the Gallagher household as they face monumental challenges that begin (after finally getting an accurate diagnosis) with managing expectations: "with one simple word like autism," Bobbie writes, "all dreams of having a ball player went away, and are replaced with the unknown."

Her candor is breathtaking.

She exposes not only the incompetence of many self-proclaimed experts, but also the numbing indifference she and her family endured. She minces no words calling out medical professionals woefully uninformed concerning the unique needs of both children and adults with autism. Strategies matter. Inferior interventions breed minimal—or even catastrophic—results. She tells us how bad decisions by "experts" triggered Austin to become violent and self-abusive. Things got so bad, Bobbie tells us, that both she and an aide resorted to wearing Kevlar sleeves to protect themselves from Austin's biting and scratching.

On the other hand, Bobbie explains how other professionals were spot-on, compassionate, and extremely competent, including the life-savers at Kennedy Krieger Institute (KKI) of Baltimore. She explains how KKI employed Functional Analysis, a "very detailed experiment in the field of Applied Behavioral Analysis," which helped as part of a comprehensive strategy to reverse Austin's harmful behavior. "They saved him," she says. Gone were the Kevlar sleeves.

All parents of children with autism face hardship. Bobbie speaks of the frequent tears, the agony, the sheer physical, emotional, and spiritual exhaustion, and questions her own existence and that of a higher power.

She tells of the moment when she learned why she was on this earth: "I was here to fight for children with autism," she writes. And fight she has.

She recounts the big moments that she treasures deep within her heart. Like when, at age eleven, Austin finally called her mommy for the first time: "It was slow and deliberate, mmaameee, and it was beautiful."

On another occasion, Austin asked for a cookie—a landmark step toward learning how to communicate his wants and needs to others. "This is the first time in his life that he said cookie without having any cookies in sight," Bobbie explains. "I was overjoyed. He was learning that words would get him what he wants." She rushed to the kitchen and couldn't get a cookie into Austin's hands quickly enough. Jokingly, Chelsea, who doesn't have autism, then asked for a soda. "We both laughed," Bobbie writes, but it was also a poignant moment illustrating the challenging inequalities between the siblings.

Bobbie takes us into the New Jersey court room where the Gallaghers fought a financially and emotionally draining three-year legal battle to achieve the best educational outcome for their son and avoid a residential placement. How would any parent feel to have a high-ranking official in your hometown say that your son can be taught "anywhere in the United States of America…just not here"? Backed by an amazing legal team and a plethora of expert witnesses, Bobbie and Billy refused to back down or go quietly into the night.

The Gallagher children "aged out" of childhood support programs at 21 years old. At that age, they ceased to be minors and were thus rendered ineligible for education and other programs. Bobbie expresses her shock, fear and dismay over the rapidity of regression she observed in her children once the support stopped. Suddenly, much of both Alanna and Austin's progress began to deteriorate.

It is a credible fear shared by many parents today. Each year an estimated 50,000 children on the autism spectrum age out, creating a crisis that requires urgent, rigorous analysis and robust strategies to face this new and largely unmet need. To that end, in August of 2014, I authored the Autism Collaboration, Accountability, Research, Education and Support Act (Autism CARES) to not only authorize $1.3 billion in autism research, but also to mandate a government-wide assessment of existing programs to begin the process of addressing those concerns.

A Brick Wall is a must-read for parents of children with autism. They and their families must know they are not alone, and that they can benefit from the trailblazing example, insights, and inspiration of the Gallaghers. And A Brick Wall ought to be mandatory reading for health care professionals, educators, academics, social workers, journalists, law enforcement, and policy makers at all levels of government. The Gallaghers are remarkable people. This is a remarkable book.

Chris Smith

Preface

"Murder-Suicide Note Saying She Could No Longer Care for Severely Autistic Son"
"Mother, Caregiver Charged with Autistic Teens Murder"
"Autistic Teen's Mom Charged with Attempted Murder"

"Better off dead than disabled," said an autism self- advocate when interviewed about what the parents in these headline cases might have been feeling.

"Better off dead than disabled."

His words haunted me and catapulted my need to get this story into print.

"Better off dead than disabled," could only come from someone unaware about what families like ours experience. In no way do I condone the actions of these mothers. Although I can sympathize with the pain of these parents, punishment for murder is necessary. But who should be punished?

Certainly there are laws against murder, but what about all the events leading up to the day when a mother decides she has no other choice but to take her child's life? Why is no one held accountable for all the mistakes that led to the breaking point? Why aren't there laws to prevent this?

Professionals who provide subpar services outside their scope of practice…shouldn't they be investigated, like any doctor who provides prescription drugs to a patient that overdoses? School officials who insist a child must fail within their program before being permitted to attend a specialized school…didn't they play some part in this child's demise?

It was not "better off dead than disabled" for these mothers. It was "better off dead than suffering." Not suffering by a disability, but suffering at the hands of those who presume to be helping. The experts who come into our lives with degrees that tell us they have the answers, only to leave us with our children unchanged or even worse than when they arrived.

Somewhere within the news interviews that occur after such a tragedy will appear a medical professional explaining that autism is a challenging disorder and that some children can be violent. But they will neglect to mention that this violence is often learned through inappropriate teaching by inept professionals, and that it can leave parents struggling to keep their children from hurting themselves or others every day.

Our children suffer and regress in their school programs because no laws dictate the level of training a paraprofessional needs to provide instruction. They suffer when the adults who control their education disagree on interventions and decide to provide what they see fit, not what is researched based. In what other group of children would this be allowed?

I planned to write this book shortly after our legal battle with our school district, but time seemed to slip by. With each news story of a tragedy involving a child with autism I felt more compelled to get Austin's story out. These sad stories read so similar to our lives. And there are more children with autism and other disorders whose parents are struggling like these parents were.

During our journey, I fell into places of darkness so deep I couldn't see a way out. Meanwhile, professionals continued to give advice that didn't work and treated our son like an experiment gone wrong. How many people can hurt a child before it is too much? What is the breaking point for a parent whose child cannot say, "Mom, I don't want to do this?" "Daddy, they are hurting me?" "Someone please listen, I am in pain." How do we ensure that our children are at the forefront of every decision?

Austin struggled with the teaching strategies of one nationally known expert in the field of autism. He plummeted behaviorally, biting himself over a thousand times a day, aggressing toward others, eventually requiring placement in an institution hundreds of miles from our home in order to get the help he needed. In that horrendous place of darkness, I found my calling. Because of Austin, I am now a Board Certified Behavior Analyst who hopes to ensure other families never have to experience that level of pain, frustration, and regression.

Recently a medical condition nearly cost Austin his life. Pancreatitis necrosis caused him to go into respiratory distress and renal failure. It took almost a year for him to finally heal, but not without some permanent effects. Austin now lives with seizures, diabetes, and other gastrointestinal problems, all in addition to autism.

But Austin lives, and that is what is important. Through his struggle I have learned that there is a critical need for education in the medical field about how symptoms of autism can make routine medical procedures difficult. It is a project in the making, and I hope to develop it further soon.

Austin has taught me to be a better listener and a more patient person. He has made me discover just how strong I am. My love for him is the endless reservoir I pull from to make the difference in his life and to help others in the autism community to realize that families can emerge from the toughest struggles. He has taught me far more than I can ever hope to teach him.

I love you Austman. I hope I have made you proud.

Prologue

I KISSED AUSTIN on the top of his head to say goodbye, knowing I could never explain why we were leaving him. I turned away and started toward the main door of the unit. Once it closed, I would not be able to re-enter without being buzzed in or having a swipe key. I just *had* to be the first one out because I would not have been able to shut that door. I left that task to Billy, he was much stronger than me.

As I looked back to make sure Billy was behind me, I saw Austin attack the staff person assigned to him that first night. She was trying to keep him from following us out the door. Austin had a hold of her clothing and was pulling her face toward his, trying to bite her. The door closed and my view was limited to a small rectangular window, but nothing could block out the sounds of his rage. I didn't need to see him to know what was happening. I had been in the same place as her before. My arms were covered in bruises from defending myself from my own child.

"Turn around, don't watch that," Billy said gently. We turned the corner and pushed the button for the elevator. The pain in my gut caused me to buckle over. My knees were so weak I could barely move. The doors to the elevator closed and Austin's horrific sounds were muffled as we descended to the first floor; eventually they became non-existent. But the sounds of the two people inside the elevator were equally wrenching. We were in so much pain, so unsure whether this would be the answer we were looking for. It had to be. We had nowhere else to turn. I couldn't help but wonder how we got here. How did our ten-year-old son reach the point of requiring placement in an institution?

Here's how.

It's a Boy

August 1991 to May 1992

It is said that you cannot feel the conception of a child. The moment when egg and sperm join, although miraculous, is so fleeting that no physical sensation can accompany it. People spend millions of dollars annually on test strips to confirm their suspicions. I didn't need to see colorful lines or a plus sign. I knew the very moment I got pregnant with our third child Austin.

It was the summer of 1991, and my stepson Shaun was down for a visit. Shaun lived in Canada and came to New Jersey so rarely. My husband Billy would take a nine-hour drive up to Canada, stay one night, and drive back with Shaun. He'd do the same when he brought him back home. We always attempted to pack these visits with activities to ensure that Shaun had fun and got to see all of his extended family. Shaun often came with "messages" from his mother that would be just enough to tick his dad off. But Billy would walk a fine line, not saying anything in order to keep the peace. If you know Billy, you know that not saying anything is a difficult task for him.

Billy is strong and confident. He was voted most popular in high school, was captain of the basketball team, and quarterback of the football team. He would often push back or question authority as a teenager, but he had a personality that always got him out of any possible consequences. When Billy walks into a room, he commands it and feels right at home.

He will talk to anyone and everyone, and without a doubt if you have met him, you have laughed. He was a commercial fisherman, a job with a romantic connotation whenever mentioned in conversation with other men. It seemed to bring out an innate hunter in them all, fulfilling some desire for danger. But Billy is creative and sensitive as well. On one of our first dates he took me to a studio where he recorded a song he had written with hopes that singing would be his new career.

When I became pregnant with Austin we were in the process of buying a bigger home here in Brick Township. Prior to Shaun's visit Billy had worked nearly three months straight to get the down payment money so we could buy the new home without selling our current one. Our plan was to become landlords. We saw very little of each other. Billy would get home from a fishing trip, take a shower, give me a kiss, and head right back out. He desperately wanted to make this work. There was always the hope he would get out of fishing, and we envisioned real estate could one day be that avenue. Fishing is a tough job and makes for an unusual family life. He wanted something different, but with only a high school diploma fishing was what he could do to support us.

That night, after a long day spent with Shaun on the boardwalk that left Billy feeling more and more like a divorced dad who just couldn't make his child happy, we settled into bed. Our daughters Chelsea and Alanna were asleep in their room and Shaun was on the living room couch. Just as I got comfortable, I realized I had forgotten to take my birth control pill that morning. I was just too exhausted to get dressed, pass Shaun in the living room, and get my purse from the kitchen, so I resigned myself to taking it in the morning. We made love that night in a way that was a release from the stress Shaun's visits could bring, with an effect that was better than any sleeping pill for Billy.

I rolled to my right side and felt a sparkle inside of me. There was a slight twinge of electric activity, a flutter that brought an internal tickle and a warm glow over my entire body. I knew I had just conceived a child. My conflicting emotions at that moment kept me awake. I felt something I'm told is impossible to feel, something that was amazing and almost spiritual. But I had two children in the other room, one only six months old. I couldn't have another baby now. I told myself not to panic, that I couldn't possibly be right, that something else caused the feeling. I thought to myself, "Business as usual when you wake up. Don't tell Billy what you think, he has enough going on right now."

We spent the next few weeks prepping our new home. About two weeks later, all the white pills were finished in my pack. So I waited for Tuesday. My period always started on Tuesday. Tuesday came and went, and I went to buy one of those strips to simply confirm what I already knew. I took the test, waited five minutes, and looked. Two solid lines. I wondered how to tell Billy. How could I tell a man who gave up so much to start this family that he will have to give up even more, postpone his chance at a singing career again, with one more mouth to feed? I knew I wouldn't be able to help financially for yet another year until we could get the kids into daycare.

I still remember his disappointed face when Alanna was born. Sure, we all wish for a healthy baby, and if you wish for more than that, you are selfish. But let's be honest, it's human nature to want what you want, society just happens to frown on us for vocalizing our preference. We already had Chelsea, a beautiful baby girl. Billy could not have been more proud, bringing Chelsea down to the dock to show her off, taking her to a photographer to get her hospital baby picture redone (he didn't like the fact that they didn't clean away the mucus in her eyes in the original). Although he had wanted a boy, he was doting and thrilled when Chelsea arrived.

After Chelsea we planned to get pregnant again quickly with the intention of having our children close together. We wanted to have two children and be done. Unlike today, we couldn't find out the sex of the child during pregnancy; it just wasn't common practice. I know Billy wanted a boy. I wanted a boy. I grew up with three older brothers and girls were a foreign species to me. I just don't know how to do sparkles and makeup. I always felt I let Chelsea down by not being a mom who enjoyed the tasks generally assigned to girls.

On her due date, February 24, 1991, Alanna entered our world. The moment the doctor announced, "It's a girl," I saw Billy's face drop. It was an unconscious reaction to not getting what he expected, and the moment quickly passed, but there it was. The nurses cleaned her up and brought her to me. I thought, "Oh my! This baby is homely." I know that sounds awful, but she was so ugly with her bright red hair just long enough to stand straight up, red eyebrows and eyelashes, and pink skin. Her nose was wider than her mouth. My very first thought was, she is so homely, her sister is so beautiful, and her father wanted a boy. I will have to love her *twice* as much as anyone.

Alanna's delivery was much smoother than Chelsea's and my recovery was faster. Billy went back to fishing in just a few days and I was home with two babies. Six months later, I was pregnant again—this time unplanned—and we had just bought a house. All I could think was that Billy was going to be furious, that I was the reason he would never have a music career, and that I had ruined it all for him. I was already exhausted from caring for Chelsea and Alanna. I felt like I simply couldn't do it again.

That night Billy came home and I made dinner. Billy sung at the table like he did every night he was home to teach Chelsea a new word of the day. "It's new word time, it's new word time, time to learn a new word today," he would sing. He would end the song with a new word like "cater-pillar." Chelsea loved this interaction and the two often sang and laughed at the dinner table. Everything seemed so normal, but I couldn't contain my news. We were putting the dishes into the dishwasher when I blurted out, "I'm pregnant." Billy, joking as usual, said, "Well it's not April 1st…" referencing a prank where his ex had once claimed to be pregnant as part of an April Fool's joke. I walked away crying and flopped onto our bed, sobbing so hard I could barely breathe.

My reaction puzzled Billy. He followed me into the bedroom and laid down with me. He couldn't understand why I was so upset. As my tears fell onto his chest and my dripping nose rubbed into his shirt, I did my best to tell him all I was thinking: I couldn't have another baby, this would ruin any chance he had of a music career, we couldn't afford this, and what if it was another girl?

In his usual calm, almost amused manner, he asked me why I was so upset and why it would matter if it was a girl? I told him he would resent me later in our marriage for getting pregnant again and ruining his chances at a new career. I feared he could only be happy if the baby was a boy. Mostly I just rambled.

Billy assured me that there would be no resentment, and that he knew music was not in his future except for being able to play locally once in a while. We could deal with the financial issues, it would just add a year to our plan for me to return to work. And as for whether it was a boy or girl, he couldn't even imagine that I thought it mattered to him. In just a few minutes, what I thought was the most devastating news of our marriage to date turned into what it should have been all along: a joyous announcement that we were going to have another baby. He held me throughout the night and let me know everything would be more than fine.

At that moment, I realized the type of man I had married: a strong man who would stay by my side no matter what. That may sound immature, but our relationship was immature at that point. I was twenty-four when we began dating. We had dated only thirteen months before being married in January 1989, and six and a half months later Chelsea was born (yes, do the math). Now less than three years after her birth, at the age of twenty-nine, I would be delivering baby number three.

I went to the doctor regularly, and when I was around four months pregnant they decided to do an ultrasound to check the baby's heart. Because I was on the pill when I conceived, they wanted to be sure all was okay. Billy and I drove to the appointment separately, as he was at the dock packing out the catch from the night before. I waited for Billy to arrive while I lay on the table in the ultrasound room. The clinician began the process of putting that awful cold blue jelly on my abdomen. She found the baby and could see that the heart was working fine. She printed me a profile picture of the baby. I asked if she could tell the sex. She moved the scanner to another position, and pointed out two tiny bright white ovals on the screen. "Those are his testicles," she explained. I was thrilled. We were going to have a boy, but where was Billy?

The clinician cleaned off the jelly, and there was a knock on the door. He was here. I excitedly told him all was well and that we were having a boy. Billy was skeptical. The clinician said she could show him, so I laid back down for more cold jelly. However, the baby had opted to move into a new position, and we just couldn't get a good picture. Billy chose to remain neutral until the birth.

On May 21st, nine days past my due date, our third baby was ready to see the world. I called my mother to come over to be with me and to stay with the girls when I had to leave for the hospital. Billy went outside and began to build a large wooden planter. Sympathy and doting are not Billy's forte; instead, he seized the moment to work on a project he'd wanted to complete. My mother cared for me until I asked Billy to call the doctor. The doctor told me to come to the office first and he'd check to see how far along I was before sending me to the hospital. This was the point where I began to cry. The overwhelming realization that this baby was about to come and the anticipation of the upcoming hours of pain made me want to delay the process. It would be okay if I was pregnant a little longer. I was already nine days late, what's a few more days?

The staff at the doctor's office confirmed that the baby was coming soon, and my doctor told us he would meet us at the hospital. Billy asked if we had time to stop next door and shop for a swing set. You may think he was kidding, but Billy was serious, he really wanted to check that off his to do list as well. The doctor told him no, so we drove to the hospital and checked in.

After hours of labor, it was time to finally push. Billy sat facing me with his arms wrapped around me, pressing his fists into my back as hard as he could in an effort to ease my back labor pain. Austin Gallagher arrived into this world quite differently from the sweet electric sparkle I felt the night of his conception. Instead, he entered with a painful burning sensation as his head ripped me open and his body slid across the cut, stinging all the way until his head was out. I was in such pain that my voice reached an octave I am sure caused permanent damage to Billy's ear. But Austin was here, and he was a boy.

The next day, I was wheeled down to the operating room. The orderly pushing my bed through the halls of Monmouth Medical Center commented, "I've never seen anyone smile on their way into the operating room." I explained, "I am getting my tubes tied, and I will never be pregnant again." My doctor was not comfortable with this. He wanted Billy to get a vasectomy, he wanted me to wait six weeks, he wanted me to be older than twenty-nine; there were so many conditions that I didn't meet before he usually suggested this procedure. I insisted that I was not leaving the hospital until my tubes were tied. If Billy's underwear passed mine in the dryer, we'd be pregnant again. I had birthed three children in thirty-four months. I needed to have this surgery.

Once back home it was life as usual with a few twists. I now had three children in diapers, because Chelsea reverted back once Austin came home and I just didn't have the strength to fight her on it. Besides, pull-ups were easier when I had to take everyone out of the house for a shopping trip or a doctor visit. I remember looking at Austin and feeling overwhelmed. I fed him, I bathed him, and of course I held him, but I found myself crying often. Fortunately, the feeling only lasted a few weeks, and then those green eyes and huge dimples just took my breath away. He was so adorable.

The next few months were a bit of a blur, but there was a blessing. Austin slept through the night by the time he was just five weeks old. During the day he was content to sit in his baby swing and watch his sisters play. I thought he somehow must have known how tired I was. Little did I know this was one of the first signs that something was wrong.

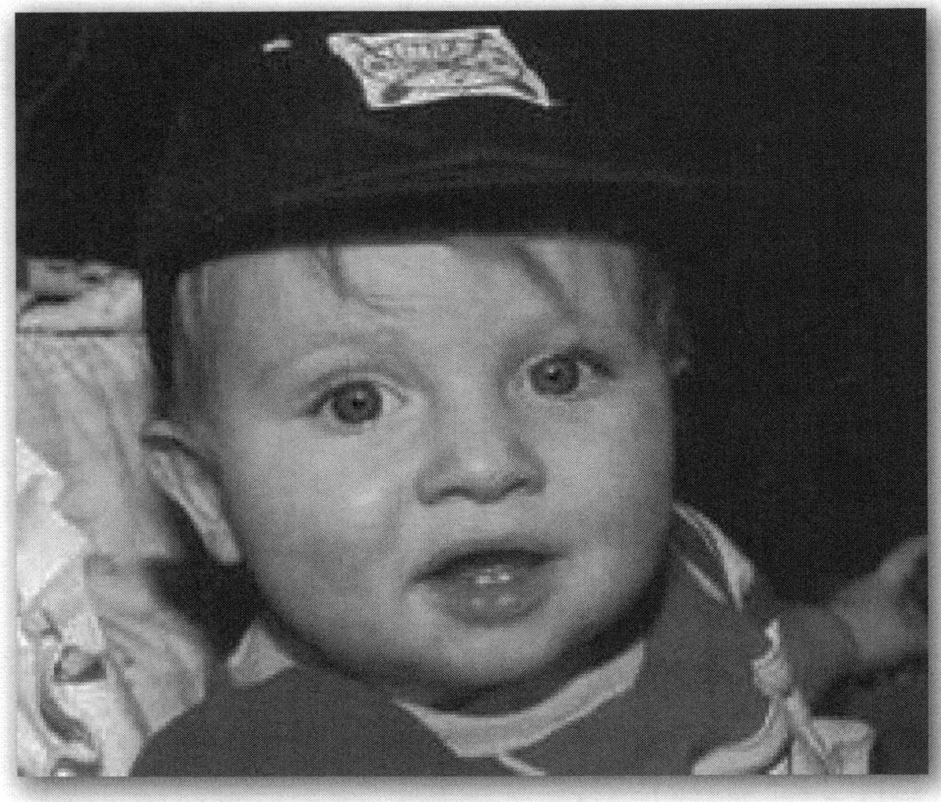

The "A" Word

May 1992 to August 1993

We began to fall into our new routine. Chelsea went to daycare a few days a week for the entertainment and social interaction that I couldn't give her while caring for her siblings. I stayed home with Alanna and Austin. Simply feeding, changing, and holding them seemed to take up the entire day. As a result, we did not have the neatest home. There were always plastic Little Tykes toys to step over.

When Alanna was around sixteen months old we realized that she was not advancing the way her sister had. She was not yet walking and had little language. Family, friends, and doctors repeatedly told me not to compare Alanna to her sister, for Chelsea's language had been exceptional at a young age. During a doctor's visit for one of many ear infections, he said, "if she isn't walking by the time she is eighteen months old, we'll investigate her development further." Of course, she walked at seventeen months old. It was soon enough to squash the concerns, but I still had worries about her language. Alanna was not babbling and had no steady sounds or names that she would use for me or Billy.

On the rare occasion when she did say words, they were beautiful and clear and beyond age-appropriate. Every night I would hold her, walk around her bedroom, and tell her the names of the items in the space. One night out of the blue, she said clear as a bell: "butterfly," never to be heard again. Every evening I would put her in the crib and kiss her between the slats three times, once at the top of the rail, once in the middle, and then at the bottom. With each kiss I would get her closer to lying down, and after the very last kiss I would say, "thank you!" One night she said "thank you" back to me. She had the ability to speak, but she wasn't using it. These small glimpses of normalcy kept delaying any investigation into her development.

Alanna's ear infections became more severe and more frequent. She spent months taking antibiotics and the eustachian tubes in her ears collapsed. Her doctor eventually decided we should put tubes in her ears. All the usual concerns about putting my child under anesthesia were present, but I had heard so often that she would start talking once the procedure was done. The collapsed tubes could have caused her lack of language because it was like hearing underwater, or so I was told. She was two years old when we had the tubes placed, and we were told that she would be speaking within six months.

But it wasn't just her speech that concerned me. Alanna had some very strange behaviors. She would take her stuffed animals out of the playpen and strategically line them up on the floor, and then one by one place them back into the playpen and line them up again there. She seemed content to entertain herself with this activity. If I tickled her on the bed and she wanted me to do it again, she would get off of the bed and start everything over by going back to the entrance of the room instead of simply asking for "more." She would always recommence play by starting at the beginning. Alanna would touch the warm bulb of a nightlight and appear to say "ow," only to reach down and touch it again. Pain did not seem to affect her. She was once stung on her lip by a bee and had no reaction. I only knew it had happened when she turned toward me with her lip three sizes bigger, the black stinger still in it.

She could often be found in the corner of a room with books, but she would not look through them. Instead, she would peel the covers off of them if she found the slightest imperfection. Any attempt to distract her went unanswered. She behaved as though she was deaf, but we knew better. She could hear the opening refrain of a Disney movie from rooms away.

Naptime was the worst. Alanna would easily lie down to sleep, giving me a short break I usually enjoyed because it meant I could get something done. But I learned to dread it because she would wake with a blood-curdling scream, as though she was being stabbed, followed by extended inconsolable crying. I would open the bedroom door and there she would be, red in the face with tears pouring down. I couldn't imagine what caused this distress because she appeared to have a high tolerance to pain. I wondered if she could possibly be having dreams that frightened her at such a young age, and if they could happen every day? I would hold her, but each time it seemed I had to hold her longer and longer to console her. One day this lasted for four hours. I couldn't take it any longer so I put her back in her crib—still screaming—stepped outside onto our deck, called my mother, and just cried. My mother was supportive and Alanna finally calmed. For the next few days I refused to open the door until she was quiet. It was hard but it worked, and she started to wake and wait for me to come get her. She could be heard babbling and playing.

Yet, still no words. Six months was too long to wait, but we did. With some hesitation the doctor made a referral to an audiologist, but he really felt we were worrying over nothing. Alanna was twenty-nine months old when the audiologist completed the hearing exam and reported that all was within normal range. She referred me to the speech therapist at her practice for another evaluation.

As a speech therapist, Cynthia Matthews wasn't qualified to diagnose Alanna. No one wants to make the diagnosis of autism, but at least Cynthia was willing to tell us to keep looking for answers. She gave us information on how to get services through the Early Intervention System. And she said something that stuck with me. In an effort to get me to focus on

Alanna and not listen to the naysayers, she told me that in her experience, if a child can speak she will, because speaking gets her needs met and it's easier than trying to get what she wants using other methods. No child would make things more difficult for herself on purpose.

What no one knew was that Alanna wasn't the only one I was concerned about. Austin was fifteen months old, and although he walked on time, babbled constantly, and absolutely loved to watch his sister Chelsea, I still felt something wasn't right. I just couldn't put my finger on it.

October 1993 to March 1994

I made an appointment for an evaluation with the Early Intervention program in Wall Township, New Jersey. Alanna qualified for services because she was at least thirty-three percent delayed in speech. In the early 1990's, Early Intervention programs were minimal at best. We received one hour of center-based services, meaning we had to bring Alanna to a facility in order for her to receive any intervention. We also had our choice of one half-hour session in a related service, such as computers, speech, or occupational therapy.

Shortly after starting Early Intervention, I heard the "A" word. Autism. I held on tightly to that word, hoping it might provide some answers. Early Intervention staff suggested that Alanna had "autistic-like tendencies." When I got home, I began to research "autistic" on the internet. There was little information beyond a definition and a list of characteristics. Some of the tendencies did seem to match Alanna: lack of eye contact, delayed speech, and unusual play. But others, such as "not affectionate or avoids being touched," just weren't her. I couldn't believe she had autism, and I was desperate for answers. I kept looking.

Every Tuesday, I prepared all three children for the day's adventure. I packed two diaper bags: one to take to the center for Alanna, and one filled with everything Austin would need to spend the day with Rita, Billy's stepmother. Early Intervention started at 9am and Chelsea needed to be dropped off at preschool, so all three kids needed to be dressed and in the car by 8am. I had no time to argue over details like outfits, but Chelsea would challenge me on a regular basis. She went through a long phase where she would only wear dresses. Not just any dress, but only dresses that had no waistbands and flared up when she spun in circles. Despite my pleas and her school's insistence that she dress appropriately for class trips, she had excellent counter points; to this day I am shocked that she is not an attorney. So I sewed swirly, flare-worthy fabric to the bottom of her school t-shirts for those class trips and I relished in her independent thinking. In the grand scheme of our lives, childhood challenges like these fell into the category of "I'll deal with that another day."

Each Tuesday I packed the car, wrangled the children, checked a hundred times to be sure I had everything, and got on the road. First I would take Chelsea to preschool in Sea Girt. Then I would back track a bit to the Manasquan circle and down Atlantic Avenue to drop Austin off at Rita's house in Farmingdale. Finally, I'd make it just in time to get Alanna to the center in the town of Wall. Early Intervention was held in a business development where you could also order custom window blinds or find someone to file your taxes. It was a series of brick buildings meant to look like a small village of shops, and there was nothing child-friendly about the environment.

At the center we were joined by four other children and their parents. The staff consisted of four to five professionals with varying backgrounds, including a psychologist, a special education teacher, a speech therapist, and an occupational therapist. Each child faced a different challenge: one of the boys had Down syndrome, one little girl had physical difficulties. Then there were Alanna and Joey. They were not at all alike, but they were given similar labels. Joey was not responsive to affection from his parents. He would scream, pinch, and flop when asked to participate. He ate only two foods: yogurt and milk. Joey had been diagnosed with autism.

I would watch him carefully to see what he was capable of, but mostly I would watch for what he *wasn't* doing. I wondered why "autistic-like tendencies" had been attributed to Alanna if this was what autism really looked like. Joey's parents were a very sweet couple who had decided to have a baby well into their forties. They looked nearly sixty, and I can only imagine that the stress of their child's disability had caused some of their wrinkles and grey hairs. They faced a challenge that would last far longer than I'm sure they had ever anticipated.

Alanna was so different from Joey. She ate everything, and her desire to be affectionate helped me through many difficult moments. When Alanna gives a hug, she gives it her all. The two of us almost become one. No one turns down a hug from Alanna. She has an energy that others have described as "therapeutic" and "spiritual." One friend swears her blood pressure drops 10 points after one of Alanna's hugs. So, except for the lack of language, I wondered how Joey and Alanna could have the same diagnosis. The vagueness of the phrase "autistic-like tendencies" gave me something to hold onto. "She's not *autistic*," I told myself, "just autistic-*like*."

The Early Intervention staff attempted to get the children to engage in a routine of movement. The staff would create an obstacle course from mats, wedges covered in vinyl, a tunnel, and a toddler-sized wood slide. If we held Alanna's hand she could make it through most of the obstacles, but on her own she became distracted and would not complete the course. She really didn't like the tunnel and would only go through it if I was behind her. When she reached the top of the steps for the slide, Alanna would sit, and sit, and sit, and no amount of encouragement could convince her to slide down like the other children. Without a nudge from an adult or another child, Alanna would not independently go down the slide. She had little interest in any of the movement routines. Instead, she would attempt to slip behind the mats to watch herself in a tall mirror, where she would spin in circles. If she was made to join the group, she would complete one task and make her way back to that mirror.

No one at the center was permitted to diagnose a child; they could only suggest I make an appointment for further evaluation. Lisa Lynch, the center's psychologist, stressed the importance of scheduling a neurological evaluation and explained that Alanna would likely qualify for special education services through the local school district when she turned three. There was suddenly so much to do before she aged out of the program, and time was short. I was excited because I hadn't known there were other programs for children with special needs as young as age three. I knew I needed to get her to a neurologist. I knew I had letters to write. I had a purpose and a direction. This was what Alanna needed.

I brought Alanna to her pediatrician. Desperate not to miss anything important in the short timeframe of the visit, I rambled to Dr. Richard DeGrappe about the services she was receiving through Early Intervention, and told him that "autistic-like tendencies" were mentioned. I asked for a referral to a neurologist so she could receive more services in school programs. Dr. DeGrappe disagreed with the label and instead attempted to explain why Alanna's behaviors were actually my fault.

Alanna was always incredibly stressed by doctor visits. She would scream throughout the examination and get herself so worked up she could barely breathe. During this particular visit she began to choke on her own phlegm and her face turned a dark shade of purple. Dr. DeGrappe told me she couldn't possibly have autism, because if she was autistic she wouldn't care about the examination and would instead be sitting in a corner rocking back and forth. He went on to inform me that she was a "behavioral" child, similar to having a teenager in a three-year-old's body, and that if I didn't stop her now she would control me, ruin my marriage, and wreak havoc throughout her lifetime. He told me that what Alanna really needed was a "good swift kick in the ass." He wouldn't give me a referral for a neurologist. He didn't see the point.

Perhaps he thought someone had overstepped their boundaries and stolen his thunder in finding a diagnosis for this little girl. Maybe he needed it to be something other than autism because he couldn't bear that a psychologist from Early Intervention suggested a diagnosis for a patient he had been treating for nearly three years?

His words made me question myself. I wondered if I had allowed Alanna to play me and whether I needed to be more strict. Was she simply choosing not to talk to me? So many people had offered opinions about Alanna's behavior over the months, and some of their comments had been similar to Dr. DeGrappe's. My personal favorite was that this was all happening because I had a third child. Someone actually suggested that Alanna decided not to speak to me while I was pregnant with Austin because she somehow knew that there was a baby growing inside me and she could completely comprehend the impact the baby would have on her once he was here. "Well, if that's the case," I thought at the time, "she is one freaking genius of a toddler."

As soon as Billy returned home that night I began to cry. He sat next to me on the end of our bed as I relayed the doctor's comments. Always my rock, he responded, "You believed him? Apparently he hasn't gotten laid in a while and his wife must have chewed him out today and he decided to take it out on you." It's true that it was the most unprofessional conversation I'd ever had with a doctor, but if it wasn't autism, and wasn't my parenting, then what was it?

I wrote a letter to the school district asking them to evaluate Alanna for services. Within a few days we had scheduled an evaluation by a social worker, a speech therapist, and an occupational therapist at the Early Intervention center in January 1994. I was thrilled. I just wanted us to get to the place where she could receive regular services, and I hoped she would meet their requirements.

On the day of the evaluation I dressed Alanna in an exceptionally cute purple outfit to show off her incredible red hair. I wanted her to be captivating. After the usual child-organizing and car-packing, I took Chelsea to preschool, Austin to Rita's, and Alanna to Early Intervention. The session started as usual with all the other children present, but shortly into it I was called over by a member of the office staff who explained that Alanna would be evaluated in a separate room. I brought her down to a small gym, where three professional-looking women immediately began to ogle my gorgeous baby. "She's so cute!" "Just look at that hair!" "Oh my gosh!" Her looks had certainly changed since the day she was born. But as beautiful as she looked, Alanna was not happy; there were no mirrors to play with in this new room. The social worker, Kristen DeRossa, asked me general questions about Alanna and our family. The speech therapist and occupational therapist tried to get Alanna to play with some toys, but she just wanted out. I sat cross-legged on the floor, and eventually I got her to at least sit with me. I got asked so many questions that my head spun. The words, "untestable" and "uncooperative" were used. The team decided that the evaluations could not be completed, but that Alanna obviously qualified for preschool disabled services. It seemed they all knew what Alanna had, but once again no one wanted to say the "A" word.

Kristen scheduled a visit for me to observe a school program at the Children's Learning Center, which was about twenty minutes away. Lisa, the Early Intervention psychologist who had first suggested a neurological consult, went with me. It eased my anxiety to know she had done this with many other families, and that she would know what to do and say. We drove up to a large tan brick building in an industrial park with hope that this would be where Alanna would learn to speak to us. After signing in, we were greeted by a staff person who brought us into a classroom of five children. We were told that in this "inclusion" preschool classroom, not all of the children had disabilities. We watched with joy as a group of tiny little ones performed movements to songs, answered questions about colors, sang along to the days of the week, and sat nicely in their lined-up seats. It was adorable. Kristen asked whether this was somewhere we'd want Alanna to go. Of course I was ecstatic, and as I looked to Lisa she gave her approval as well. Kristen explained, "If we can get the Individualized Education Plan (IEP) done, Alanna can start March first," just a few days after her third birthday. But first we needed to get a formal diagnosis.

Kristen asked if we had scheduled a neurology appointment. I explained that our pediatrician felt we were overreacting and wouldn't provide a referral. Kristen offered the school's neurologist instead, explaining that the school contracted with a doctor to complete evaluations for children who needed them for placement. She promised to contact me with dates the neurologist would be in our area.

A few days later I got the call. Kristen explained that the room where the neurologist usually completed the examinations at the school might be too much for Alanna to handle. Instead, she offered to bring Dr. Dorothy Weyman to our home so she could examine Alanna in a more comfortable setting. I was so pleased because I didn't know if Billy would be on shore or out fishing at the time, and a home visit meant I wouldn't have to find sitters or bring Austin and Chelsea to the school. I was deeply thankful they were willing to make this accommodation.

On February 22, 1994, just two days before Alanna's third birthday, Dr. Weyman and Kristen arrived at our home. Luckily, Billy was on shore that day. Dr. Weyman had a strong presence and a direct manner that I would later learn to appreciate, but at this first meeting I was not prepared for her. She began the evaluation tersely: "How are you? Which child are we looking at?" I pointed to Alanna.

Dr. Weyman sat in a chair, grabbed Alanna between her knees, and wrapped a tape measure around her head. She then released her back into the open space of the living room. Alanna began to scream, the awful scream that would wake her from naps in days gone by. It made the hair on the back of my neck stand up. Dr. Weyman asked if this was normal, and I wanted to say, "Well, yes, if a stranger just grabbed her and wrapped a string around her head without warning, she'd be scared." Instead I just stared at her and shook my head "yes."

The doctor asked additional questions that had become familiar from past evaluations: "Does she talk?" "How many words?" "What does she do all day?" She announced that our daughter had infantile autism, and that I needed to get her into a good school if I ever wanted her to talk. Dr. Weyman then packed up her supplies and started for our front door.

She noticed Austin sitting in his highchair and asked, "What about him?" I told her I was worried about him too. I explained that he didn't play typical games like peek-a-boo, imitate simple movements, flinch at loud noises, or turn his head when his name—or anyone's name—was called.

Dr. Weyman noticed how Austin laughed when Chelsea passed him and how he wanted her to do it again and again. She acknowledged that his eye contact was amazing when we talked to him. She told me she didn't think it was autism because his eye contact was too good. "Look how he looks at you. Get his ears checked." Ok, I silently thought, deaf I can do.

Dr. Weyman told me to call her when we had insurance and left in a manner that was as swift and off-putting as she had been throughout her visit. Suddenly she was gone without any explanation of what to do aside from getting Alanna into a school. Kristen turned to me and asked if I was okay. "Yea, I'm fine," I muttered.

"This is really the first time you're hearing 'autism'," she said, "are you sure you're okay?" With a strange sense of relief I told her, "We kinda thought it was this."

Autism. She had autism. Not "autistic-like tendencies." She was autistic. I was okay with that; I thought the label would at least give us some direction. Now we could put together a plan.

The rest of the afternoon went on as usual. I had to get dinner on the table and bathe the kids. But as I loaded the dishwasher I had a sudden rush of reality. *My daughter is not fine, she is autistic. I don't have a clue what that means, or what is about to happen.* For the rest of the night I battled bouts of hysterical crying.

Billy had to go to work and would be fishing for several days off shore. What was the use of crying if there was no one to console me? I decided the pity party for one was over. In the morning, I awoke ready to do battle with autism. First I decided to schedule Austin's audiologist appointment. That would be simple enough and would allow me to feel like I accomplished at least one positive thing. I could start to move forward by making medical appointments and calling school personnel. Next on the list was to research what autism was, and especially what Alanna needed.

We celebrated Alanna's third birthday at home with just a few family and friends. Kristen stopped by with the documents we needed to sign to enroll Alanna at Children's Learning Center. I didn't even review them, I just signed on the dotted line. I trusted Kristen knew what needed to be done.

A few days later a taxi pulled up. Inside were two men and a car seat. They told me they had come to take Alanna to school for the first time. I was shocked and confused. I brought Alanna back into the house and called the bus company, asking if they had really sent two men in a taxi to take my daughter to school. "Yes," I was told, "the regular driver returns to work tomorrow." I don't know why I put her in that car, it terrified me to do so, but I did. I immediately called Children's Learning Center and begged them to call me when she arrived.

Even after I learned she had gotten to her destination safely, I sat at the window the entire day and waited for her to return. I tortured myself with questions: Why did I allow them to take her? What if someone hurts her? How will I know? It seemed so unfair, how could a mother be asked to put her child into a car with complete strangers and simply accept that this was part of the process to help her? Six hours later Alanna returned home, and I couldn't wait to grab her and hold her. The next day two women arrived, and they were friendlier and more understanding of my hesitation. I had a more relaxing second day, and as each day passed I settled into the routine of placing my baby girl in the hands of others.

With all we had going on between Austin's doctor visits and Alanna's new school situation, Billy and I decided it would be easier for me if we paid the preschool transportation fee so Chelsea could be picked up and dropped off at home. With both of my girls heading off each morning with their backpacks and lunch boxes, I had more time to focus on Austin. Maybe his ears really were the issue, maybe it was just being the third child, maybe it was because he was a boy, or maybe all he needed was just a little more attention.

Austin saw the same audiologist who had evaluated Alanna. Once again Sandy Richardson led us into the booth and the sounds were filtered in. First they came from one side of the room, then from the other, in varying tones and at different volume levels. When most of the session was complete, Sandy said she had one more test. She was going to introduce an exceptionally loud sound into the room to see if it startled Austin. She asked me to stay near him but not touch him, and to cover my ears. I followed her instructions, and she blasted the room with a loud BOOM. Austin remained unfazed.

Sandy explained that, based on her results, it appeared Austin was not able to hear. She wanted to retest him on another day to confirm. We returned to the office for a second visit with the same results, and we left with the diagnosis that Austin was deaf. Sandy put me on the path to Early Intervention paperwork once again.

This time we were sent to a program in Neptune, New Jersey that was specific to the needs of the hard of hearing. The staff could not have been kinder as they began their evaluation process. They had a bit of information about our family history. They were sympathetic to Alanna's recent diagnosis and were being ever so gentle with us regarding Austin. Different people interacted with Austin throughout the evaluation. One woman brought him over to a computer that had a microphone attached. If he made noise into the microphone, it was represented by color and movement on the computer screen. She tried to get Austin to make some sounds to see if he had any interest in the cause and effect they would have on the screen. Austin did not make any sounds, but he did enjoy the visual effects; he wanted her to make sounds while he watched the screen.

He started to move around the room and attempted to climb up on the radiator. Each time he would be instructed to get down, but he would find a new route. While I spoke with one evaluator, another began to play music and noticed that Austin turned. She grabbed a toy keyboard and began to push keys. Austin followed the sounds. Tina Burden, one of the evaluators, asked me about his usual routine. When I explained how good he was, especially because he slept so much, she asked if I was concerned about his sleep. I didn't understand the need for concern. I felt I was blessed to have such a good child. After having three children in thirty-four months, I believed that someone was watching over me and had given me a good baby this time.

But Tina explained that babies can sleep too much, and that it could be a warning sign of more serious issues. *Seriously?* Our pediatrician had never expressed that a baby could sleep too much. I'd never heard such a thing before in my life. What was this a warning of? None of the evaluators wanted to say it, but they all knew it wasn't his ears. I was told to schedule a BAER test at a local hospital, which would check Austin's brain wave activity in response to sounds. We couldn't get in for two weeks.

While we waited for the appointment, I began to notice just how many "autistic-like tendencies" Austin had begun to demonstrate. He was walking on his toes and flapping his hands. I remember Billy's stepmother Rita telling me about Austin's incredibly infectious laugh every time he heard the opening of an episode of Disney's "Spot the Dog." I didn't get to see that at home. We didn't have the Disney channel, he only got to watch the show at Rita's. He would hear the show's theme song and run to the television. The program would hypnotize him, and he would laugh a laugh that came from the gut. He didn't point to objects and had no interest in toys, he only cared about the television.

He was an angel, almost too good. He would sleep all night, nap during the day, and stay in the baby swing without a single complaint. He could get that wind-up baby swing going with such force that the back legs would lift off the floor and come slamming back down. When he was in the jumper, he would get so high his feet would nearly come out of the seat and he would make every attempt to get it to spin. I already knew what the next appointment would bring, but I held onto the hope that the audiologist was right. It was his ears. It had to be his ears.

Austin was twenty-two months old when I took him to the hospital in Toms River to have the BAER test. The staff gave him a sedative to keep him still. Austin lay on a large table looking so small. The room was silent. The doctor put electrodes on Austin's little head and headphones over his ears, then stood behind the equipment turning and pushing knobs. Once the test was complete, the doctor handed me a printout. It looked like a long receipt from the grocery store. He told me that Austin, "may have some difficulty processing soft consonants, but that is all. I don't know what is wrong with him, but I can tell you it's not his ears." I grabbed Austin off that table and held him tighter than ever before. I knew what it was. My son, like my daughter, had autism. I made it all the way to the car before I broke down.

A subsequent appointment with a neurologist simply confirmed it. We were a family with three children, two with autism. I wondered how to break the news to Billy.

Armed and Ready

March 1994 to May 1995

Billy certainly knew I was concerned that Austin also had autism, but he was hanging on to the possibility that Austin was deaf. When Billy came home I told him what the audiologist had said. We reviewed the classic autism behaviors Austin was exhibiting: no words, not playing with toys appropriately, and flapping his hands. For each characteristic, Billy tried to find reasons why it could happen in a household like ours, and why it might not be autism. If I insisted, "Austin has no words," he'd answer, "We don't make him talk." With each example I gave, he went on. "Maybe if we read to him more. Maybe if we spent more time with him. Maybe if Alanna didn't take up so much of our time, and Austin wasn't being bounced from grandparent to grandparent while we go to therapists and doctors..." He believed that with Alanna settled into a school program, we could now focus on Austin.

But whenever Billy said "we" weren't doing enough, all I could hear was, "maybe if *you* just did a little more, our son would talk." There was no "we" in our marriage when it came to the kids, or the housework, or the chores. I loved my husband, but he was not always present and all of the "we" stuff really meant me. He would come home from days of fishing and get to play husband and daddy for brief stints. Then he would return to the fishing boat. Like others, he saw our situation from the outside in, and like others, he judged my performance.

I was home alone with our three children most of the time, trying to do the best I could. This mom thing was hard. I wasn't sure I was fit to do it. I didn't enjoy getting down on the floor and playing the way other parents seemed to. I went through the motions, but just couldn't make myself attend for long periods. But I wondered whether I disliked it so much because my children didn't care about it and gave me no feedback. Should I be doing more? How much more is enough?

Accepting that another of our children had autism was difficult, much harder on Billy than on me. My guess was because it happened to our son. This was Billy's chance to have a son that he felt he could influence, one that would follow in his footsteps and the footsteps of all his friends' male children. Someone to do guy stuff with. With one simple word—autism—all his dreams of raising a ball player went away and were replaced with the unknown.

Taking care of a daughter for the rest of her life didn't seem to be such a hard future to imagine, and in a way it comes with some noble concessions that people admire. But taking care of your son? That was different for Billy. He would say that his lack of acceptance came partly because it was almost unbelievable that this was happening again, and partly because he just wanted my life to get easier, not harder. He was convinced he must have done something wrong in his past to deserve this sort of punishment as a father.

I took Austin to a developmental pediatrician, Dr. David Vanwick, instead of returning to the neurologist. As we sat in the waiting room, I noticed the other babies there. I listened intently to the conversations they had with their mothers, and my heart ached at their desire to show their mothers the toys in the room. I was in awe of their speech, and I smiled when they came near, but I was so jealous.

"Austin Gallagher," called the nurse. I lifted him from the floor and carried him into a very adult-looking office. Dr. Vanwick sat behind a large professional desk and gestured for Austin and me to sit in the leather chairs opposite him. Austin immediately hopped down and attempted to climb onto a shelf near a window with vertical blinds. The doctor watched as I attempted to control Austin before he destroyed something. I held onto Austin as Dr. Vanwick asked several questions, all of which could have been answered without Austin present. We went over all the usual queries: Does he babble? Does he have any words? Does he walk? On and on and on. I was so frustrated. Dr. Vanwick had Austin's records from his regular pediatrician, why was he asking me all these questions again? Couldn't he see how I was struggling just to keep Austin in one place? He told me to make an appointment with a neurologist named Dr. Ron Karas. Another doctor, another appointment, and yes, another delay.

Dr. Karas was a kind man with a gentle nature. He got on Austin's level and attempted to engage him. We reviewed all the same topics every other professional had asked about, but I was not as annoyed with Dr. Karas because he at least showed an interest in Austin. As the visit was coming to an end I asked him about the diagnosis, and specifically asked if he thought it was autism. He gave me a response I did not expect. He wanted to wait and see, and told me I should bring Austin back in six months. Dr. Karas explained that he didn't like to give a diagnosis of autism before the age of three because so much could change.

He attempted to tell me to give Austin time, that boys are slower to talk. He went on, "Perhaps you are more focused on this because of your daughter. The likelihood of you having two children with autism is so slim." Slim to none, I was sure, but why were we talking percentages and possibilities, instead of focusing on the child in front of us? In that moment I realized my appreciation for Dr. Weyman's exceptionally forward manner. I learned that I was not the type of parent who needed to be spoon-fed. I preferred to be hit over the head with a sledgehammer and knocked to the ground with all the overwhelming information I needed, because I would get back up armed and ready to do battle. This man had wasted my time. More importantly, he wasted Austin's time.

Austin was evaluated by Early Intervention and clearly qualified for services. Once again, we started the process of going to the center one day a week. Every Wednesday I sent the girls off to school and packed up Austin. I brought him to the same center that Alanna had gone to, and the same staff was present, but now there were new parents and children. All five children in the group had autism. When I brought Austin into the room, he immediately went over to the wooden kitchen stove and climbed inside the cabinet to hide. He wouldn't come out for most of the hour. Toward the end of the session, the staff asked all the parents to gather up their children and sit in a circle so we could sing a goodbye song together. The goal was for this to be a signal to the children that the session was ending.

I was the mom that all the other mothers pitied while silently thanking God that their child wasn't as challenging as mine. I pulled Austin out of the miniature cabinet beneath the wooden stove and dragged him to the circle. Once there, I sat on the floor with him wedged into the pretzel-shaped space between my legs and attempted to keep him there while he screamed, cried, and clawed his way up my shoulders in an attempt to escape. The staff told me to keep him in the area as best I could, so I pulled him back down, sat him with his legs straight out, and wrapped my legs on top of his. This only caused him to butt his head into my chest and fight with everything he had to get away. The song finally ended and we all left. I could barely move my arms after that workout. Every week it was the same. Austin had no interest in the other children or the activities, and all he wanted to do was hide.

Because Austin had such a difficult time, the staff suggested that he not complete the entire one and a half hours in the same day. Instead, I could bring him back on a different day for the additional half hour of service.

At least it was another day to get out of the house. So on Thursdays I would pack him up again, drive twenty minutes in order for him to engage for thirty minutes on a computer, and then twenty minutes back home. During the thirty minutes at the center, Austin would interact with a cause and effect game on the computer. It allowed him to use the mouse and scribble on a blank page, then click an eraser that would "blow up" the picture using a black and white spiral and some sound effects. Austin loved it. His ability on the computer would often shock Barbara Atkinson, the special education teacher. We would watch him navigate the mouse and keyboard to get his needs met. But as soon as someone would try to show him how to do something else, he would scream and refuse to follow directions. All that Austin learned he learned by trying on his own.

During the final weeks of Early Intervention, Lisa Lynch suggested that I bring Austin out into the hallway when the group sang. Her reasoning was that the distance might help him to tolerate the song while still hearing it and learning that it signaled the end of the session. I wasn't sure if this was for Austin's benefit or the benefit of all the other children and mothers who had to see and hear our struggle. I couldn't help but think that some parent did not want to witness what we went through and spoke up about it. At each visit I hoped that, finally, Austin would understand that all this was happening to help him. But in all the months we attended Early Intervention, Austin did not adjust to the events. He was as strong in his refusal to go to the song circle on his very last day as he was on his first. He never came out of the child-sized kitchen cabinet, and he never spoke a single word.

Austin would soon be aging out of Early Intervention and starting a preschool program like Alanna. We had sent our letter to the school district and once again started the process of having him evaluated. I spent a lot of time on the internet researching the needs of children with autism. I read a book by Catherine Maurice titled *Let Me Hear Your Voice*. It was the story of a woman struggling with two children with autism, one boy and one girl. It was my story.

I absorbed every word and couldn't put it down. It gave me the blueprint I needed to help my children, the strength to face those who stared, and the words to use when others tried to tell me what was best for my children. This woman had felt exactly what I was feeling. I needed to know that her story ended happily, that there was hope for my two children. She described the applied behavior analysis (ABA) teaching sessions her children participated in and the many hours of work and tears it took to get them to complete simple tasks. But they learned to complete those tasks. I decided I had to learn more about ABA, and I needed to find out how to make it happen for my children. Her children were a success story, and I needed my children to have the same outcome. This information was another brick in the wall as I built a support structure for our children, and I was energized to move forward.

I joined Parents of Autistic Children (POAC), a support group moderated by the Center for Outreach Services for the Autism Community, or COSAC. COSAC offered a seven-week training in behavior analysis, and I signed up as soon as it became available in my area. The group also provided a one-day seminar about advocacy for parents, including how to help other parents of children with autism. I knew I absolutely needed to attend that event, first to make sure we were doing everything right, and second to possibly help others.

At the seminar one of the COSAC staff asked, "What is happening in Brick? We've had three calls this week." Billy and I had also noticed the number of families from Brick we were meeting as we navigated this new world of autism, but for now we were focused on Alanna and Austin. We were trying to connect with any available agencies and learn all that we could. We found a conference at SUNY, in Westchester, New York, where Catherine Maurice would be speaking. Dr. O. Ivar Lovaas, a professor of psychology at UCLA, would be also giving a presentation there. Everything we read about ABA after first learning of it in Catherine Maurice's book led us to the research done by Dr. Lovaas. We had to get to this conference to see them both.

May 1995

With babysitters in place and excited to learn all we could, we made our way up to the SUNY campus and signed in. A light breakfast was served to a capacity crowd of parents and professionals affected by autism. Actor Aidan Quinn was there, and of course there was a bit of a ruckus around him. The poor man was coming to an event to learn more about treatment for his daughter's autism, and he still got bombarded with star-struck fans. But Hollywood stars and average parents alike were all shuffled into the same packed auditorium. I remember simply wanting to hear every word.

After a welcome speech by the president of the organization hosting the event, Dr. Lovaas was introduced. The man we had all come to see stepped up to the podium. He discussed his research and shared cases of individuals with whom he had worked. Throughout the presentation he occasionally showed brief video clips to highlight the points he made. One in particular stood out: a young man rocking back and forth and smiling to himself. This was Dr. DeGrappe's image of a child with autism, and it was playing before my eyes.

Dr. Lovaas described the children who were part of a study conducted within his program at UCLA. His data illustrated that forty hours per week of ABA services could dramatically change the outcomes of children with autism and make them "indistinguishable" from their peers by teaching basic stills and decreasing challenging behaviors. He showed before and after videos as evidence.

As further support, he then brought some of the students from his program onto the stage. Mock therapy sessions were conducted for the audience. The children sat so beautifully, looked to their therapists for direction, and didn't seem fazed by the audience. One child/therapist team presented a simple direction-following task in which the therapist told the child to stand up, clap her hands, and so on. Another child answered some basic questions about his name and favorite colors. I was in awe of these children; they had been taken so far from their homes in California and were handling this situation so well. They were on stage, which would be frightening even for a typical child, but for children like Alanna and Austin it would be absolutely terrifying. I felt as if I were the only person in the room. These children were showing me the possibilities. Someday, my own children could speak to me.

A tiny girl bravely approached the microphone. She looked to be about seven years old, so adorable in her Sunday dress with white socks and black shoes. She played a small plastic guitar and performed the "I Love You" song from the Barney and Friends television show. She sealed the deal for me, even though I had come to hate that show because my children spent so much time watching it. At that moment I could not get enough of her song, and all I wanted was to hear it again and again.

As we exited the auditorium I was stopped by a mom I often saw at the local support group from Brick. "This all seems great," she said, "but did you hear their voices? They all sounded like robots." Once she pointed it out, I supposed I agreed a little. The responses of the children were less than fluent, but these children were not able to speak at all prior to participating in the program. For a mom who hadn't heard any language, even robotic vocalizations would be a welcome sound. I just wanted to hear my children's voices.

That evening there was a dinner, and as is the case with many of these fundraisers dinner was very late. So we wandered outside to the patio where we asked another couple, "Do you mind if we join you?" This small encounter would change our lives. Bridgette and Ray Glenn had three boys, and their middle child had autism. They were running a program similar to the one described in Catherine Maurice's book, a full ABA program from their home for forty hours a week with staff coming in on a daily schedule. Their program implemented the type of teaching that we had seen in the videos during Dr. Lovaas' presentation.

Bridgette went on to explain how they had to fight their school district to get the program funded, and that she had to train the staff and hire the experts. She was also in charge of paying everyone out of the money she received from the school. Bridgette and Ray stressed that we should not believe what the school district told us, that we needed to investigate for ourselves what we felt our children needed. This was our first lesson in the difference between what our children were getting and what they were actually entitled to, and how money always plays a part. This also kick-started our plan to stay on top of what our children needed and not listen to those in charge.

Our conversation ended as time came to move back inside for dinner and Catherine Maurice's keynote presentation. As she began to share her experience I was again captivated by the similarities of our story, except for the financial part. Catherine had the money to pay for what her children needed. We did not. Ray and Bridgette had explained that we would probably need an attorney and recommended someone they used. The importance of legal support became clear as Catherine went on to describe her fight to get services and the people who tried to stop her. Most of all, she explained that if we did not fight for all that our children needed—now—they would not make the progress we were hoping for.

Ray and Billy had left the table together for some reason, and the next thing I knew Ray was waving Billy over to meet Catherine Maurice. After a brief introduction and an overview of where our children were currently attending school, she told Billy, "You shouldn't trust your school district. It's like leading the lambs to slaughter." She went on to explain that school districts only look out for the bottom line, and that we needed to get our children out of there. Later that evening Billy met Dr. Bernard Rimland, a research psychologist and father of a child with autism. Dr. Rimland's research debunked the long-believed "refrigerator mother" theory as the cause for autism, and he had advocated for children with autism his entire life. Dr. Rimland echoed the others' warnings about how money would drive all the decisions made for our children. We needed to get our children into ABA programs and we needed to do it *now*!

Before we attended the conference, we were satisfied that the school district was going to place Austin in the same program as Alanna. Now that we knew Alanna was not getting the right type of program, we certainly weren't going to follow that path for Austin. We went back to the school board and explained that we wanted an official IEP meeting to discuss what Austin needed. By now we had learned so much about what was done incorrectly when we went through this same process with Alanna. There was no IEP meeting for Alanna except that signature at her birthday party. The district never told us that we had any say in what services our children could receive. This time we were ready for them.

Kristen DeRossa was our case manager once again. She and another child study team member came to our home for a meeting and we presented our desires: a full forty-hour ABA program in our home for both Alanna and Austin. Of course we shocked Kristen; she thought we were simply going to sign the papers to place Austin at Children's Learning Center just like we had done for Alanna. She and her colleague were unable to approve our request. But at this meeting Kristen did mention that there was an ABA program in the district that we should take a look at.

At first I was ecstatic about the news and immediately made arrangements to visit the program. However, soon after I became upset and wondered, "Why didn't they tell us about this program when Alanna was first ready for school? Why did she have to go to a non-ABA school thirty minutes away when there was an ABA program in one of our local schools?" Later, when we asked those questions, we were informed they didn't have room in the program back then and they didn't want to show us something we couldn't have. But I knew so much more by now that I didn't know then. I now knew not having room was not a legally acceptable reason to not provide the appropriate program. If the district had an ABA program in place, then they must understand the importance of ABA for children with autism. If we could get Austin and Alanna into this program, we wouldn't have to fight legally or find staff to provide programming in our home.

Our children would get what they needed, and someday we would hear their voices. We were armed with information and ready to fight, but the battle ahead was so much bigger than we expected.

Blessed Battle

"I was born to be a blessing."

—*Maya Angelou*

For most of my teens and early 20's I attempted to please everyone until I reached the point where I had no idea of who I was or what I wanted. I simply wanted whatever the person I was with wanted. I never could identify myself as someone with a goal or a future. I was just an outline, someone with no passion. I would claim to want the things society tells us we all want, like a husband and children. But I cannot remember once being able to say: I want to do or be ___________, and being able to fill in the blank.

Alanna and Austin have been the catalyst for most of what I have done in my life. Of course, the fact that I would love and fight for my children in any way necessary was always a given. But after having two children with autism, the event that sealed my destiny was entering Kathy Ramirez's classroom at the Lanes Mills School in May 1995. There I witnessed teachers and paraprofessionals working with preschool children in a way that should not have been permitted, and I was appalled at the apathetic attitude of the staff, the inappropriate teaching, and the lack of respect. That day I learned I was on this earth to fight for children with autism.

Many other events led up to that day, but visiting that room forced me to insist that my children would get better because my children deserved better. Being labeled *disabled* doesn't mean a child should be satisfied with the scraps they are thrown. By no means were my kids going to get scraps from the school board's table. I could only hope that, like Maya Angelou, I was born to be a blessing—at the very least to my own children, but maybe even to more children with autism. But a blessing to one may be a curse to another. When you fight to make a difference not everyone will agree with you, and some will do all they can to take you down.

May 25, 1995 – Lanes Mills School

I sat in the parking lot of the Lanes Mills School, turned off my car, and got my pen and pad ready. I was excited for what I was about to see. I wasn't happy that our school district never told us this classroom existed the first time we went through this process, but at least now we could move forward.

I was finally going to see an ABA program in action. I truly was energized and felt a sense of relief that perhaps soon this would all be over. Both of my children would be in a good program, they would start learning, and this autism thing would be behind us.

After I signed in at the office, it took a while for someone to walk me to the class. As I entered the classroom, Mrs. Ramirez said I was late and that she had been expecting me at 9:00. I apologized and explained, "I was told 9:30." I didn't mention that I had waited in the office for more than fifteen minutes; I didn't want to start off on the wrong foot. "But that's okay," she answered, "just take a look around. If you have any questions, please feel free to ask." She seemed to have full confidence in the classroom techniques I was about to witness.

The moment I stepped into the room I knew it wasn't a place for Austin. The walls were covered with information, clutter, and signs. The windows were covered with paper curtains that would last all of two seconds once he climbed atop the old school radiators. The children's cubbies were built of three-foot-high divider walls, each right next to the other. As I sat near one of the cubbies, it was difficult for me to concentrate. Each teacher gave directions to the student they were assigned to, but none were giving the same directions. With the cubbies so close together, it was hard to differentiate who was talking to whom. Each cubby also had lots of information posted, with personal information about the student, class schedules, speech schedules, and artwork tacked up on the walls. A window air conditioner was blasting so noisily that students needed headphones to hear the computers.

I focused on the teaching. I expected the staff to be a bit more animated and maybe even a little nervous with me present to observe the class. I certainly did not expect what I actually saw.

As I watched a student in a cubby match numbers I heard a loud exclamation from across the room. "SHAME, SHAME, SHAME ON YOU…I can't believe you did that!" An aide was yelling at a student. "What did he do?" Mrs. Ramirez shouted back. "Dylan pissed all over the place," the aide huffed. I was horrified. Not because a seven-year-old boy wet his pants, but because of the staff's reaction. Did she really just say that in front of him? In front of the entire classroom? Anyone who works with children should know not to make a fuss over such things, and should definitely know not to use that sort of language. She pulled the desk out of the way and ordered Dylan into the bathroom as she sighed over the clean-up ahead.

"His mom said he got into the refrigerator this morning and drank an entire carton of orange juice," Mrs. Rodriguez offered with frustration. As the clean-up continued I noticed the staff were prepared for the accident, with extra clothes on hand specifically for Dylan. It was clear that he was not fully toilet trained. It didn't take long for me to wonder, "If they are still training him, and his mother felt it important to let them know about the orange juice, why didn't anyone take him to the bathroom prior to the accident?"

Dylan and his aide were out of the room for a while, so I watched the others. Giacomo, a small boy with great big brown eyes, was in the corner cubby. I was told that he had a history of trying to escape. The staff had placed a table in front of the exit to the cubby, corralling Giacomo and Debbie Sewell, the speech therapist, into the space. He kept putting his head down on the table so Debbie made eye contact and shrugged her shoulders at me, silently communicating that she didn't know what to do with him. The next time I looked in their direction, he had fallen asleep and she was holding him in her arms. She placed him on the floor and quietly exited the cubby. Mrs. Ramirez agreed it would be a good idea to let him sleep, and Giacomo remained asleep for the rest of my two hour visit. The staff appeared somewhat relieved not to have to engage him.

Another little boy, Timmy, had hair was so blond it was nearly white. Each time a task was presented to him he would bang his head on the desk multiple times. His aide requested a catalog from one of the other staff members, who quickly grabbed it from a shelf and handed it to her. Timmy's aide showed it to him and immediately he stopped banging his head and began looking at the pictures. Once he was asked to work again he would bang his head, and the staff would give him back the catalog. Even an amateur like me could see that this was not healthy and that they were reinforcing his head banging behavior.

Eventually all the children, except Giacomo, were brought to a center table where they had a snack. Zaheed, a small, very thin boy sat closest to me. He was given Frosted Flakes. It took all the encouragement his aide could muster to convince him to eat them. Zaheed had no interest and ate the cereal as though he was bored.

An announcement was piped into the room: "Mrs. Ramirez, Kevin's bus is here," said someone from the office. One of the students was packed up and taken to a bus that was waiting for him outside the school. Mrs. Ramirez sensed that I was curious about why his bus had arrived so early in the day and explained that this young man received occupational therapy in another school building up the road. The children finished their snacks and returned to the cubby spaces to do more work.

Zaheed sat at his desk scraping the crayon off of pictures he had drawn. He seemed to enjoy seeing the waxy color come off the paper and fill up the area behind his nails. He would then rub the rainbow of shavings between his fingers. The aide blindly attempted to continue the work, endlessly repeating, "Look at me. Touch ball." She tried to convince him to take a Frosted Flake as a reward for success. He didn't want them at snack time and he certainly didn't want them now. Instead, between each of her demands he would go back to scraping the crayon off the drawings.

I had learned so much at the SUNY conference. I remembered how Dr. Lovaas and the instructor at the COSAC training insisted that when you teach children with autism, you must present the direction once and then require a response. It was clearly stated that teachers should not repeat a command if a response has not been achieved. But all I heard as I observed cubby after cubby was repetition: "Look at me. You need to look at me, PJ. Look at me." Or "clap your hands, clap, Kevin, look, clap your hands."

The class next gathered for "structured" play in the center of the room. The aides sat in a circle with their students in front of them. I joined them on the floor. I thought a group activity was about to begin. Instead, they gave each child a toy. This "activity" simply allowed all the adults a chance to converse while each student engaged with a preferred object.

Timmy sat with his aide, but the moment he was separated from his catalog he banged his head on the carpet-covered cement floor. The aide quickly grabbed the catalog and placed it under his forehead. When Timmy saw it, he stopped and looked at the pictures.

Mrs. Ramirez was excited to show me one of the students the district bragged about because he was on a 2nd grade reading level and was talking. PJ reminded me of Ralphie from *A Christmas Story* with his adorable round head and thick glasses. I sat next to PJ so I could hear him. Mrs. Ramirez handed him a department store catalog opened to a page with pictures of electronic equipment. I reached over to turn to a page with toys, but PJ quickly let me know—"NO!"—I wasn't supposed to do that. PJ then repeated, "VCR, VCR, VCR, VCR," and "VCR camera, VCR camera." Mrs. Ramirez became tired of the repetition and asked, "What movie did you watch last night?" He answered, "Hunwondematon." Mrs. Ramirez asked again for clarity and he repeated, "Hunwondematon." Finally, she deciphered what he had said. "Oh, 101 Dalmatians! Did you like it?" she asked.

"Yes."

"Did you watch it with your dad?"

"Yes."

She then attempted to take the catalog away and PJ screeched as though a needle had just been jabbed into his arm. She immediately returned it. This student was the district's pride and joy, their representative that this program was working for children with autism.

Meanwhile, the conversation between the aides focused on a field trip they had taken to the beach the previous day. When one aide commented to another that she had gotten quite a bit of color, she responded with, "It's not my fault I got stuck with the kid who just wants to sit and play with the sand." She gestured toward the same child she was sitting with. The little boy with a head of hair like Elvis paid no attention to their discussion, but I couldn't help but wonder whether his disconnect was due to a lack of understanding or because he understood completely that he was the topic of conversation.

"OH! GET AWAY FROM ME! He did it again!" Dylan's aide yelled as she shoved him in the back. Dylan had wet his pants again, soaking the aide's pants and the carpet as well. Dylan began to laugh, and the aide rudely informed him, "You're not funny."

I was mortified. How did this person get this job, and why was she allowed to keep it? I wondered why Mrs. Ramirez wasn't reprimanding her. The one saving grace was the smirk on Dylan's face as he was brought back into the bathroom to be cleaned up and changed again. I could feel the sense of satisfaction he had gotten from her reaction.

What I saw that day was unconscionable, and as a parent I wondered what went on in this class when it was not being observed. The teacher's acceptance of her staff's behavior was a clear indication of a major problem with this program.

As I walked back through the parking lot I angrily thought, "Put my children in that classroom? Not on your life!" Once inside the privacy of my car, I cried. I cried because this was not the answer I had wanted for Alanna and Austin, and now we had to make the right thing happen ourselves. I cried because I didn't know what that was going to take, and I was already tired. Most of all, I cried for those children and all that they endured each day at the hands of those women.

I remembered noticing the name of one child on the wall of his cubby. It was such an unusual name—Fryczynski—that there couldn't be too many of them in our town. When I got home I decided to try to find his mom. There were two families with that name in the phone book, I called one and found the mother of the boy in the class. We talked for quite some time about my observations. Shortly after that call Billy and I would meet most of the families from that room.

May 1995 to May 1996

The school district called an IEP meeting just a few days after my visit to Mrs. Ramirez's class. Billy and I needed to be prepared to argue our points. We had to be clear about why we were moving forward with our request for a forty-hour-per-week in-home ABA program. I brought stacks of paperwork, copies of the journal article that Dr. Lovaas published, and my list of concerns regarding the classroom. That class was not the type of ABA we were looking for.

Billy took off from work because I really needed him there. We walked into a room full of staff from the school, some familiar faces and some new. Our case manager Kristen and Mrs. Ramirez were there, along with Debbie, the speech therapist from the ABA class. We met school psychologist Dan Pepito, Robin McGivney the Learning Disability Teacher Consultant, and Kathleen Sipowitz, Director of Special Services.

My heart was pounding. I felt so out of my league. Mrs. Ramirez passed out IEPs for both of our children. Each was more than 80 pages long, and they were identical except for the name on the front page. As the attendees each discussed their role within the district and specifically how they would be involved in Alanna's and Austin's education, Billy and I realized that they were under the wrong impression. They thought we were going to put our children in that classroom. I tried to be systematic in my approach, but I failed miserably. I attempted to show how the IEPs weren't appropriate because they weren't individualized. The document included so many goals that didn't pertain to Alanna or Austin. We specifically pointed out one of the goals: our children, ages three and four, were to learn how to bowl and how to keep score. Mrs. Ramirez explained that it was "an ongoing IEP that will follow the children," until they completed it. After Austin and Alanna met all of these goals, the district would write new IEPs. Besides, all the children went bowling every week. For every question or concern I had, they had an answer. I was using all the knowledge gained from the workshops I had attended on the IEP process. However, I was not able to articulate our argument in a way that would persuade them, and my emotions began to take over.

We showed them the journal article and tried to explain what children with autism really need. They reacted to the article as though they had seen it a million times and had no interest in revisiting it. They told us this was an ABA classroom with an "eclectic approach." Billy and I stressed that we wanted only what would give our children the best possible future. We wanted what was in the research article. The discussion concluded with just one sentence that told us exactly where the district stood:

> "We don't have to give you the best, we only have to give you what's appropriate," Mr. Pepito said.

My eyes widened to the size of golf balls and my mouth dropped open in shock. Billy looked Mr. Pepito straight in the eyes and told him, "If what you are offering is *that* classroom," pointing to Mrs. Ramirez, "the answer is *no*!" We attempted to explain my experience in the class, but Mrs. Sipowitz would have no part of it and ended the meeting.

When we got home, we scheduled an appointment with attorney Margaret "Peggy" Maldonado, from Montvale, New Jersey. Then, after researching programs, I called the Wilson School's outreach program and spoke to Mary Cooper. I explained to Mrs. Cooper how we wanted to begin an in-home program for our children and we needed someone who could teach us how to run the sessions. She scheduled a consultation with Joanie Hurst, a special education teacher who worked with children with autism.

Unfortunately, I learned that when this level of disagreement is reached with a school district, there is so much to be done. I had to schedule training with Ms. Hurst, organize family to help us provide an in-home program, and ensure documentation of every skill we worked on. I managed all this while also scheduling experts, talking strategy with the attorney, and making appointments. I was running a business and my children were the commodity.

Billy and I gathered several family members to become our staff: my Aunt Mill and Uncle Tony, Billy's sister Donna, and Rita. We hired a young girl from a local college and agreed to pay her for her time. Our first group training session was held at our home. Ms. Hurst showed us how to get our children's eye contact and to teach them to focus, or attend, first. She gave us some basic skills to practice with each other. Then she brought in Austin and modeled the skills with him. Everyone was excited to be part of the change we were creating.

Following that session our home ran like a well-oiled machine. We set up two rooms as teaching stations, one downstairs and one upstairs, so Austin and Alanna could work at the same time. With all the help we had, we were creating a solid twenty hours per week of programming for each child.

On the legal front, Peggy had scheduled a mediation meeting for July 24, 1995 to discuss our request with the school district. However, I had already scheduled an expert evaluation for both kids with Dr. Thomas Fletcher on that same date. These types of appointments were difficult to get, so Billy and I decided that I would take the kids to the doctor while he went to the meeting. Billy and Peggy met with Mrs. Sipowitz, school district's attorney David Carrigan, and the state mediator at the school administration building. I left the house a little after Billy to head up the Garden State Parkway to exit 135.

During the drive I received a signal from Billy on my pager. I got the two kids out of the car and up to the office so I could call Billy. He said I might not need to go through with the evaluations; it looked like the district was going to settle our case and give us what we asked for, an in-home program. I was ecstatic, but decided, "Let me do this anyway, we are already here." As I hung up the phone I began to cry tears of joy and relief. My children were going to get what they needed, and it wouldn't drain us financially or emotionally.

After a short wait, Dr. Fletcher called us in. He was a gentle man who interacted with the children one at a time. Dr. Fletcher spent much of his time observing Austin engage with items in the room before attempting to step in and interact with Austin himself. He dumped pieces of a wooden peg puzzle on the floor and watched Austin put them back in using his toes. Dr. Fletcher laughed and asked if this was typical. I explained that Austin used his toes as frequently as he could if it prevented him from having to bend down or stop to complete a task; he was quite talented at using his feet. He tried to get Austin to follow some simple directions such as clapping his hands, but Austin wanted no part of it. He asked all the usual medical-visit questions, and apologized for the repetition because he knew I had answered them so many times already.

When Alanna's turn came, she found a box of crayons, dumped them onto the floor, and began to put all 64 of them in rainbow order. Dr. Fletcher asked if she liked to color, and I told him, "No, she doesn't. She just likes to scribble really hard and then touch the tip after she makes it hot." He then asked me what a typical day was like at home.

Typical. That was not a word I used to describe any day in my home. But most days started by getting all three children up and fed before the first round of ABA therapy started. Chelsea would leave on the school bus. Once a family member or therapist arrived, I would take one child and they would take the other. We would work for two hours before allowing the children time to engage in play. But play for them wasn't typical, either. Alanna would go into the playpen and grab her stuffed animals. One by one she removed them from the playpen and placed them on the floor, flat on their backs with the limbs of their bodies spread out. Once she had them all out, she put them back in one at a time and started all over. She lined up magnetic letters on the refrigerator or wooden ABC blocks on the table in alphabetical order. Austin would come along and knock down the blocks one by one, inevitably causing his sister to dissolve into tears. Alanna rebuilt the blocks again. Austin would climb on top of the mantel to sit and watch as Alanna graciously prepared the blocks for his next takedown. Lunch was served, and more people would arrive. We did this all over again in the afternoon.

In the evenings, Austin sat in the doorway between the sunroom and living room to watch a movie. But Alanna would insist that every door in the house be closed and Austin's position would prevent the door from shutting. His smile revealed that he received some satisfaction from seeing his sister grow red in the face while trying to shut the door on him. Her lack of success would lead to tears. I would let her watch a movie in my room instead. (I owe Walt Disney not only for my children's enjoyment but also for my very sanity.) Alanna watched movies by lying on my bed with her eyes facing the mirrored headboard. She looked at the television screen through the mirror. Neither of my children spoke to me, and it seemed that I spent much of my time just keeping them out of trouble. That was a "typical" day at the Gallagher house.

Those "typical" days at home made me happy that Chelsea had a place to go and have fun. In the evenings she tried her best to gain my attention through conversation. I wished I had more time for her. I convinced myself that I would after this battle with the district was over.

I left the appointment wondering if I would ever need to see Dr. Fletcher—or any doctors—again. Our children were going to get what they needed. I drove home as quickly as I could and ordered Chinese food to celebrate. Billy explained what had happened during the meeting. At the end, the district's attorney confirmed that the settlement agreement would be hand-delivered in the next day or two.

The next day we were out in the yard when an elderly gentleman in a small white car stopped in front of our home. He handed me a manila envelope, asked me to sign for it, and left. The envelope seemed awfully thin, but I ripped it open. Printed on the official letterhead of the attorney's office it read: Mr. and Mrs. Gallagher, The Brick Township School District will not agree to the conditions of the settlement agreement signed on July 24, 1995. Please proceed as you deem necessary.

Billy grabbed the single piece of paper from my hands. He read it again and again in shock. We called Peggy. She was in disbelief; this had never happened to her in the past. We had to start the process again and file for another mediation meeting.

The next meeting was held on August 31, 1995. Another agreement was signed, but now the district wasn't offering a full in-home program. This time we agreed to send our children to the in-district program as long as the district provided staff training and other conditions outlined in the settlement. It read:

1. Staff training by Wilson School. Kathleen Sipowitz will advise Peggy of the specifics after she talks to Wilson.
2. Alanna will have lunch in the cafeteria with the general education children.
3. Speech and occupational therapy will be provided in individual sessions outside of the classroom.

4. Alanna and Austin will continue to receive services at home, after school, three days per week.
5. Two days per week both children will attend a preschool handicapped classroom for students with less severe disabilities for socialization.
6. Alanna and Austin will have their own aides, and their IEPs will specify three hours per day of discrete trial training (just like we were doing at home).
7. All agree to reconvene in January to review the program and progress.

Although we had reached an agreement, several questions still remained. We refused to place our children in the program until we had the answer to number one: what was the extent of the training to be provided? While we waited for a response we continued with our home program.

Billy attended back-to-school night and introduced himself to all the parents. He was open about our children and what we were trying to get the district to do. We hoped that if we could get all the parents to make the same request, we might get the district to comply. In the big picture, this would help all the children. On a smaller scale, maybe we could save some legal costs. Most of the parents agreed to exchange emails and phone numbers.

A few weeks passed. The district was willing to provide a few workshops to the staff, but there would be no ongoing training or consultation with Wilson. We couldn't accept that answer. A few workshops, what would that do? These people needed serious training, not a workshop that would do nothing more than give them a day off.

On September 21, 1995 we filed for due process with the Department of Education. We had to meet with all involved parties again and attempt to resolve the issues. But before we could do that, we had to hire experts to review the program and make recommendations. Dr. Fletcher was one who provided his insight. In his report he detailed his recommendations and his concerns, which were very similar to ours. He state that the district's implementation of ABA strategies was not up to par. Staff needed training by someone with expertise in this area. Dr. Marshall Howard was another expert who participated; he also had concerns with the program. Both recommended ongoing consultation from Wilson.

As we waited for the court mediation date, we decided to move forward with a meeting for the other parents of children in the program. We contacted an advocate, Brenda Conine, and asked her to come to the meeting and help us. Several of the children's parents and grandparents came to the meeting. Billy had met another family who had two children with autism, the Pierre's, at back-to-school night; they came to the meeting in our home as well. This was the start of Brick POSSE (Brick Parents of Special Services and Education). I told the group about the problems I saw in the classroom, and Brenda explained that we would be stronger as a group. We discussed how inappropriate the children's IEP goals were, especially the one about bowling. The parents acknowledged they knew the children went bowling, but they were never quite sure what they did at the bowling alley. We decided to find someone who could go in and take a look without the staff knowing.

My mother agreed to the task. We sent her to the local bowling alley on the scheduled day. She sat at a table on the raised floor behind the lanes, not anticipating what she was about to see. Giacomo ran back and forth throughout the bowling alley. Mrs. Ramirez grabbed him and sat on him in an effort to keep him still. My mother was so flustered by this that she had a hard time concentrating. Luckily, not much else happened besides the aides helping children with little interest in bowling to roll a ball down the lane. These children could barely speak. This was a waste of educational time.

We contacted Mrs. Sipowitz immediately, and as part of her duties she had to call the Division of Youth and Family Services (DYFS) to investigate. DYFS interviewed me, Billy, my mom, and the school personnel. Even though Giacomo had bruises on his spine, no charges were filed. Giacomo's parents never came to another meeting of Brick POSSE, and Giacomo was no longer in that classroom.

We needed the other parents to make noise and demand that changes be made. Each family came forward to request that the district provide training or other changes to their child's education. The district would then ask to meet with them individually. They were warned not to become involved with our family. It was a true divide and conquer strategy. Some listened; some didn't.

Resolution took many meetings, lots of letter writing on the part of the attorneys, and much money spent on legal fees and experts. Finally, the district agreed to train their staff using the Wilson School's Outreach Program with the oversight of Joanie Hurst. We could not have been more thrilled. In January 1996, our children would go to school. I thought we would be able to take a breath and start to enjoy a more "typical" home life.

We were blessed with another victory a few months later when we finally heard a sound we had been longing for: Alanna's voice. On occasion, Alanna spoke a word or imitated a sound. But for the first time Alanna was regularly asking for items like pretzels, cookies, milk, and so much more. We knew the fight had been worth it, and we were on our way to getting her to talk.

We hoped Austin would soon follow suit. He babbled on a regular basis, but he did not form words. He had such a difficult time getting his needs met, and it caused tremendous anxiety for me. If Austin wanted something to eat from the kitchen cabinet, I would start to panic. My interactions with him were not always positive. He would lead me to the cabinet and throw my arm up in the general direction of the items on the top shelf. If I was lucky enough to pick the right item the first time, all was grand and I felt as though I had avoided a land mine. If I picked the wrong item on my first choice, I was in for a battle. He would flop to the floor in tears. It didn't matter what I offered him after that. The fact that I didn't get it right the first time was all it took to set off the tantrum. I tried to pick him up and let him make the choice, but he would still want to use my hand instead of his.

But then one day Austin brought me a coupon for Waffle Crisp cereal from the Sunday newspaper flyer. I knew we had some in the cabinet. We walked to the kitchen and I grabbed the cereal from the top shelf. No tears, no flopping to the floor. I poured it into a bowl and handed it to him. He walked away satisfied.

Later I signed up for a workshop by Lori Frost on PECS, the Picture Exchange Communication System. We knew this was going to help Austin. Ms. Frost explained how to get a child to communicate. Essentially, you make pictures of preferred items and have the child hand you a picture in exchange for the item. We immediately began to implement the program at home. Austin's home therapist taught him to request fourteen foods and eight toys in just two weeks. We put pictures everywhere: on the inside of our cabinets, on the refrigerator, on shelves, anywhere there was something we thought he might want. The dread I felt when reaching for something on the shelf was over.

Austin quickly became resourceful at using the pictures. He once lost a picture of a box drink, so he brought me a picture of a box of cereal and a picture of a glass that said "drink" on it. He tried his hardest to make it perfectly clear what he wanted: a drink in a box. Austin did it through pictures, but now both our children were talking to us.

May 1996 to January 1997

What we thought was one for us in the win column turned out to be an everyday fight for our children's education. Joanie Hurst was hired to train the teacher and paraprofessionals assigned to Alanna and Austin. She also continued to consult in our home program. Joanie would often face struggles in the classroom. The teacher would constantly disagree with the presentation of tasks, from the words used to the seating arrangements chosen.

Even though everyone had agreed that consultation would occur, we soon learned that didn't necessarily mean consultation would actually be followed. The teacher technically had the right to deny the recommendations as she saw fit. If that was going to be the case, why had we even bothered to fight for training? I couldn't understand why this all had to be so hard. We were asking the district to teach our children in the same manner we had been teaching them. The consultant was part of an agency that had a track record of success for children with autism. Why wouldn't a teacher want to learn more? Because ego will always impede progress.

We tried to convince the district to implement the recommendations made by Joanie and Mrs. Cooper. We brought in our experts to help better explain our side without the emotional involvement I struggled with. Nothing seemed to work. Then we received a letter from the district requesting another IEP meeting in May 1996, even though the current IEP was only 5 months old. I wondered why the district would want to hold another IEP meeting so soon. We asked to have it rescheduled for January, when it was due for annual renewal. They insisted it be held in May.

At that meeting, the district announced that they would discontinue the home program and all consultation from the Wilson School. I didn't understand how they could be allowed to do this. My children needed these programs. They told us that Alanna and Austin would be given spots in their program, and that services would be delivered as the district saw fit. We had fought for nearly seven months and paid over twenty thousand dollars in legal and expert fees, and all we got was five months of non-compliance with the consultants. We had no recourse; the district simply stopped paying for the services. Wilson wasn't going to work for free. We made the necessary phone call to the attorney and went back to self-funding the home program. Peggy was taking time off from her practice due to personal reasons, so she referred us to Herb Hinkle's office in Lawrenceville, New Jersey.

Here we go again, I thought. We scheduled a meeting with Herb to have him review our case. We arrived at Herb's office with a stack of beautifully organized binders filled with tabs to separate the documents according to their focus. "You can always tell the families of children with autism," Herb commented. "They always come with so much documentation." He didn't even open the binders. Although we felt we were the only ones being tortured by our school district, Herb assured us that from his experience our story was common throughout the state.

He explained that what the district had done was unfortunate, but within their rights. We could file for "stay put," which would mean that our children would minimally get back the services they had before the district pulled the Wilson School out and discontinued the home program. However, he wanted us to think hard about taking that step. If we moved for a stay put order within the court, our children would end up in a program where the staff had been less than receptive to the consultation. Did we really want them to stay at this program, and in this district, with these same people in charge? We would always be at the mercy of the district, which could discontinue the program at any time.

Or, he asked, did we want them out of the district and in a program that would provide them with the type of teaching we had been asking for? Of course we wanted the latter. But we learned we were unprepared for the sacrifices that we would have to endure to make it happen.

Herb spelled out the strategy he wanted us to follow. First, we needed to discontinue the home program. I didn't understand how he could ask us to do this. This was the only part of their education where Alanna and Austin were making progress. But Herb explained that we needed to show that the district's program on its own was not appropriate. The children would continue to show positive outcomes if the home program continued, and the district would take credit for that progress. It didn't matter if we had data and documents that indicated otherwise. He wanted us to understand that we had to prove beyond any doubt that the Brick Township School District was not helping our children. So we followed his recommendations. Had anyone told me how long it would take, I never would have agreed.

During the summer of 1996, Alanna and Austin continued to go to the program at Lanes Mills School. At home, they received no therapy. We watched Alanna regress. Without the home program, she quickly began to lose the language she had started to develop. Although she had unusual play habits, she at least had habits, but like her language these faded too. Each day after school she would sit in the corner of our dining room. As the days passed, the items that she brought with her would grow. Eventually she would bring all of her stuffed animals and a blanket, and then she would hide under the blanket. She stayed there unless forced to come out or when it was time for dinner, a bath, or bed. I took a picture every day to document her regression. Each time I clicked the shutter I would cry. I understood the process of trying to win a case. What I couldn't understand was why *this* was necessary.

I'm losing her, I thought.

Because Alanna was now five years old, she aged out of the preschool disabled program. Starting in September, she would attend a program at the Drum Point School. Austin would remain in Mrs. Ramirez's class, though the class had moved to a new building. Alanna had to adjust to a new classroom, new staff, and new students. Her new school psychologist was Dr. Alan Hoffman, the husband of Alanna's new classroom teacher Linda Hoffman. We met with Dr. Hoffman as part of the re-evaluation process. I expressed my concern for Alanna and her recent regression, specifically in the area of language. Dr. Hoffman said, "Maybe it's selective mutism." I lost it. "Selective mutism? What are you talking about? She has autism, and she was starting to speak and now she isn't. There is nothing selective about this. The program she is in is causing her to regress." How could I possibly expect him to own up to the fact that his wife's classroom was failing my daughter? Dr. Hoffman disagreed, of course, and he assured me that he could be unbiased when assessing Alanna.

Back in Mrs. Ramirez's program, Austin challenged the staff and was not progressing. I scheduled appointments to observe him. In the new building, the school had built a "viewing window" for parents and others to watch the class through. During one of these observations I saw Austin work in the cubby area directly beneath the window. Mrs. Ramirez stood with me to explain what the staff member was doing. I watched as Austin struggled to respond to simple one-step commands like "clap your hands." He refused to match letters of the alphabet, yet at home he would type letters on the computer. His ability to type had been evident at a young age. At first glance the documents would look like word search puzzles. But closer inspection would reveal that he had placed the titles of movies or characters he enjoyed amongst the letters. He would fill up multiple pages with lines that looked like this:

AGFTEUTJU***WINNIETHEPOOH***LMBUYV
LQRSOLMXUI***MUPPETS***HERSIKJRUASE

Austin wouldn't complete the task at hand, so the speech therapist, Debbie, stepped in and brought out an ABC puzzle. Austin flopped to the floor, and Debbie tried to wrestle his stiff body back into the chair. Eventually she gave up, left him on the floor, and brought the puzzle to him. Once it was on the floor, Austin completed the puzzle with much prompting from Debbie. Mrs. Ramirez was so pleased. I couldn't muster up the courage to tell her just how awful I thought this program was. I thought she would become defensive if I told her that many of the common errors of ABA programs highlighted in the trainings we had gone to were occurring in her classroom. I treaded lightly, I had to leave my son in her care. I worried that if I told her what I really thought, she would somehow take it out on Austin when she got back in the classroom. Instead, I told her I disagreed that he was making progress and I didn't understand why she wouldn't take the advice of the consultants. She tried to defend her stance and told me that what she did was similar to what the consultants showed her. She claimed that ABA can be interpreted differently but still be effective. I just wanted out of that viewing area, and I desperately wanted my children away from those people.

During the next four months we went through the motions as instructed by our attorney. We met with school administrators, teachers, and experts. We documented everything. We placed all our faith in what we believed to be right for our children. All the while we watched them regress and felt painfully helpless.

Kristen DeRossa was leaving the school district and we were assigned a new case manager, Ellen Luminas. She read the entire history of our case and reviewed all the reports from the experts. She met with us and attempted to understand our position. Ellen contacted Mary Cooper and worked out an amazing alternative.

Ellen had us meet her at Mrs. Cooper's office. She told us Mrs. Cooper would be willing to provide the children with a program in an old dorm room on the Wilson School campus. At first we were a bit confused. Ellen explained, "We are going to give you a home program, but here in this building." The children would have to travel over an hour away from home, but at this time Alanna was already on the bus for forty-five minutes anyway. An hour of travel to get the program we wanted, or keep them close to home in a program that was a disaster? We didn't have to think twice.

In January of 1997 Alanna and Austin started school at the Wilson School's Outreach building. They had staff trained in ABA, Joanie Hurst as the lead teacher, and Mary Cooper right down the hall if anyone needed advice or support.

We had a meeting to discuss the IEP goals. The attendees explained their backgrounds and the roles they would play in Alanna's and Austin's education. I couldn't help but notice the contrast to what we had heard in previous IEP meetings. For the first time, I was in a room filled with people who knew what Alanna and Austin needed. For the first time, people were telling me how they were joining forces with us to make a change in our children's lives. That night, for the first time in a long time, I slept without worry of what the next day would bring.

Inconclusive by Design

January 1997 to April 2000

Our children were finally settled in a program with practitioners who would do all they could to help them. You might think this would finally be a time for us to rest. But ever since Austin's diagnosis, I couldn't help but wonder how we ended up with two children with autism, a condition we had never heard of before. There was no family history of anything even close. Most of the experts and doctors we spoke to also pointed out how unusual it was. And the comment from the woman at COSAC kept playing in my head: "What's going on in Brick?" I needed to know why or how this happened. If this was genetic, Shaun and Chelsea deserved to know. If this was environmental or had some other cause, everyone deserved to know.

In February of 1997 I attended a POAC parent support group meeting. The group met monthly in a small room above a thrift store in Point Pleasant. This month yet more moms of newly diagnosed children were in attendance. My friend Angela and I could not help but wonder how many more of us there were. The parents who started this group had children a bit older than ours, and they told us stories of how limited services were when their children were young. In order to fill a classroom of six, the Brick School District had to bring in children from other towns like Point Pleasant and Seaside. Angela and I looked at each other in surprise. "They have no problem filling up the classes now," I said. "They are even sending children out of district to private placements. Why do you think there are so many?" Some speculated that word had spread that Brick offered programs for children with autism and people were moving here to take advantage of them. But I didn't move here for the programs. Neither did Angela. None of the families that had come to our home from Mrs. Ramirez's class had moved here for the programs. Our children were all born here.

I needed answers. Were families moving here, or were these children born here? If they were born here, was it so farfetched to think that something environmental was causing the autism? The town next to us was fighting to stop a rare form of cancer that was plaguing their children. Why couldn't autism also have an environmental cause?

I developed a survey. It wasn't anything scientific, just some basic questions: Do you have a child with autism? When is his/her birthday? Where did you live when your child was born?

We handed the survey out to parents we knew and asked that they forward it to anyone who might participate. We asked the Brick school district to distribute the survey to families by placing it in the children's backpacks. The district refused, even though other organizations often sent home flyers in our children's backpacks. They cited some regulation, but when we asked to see a copy of the regulation it was never supplied.

Support from others helped us get the word out. One mom copied the survey, got onto her son's bus, and placed it in the backpacks of every student going to the private school her son attended. But others tried to squash our pursuit. Angela placed copies in the community bulletin section of the local library. Each time she went back to refill the bin she would see that they had been moved from the top center spot to the bottom, sometimes even behind other documents. Each time, she moved them back.

I don't know what I expected, but my excitement grew each day I went to the mailbox. I wasn't excited to see that there were more children with autism than we ever could have imagined, but it appeared we might be onto something that would lead to answers. Forty-two families answered the survey, and thirty of them had children born in Brick between 1990 and 1995. Thirty children in five years that we knew of, how many more could there be? I just knew I had to do something with this information. I knew it was going to lead to some answers. I called COSAC and asked them where to turn. They told me to call NAAR, the National Alliance for Autism Research.

Dr. Eric London from NAAR took my call very seriously. He asked me several questions about how I had gathered this information, then offered to come meet and discuss what we might be able to do with the results. We placed an ad in the local paper to announce the meeting.

In July of 1997 Brick POSSE held a meeting at the same library that hid our surveys. Sixty-three people attended, most were parents of children with autism. Some had answered our survey, some were just now finding out about why we were gathered. There were a few local officials who tried to blend in, but when three men in suits sit together in a single row, they tend to stand out in a room of people wearing the typical mom and dad uniform.

Dr. London brought two scientists, Micki Bresnahan and Dr. Craig Newschaffer, to the meeting. Ms. Bresnahan opened by describing how difficult it can be to move forward with any type of investigation. Funding was needed to start any project, especially one of this size. Although some recent studies had been conducted, the cause of autism was a very new topic in the world of epidemiology and research. When I explained that Toms River, the town just next door, was receiving money from the government to investigate a childhood cancer study, she said, "cancer is sexy in the world of science." An odd choice of words, but we understood what she meant. Cancer got the big bucks because there was big interest and big money in finding a cure.

By the end of the evening, Dr. London, Dr. Newschaffer, and Ms. Bresnahan had helped us prioritize our next steps. Dr. Newschaffer would schedule a meeting with the New Jersey State Department of Health (DOH), and Billy and I planned to present our information to Congressman Chris Smith. It just happened that these appointments fell on the same day. There was a chance we actually might have enough information to move this to the next level. I couldn't sleep a wink; I just knew we were onto something huge.

Congressman Chris Smith greeted us and asked us to join him at a small round table inside his office. He listened intently as Billy and I explained all that we had done in the past few months. He suggested bringing this information to the New Jersey DOH. We explained the support we had from NAAR and told him that Dr. Newschaffer was at the DOH that very minute. We were hopeful the doctor would emerge with a positive response from them, but we wanted to know we had the congressman's support just in case the state didn't agree to help. Congressman Smith assured us that he would investigate this further and reach out to the DOH to see what the next steps would be.

Dr. Newschaffer contacted us later that day to let us know the DOH had punted us to a higher level. They did not feel equipped to complete such a study and recommended that the National Institutes of Health (NIH) be brought in. Congressman Smith got the same response. Billy and I were ecstatic. A congressman had taken the story of a commercial fisherman and a housewife and not only listened, but did something about it.

On April 1, 1998 we were on our way to the United States Capitol in Washington, D.C. Senator Robert Marrone and Congressman Smith had arranged a meeting at Senator Marrone's office to discuss the next steps in the investigation. On our drive down to D.C. Billy and I prepared ourselves to fight if necessary. When we arrived at Senator Marrone's door we were told that the senator wanted to meet with us separately first, so we were escorted to a reception area outside a prestigious office. Meanwhile, Congressman Smith was brought to a conference room. Senator Marrone stepped out of the office, shook our hands, then turned and led us into the conference room. Meet us? He barely heard our names before he gestured for us to follow him. The senator simply wanted a staged entrance into the conference room where everyone had been waiting.

We opened the double doors and entered a room filled with people. Not everyone could fit at the table; some of the representatives had to sit against the wall. It was hard not to feel small in a room of this size, in a building of this importance, surrounded by a senator, a congressman, representatives from the NIH, the Agency for Toxic Substance and Disease Registry (ATSDR), and the Centers for Disease Control and Prevention (CDC), and someone standing in for New Jersey Governor Christie Whitman. The title "doctor" was announced more frequently than not. Some of the attendees were wearing military uniforms. To say I was in awe would be an understatement.

When it was time for Billy and I to introduce ourselves, all I could get out was, "I'm Bobbie Gallagher, from Brick." I had no title to offer, no background or area of study. I often went by "Chelsea's mom."

Dr. Bruce Johnson from the NIH explained that after review of the information, they had decided to call on the CDC and the ATSDR to conduct the investigation. The CDC was already conducting an epidemiological study of autism in the counties surrounding Atlanta, Georgia. They had the blueprint for how to move forward. We were each given a folder that spelled out the two agencies' upcoming involvement in the investigation of a cluster of children with autism in the Brick Township area. If I could have high-fived my husband I would have, but I was trying to appear professional. We had made it to the big leagues, and these people were listening to us.

The months that followed were filled with interesting moments. Being new players in the game of politics, we were in for a rude awakening. Representatives of the federal government had arrived to investigate the number of children with autism in our town. One of their first meetings was with our mayor, Joseph Carcere. We were invited to attend and were told it was intended as a courtesy to the mayor. They would explain the intentions of the federal agencies and get the mayor's take on the matter before proceeding with the study.

The mayor welcomed us, Senator Marrone, Congressman Smith, and a few representatives from the CDC and the ATSDR into a large paneled room. He expressed some hesitation about this investigation starting in his town. We tried to explain all that we already knew, but Mayor Carcere was worried that the situation would be similar to the childhood cancer investigation in Toms River, and that people would leave the town as fast as they could. My blood pressure climbed as I silently raged, "*That's* what you're worried about? Not about the number of children? About even one child? You want to make sure that the property values remain at their current level?"

Maybe his real fear was that the investigation would reveal the part he played in decreasing the requirements set by the Environmental Protection Agency for the superfund site in our town. Instead of putting a cement cap on the entire chemically contaminated property, he negotiated the requirements down to two feet of sand. How was sand going to keep the toxins out of our ground water? According to news articles, he was proud of himself for saving the taxpayers ten million dollars. That wouldn't be such a savings if we found out that it contributed to the rise in autism here.

The conversation moved to the topic of accessing school records to help identify children with autism. Mayor Carcere disagreed with the practice and insisted that families grant permission first. One of the CDC representatives explained to him, "We aren't asking you, we're telling you." When the CDC does a study to investigate a cluster it is a health concern for everyone in the area. They do not need permission to review public records.

Several more meetings were held with local politicians to ensure they had adequate information to share if they got calls from constituents. Once all of those preliminary meetings were complete, we were able to announce the plan to the general public.

On January 19, 1999 the CDC and the ATSDR held a press conference at the Brick Township High School to announce their investigation into a possible cluster of children with autism in Brick. The turnout was good, but not great. There were reporters from local and national papers, most importantly the Associated Press was there.

The CDC representatives described the format of the upcoming investigation. First, they would evaluate children who had received a diagnosis to ensure they met the criteria of autism. Families would be contacted and asked to participate. For those that chose not to, a determination would be made based on the child's school record. Next, they would conduct a research investigation into the possible environmental causes of autism. Last, they would evaluate potential sources of toxins in Brick Township and identify pathways through which harmful materials might reach the families of children with autism. The CDC representatives closed the meeting by taking questions from the audience regarding possible environmental causes in Brick and whether vaccines played a part.

It would have been nice if someone from one of the government agencies gave us a hint about what to expect after the Associated Press ran an article about the announcement. We were thrown into a media whirlwind. The next morning there were three news vans outside our home and telephone calls coming in from many other media outlets. They all wanted to interview the family who started this investigation. Unfortunately, we approached this responsibility naïvely. We thought the best thing we could do was to agree to the interviews. In some way, we felt it was our duty. We had started this, and we needed to talk about it to ensure that the information got out there. We needed the national attention that could help provide the funding Congressman Smith was working to secure. But we underestimated the strong desire for salacious sound bites and the editing process used to achieve them.

Chelsea was home from school and decided to act as our agent. She took down names and gave each news crew a time slot for their interview. She could often be found in the dining room entertaining one station's crew while we were being interviewed by another in the living room. It was amazing how, at the age of nine, she simply rolled with the events. She was not at all impressed that CBS News with Dan Rather or Good Morning America was in our home. To her this was simply an audience of adults to impress with her organizational skills and her remarkable maturity.

Some of the crews were incredibly gracious when we opened up our home to them. Others acted as though we were inconveniencing them by not permitting unlimited access to our children. One crew fought with another over who had gotten there first. Some eavesdropped on the interviews to hear the other reporters' questions. We had salsa and chips for dinner because there was no time to shop or cook, and certainly no time to eat. The next day there were more of them. Billy had to go to work and I had to get the children ready for their bus, but the reporters were waiting for us in the front yard.

We would watch each piece when it aired. We quickly realized how out of our league we were. Responses were edited for sound bites. In one case, I was asked, "What do you think is the cause?" My full reply was, "We don't know. It could be the water, the air, anything. That is why we need this investigation. No one knows." But my response was edited to, "It could be the water." Another show introduced our family as having moved to Brick after Chelsea was born, which wasn't true. Chelsea was conceived and born in the same home as her siblings. Yet another cut Chelsea out of a family vacation photo entirely and only spoke of our two children with autism. That one hurt when Chelsea saw it. She wanted to know why it had happened, which was difficult to explain to a nine-year-old who had been deeply involved in this process. She deserved to be mentioned. All of this affected her as well.

CDC and ATSDR personnel were also interviewed. The news pieces would typically include a combination of sound bites from us and from one of the agencies in attendance, as well as someone from the town disputing any chance that there was a problem. The news crews managed to find a few parents of children with autism to go on record saying they didn't feel there could be an environmental cause, in particular Bob Riccardi and Carrie Riley. It seemed that whatever show we did, Bob and Carrie were either featured in the same piece or in one aired the next day. Bob had two sons, one with autism, and Carrie had two children with autism. Both made a point to say that they did not believe in an environmental cause. They thought we were just stirring up hysteria, but they never explained why they thought that was our agenda. What could we have gotten out of stirring up hysteria? Why would federal agencies listen to us if this wasn't truly a concern? Did Bob and Carrie really think the NIH, the CDC, and the ATSDR needed Billy and Bobbie Gallagher's attention?

But we had support from local parents as well. Angela and Kevin Fryczynski interviewed with us. They too wanted answers about autism and what was going on in our town. They had purposefully moved to Brick to own a home and start a family in an area away from the city. Now they questioned whether they had made the right decision.

Phone calls came from across the nation. Some were from people offering support. Others wanted to share their opinions about the cause of autism. Many felt we should be suspicious of childhood vaccines. We did not receive a single call that was derogatory, but we did get a few that were interesting. A man claiming to be a priest from upstate New York informed me that my children were possessed and offered to perform an exorcism. "My children are a blessing," I replied. Another call came from a psychic who claimed there was a "black cloud over Brick Town." She said she knew this was going to happen, just like she had known the Kennedy assassination was going to happen. She also claimed that she had been abducted by aliens when she was younger. If nothing else, she provided me with a good chuckle from time to time when I remembered her call.

The media hype eventually died down, like all breaking news stories do. We had one last major interview with Nightline in March. They could not have been more kind and even provided us with information to use if we found ourselves in this same situation in the future. The reporter explained that we could ask that one station do the "B roll," or shooting of extra footage, and provide it to all the others. This would at least give us some control over what was used. He also explained that he was only telling us this after he got his own footage, of course.

During the next year there was the occasional interview request from a local studio or newspaper that wanted to portray a local family in an Autism Awareness spot. Billy and I recognized that we had put ourselves out there for the media and that there might be repercussions, but we also knew that many families were unwilling to be the focus. "How could the autism community make change," I thought, "if no one wants to be the face of that change?" Each time we were interviewed, Bob and Carrie would be featured right behind us. It was unclear why they felt so adamant about stressing that it wasn't the environment. How did scientifically investigating the possible link between autism and the environment become some sort of personal agenda for them to stop? Carrie said she had a brother with autistic symptoms and therefore she believed it was genetic. Bob had no idea, and even mentioned in one interview, "it could be something the mother ingested," without understanding that meant the cause could be environmental. If it turned out their children's autism was caused by genetics or something else, fine. Why try to hinder this investigation?

Regardless of anyone's opinion, the investigation began. Each child identified by the CDC was evaluated to ensure they met the requirements for a diagnosis of autism. Dr. Jacqueline Vago and Dr. Audrey Jupiter conducted the reviews, and Alanna and Austin were the first children to be evaluated at the Ocean County Health Department. The other children's evaluations would be conducted over the next several months, with Dr. Vago traveling to New Jersey a few days each month until they were completed. By the end of the evaluations, sixty of the seventy-five identified children were confirmed to have autism according to the process used by Dr. Vago and Dr. Jupiter.

ATSDR conducted their portion of the investigation by looking into pathways by which toxins may have reached families. They were specifically interested in whether mothers had ingested any toxins during their twentieth to twenty-fourth days of pregnancy. The hypothesis was based on the research of Dr. Patricia Rodier, which showed a link between the presence of toxins during those five days of gestation and injury to the brain leading to autism.

On April 18, 2000, two years after our visit to the United States Capitol, the CDC returned to Brick Township ready to announce their findings. But the events leading up to this day were odd. We had already been informed that the study was completed, but several members of the CDC let us know that there were delays in publishing the results due to a review of the study by those in charge. One explanation for the hold-up was that Donna Agene, the United States Secretary of Health and Human Services, had issues over the wording in the document. We were told there was dispute over using the word "high" to describe the number of children with autism in our town; apparently Dr. Agene did not want the word "high" included in the document. When I questioned whether that meant they were trying to change the numbers, I was assured that the data would not be altered. However, "Hillary [Clinton] is deciding on a run for Senate in New York, and you know how political these things can get," Dr. Vago said. But I didn't have a clue what she meant by that. What did Hillary's run for Senate have to do with announcing the results of this study? Eventually the word "high" would be revised to "elevated." We would later discover that the numbers weren't changed, but they were certainly manipulated.

When the day finally arrived, the professionals involved in the study came to our home to present the results. Some of them we recognized, like Frank Lotta and Robert Knappe of ATSDR, and Christine Doyle of CDC, having worked with them over the past two years. Some we had never seen before. We would later learn that the new faces were the agencies' damage control team. The representatives we knew acknowledged that they wanted us to hear the news first, and asked if we would refrain from any interviews until after they could announce the information to the public. The numbers were much higher than we had imagined. At this time the national numbers were thought to be one in five hundred. Brick had a ratio of nearly one in eighty-eight children with autism. I'm not sure who spoke after that, I became somewhat numb. I remember someone mentioning that we had more children with classic autism than would be expected as well. Traditionally, when data were calculated in similar studies, children at the higher end of the spectrum, or those with Asperger's, were typically the ones that led to the higher rates. That was not the case here in Brick.

That evening we attended the press conference at the town hall. The federal agencies decided to break the delivery of the news into two sessions: one two-hour session for news media, and one two-hour session for the community. We attended the one for the community, Billy and I arriving separately due to babysitting challenges. Long tables lined the perimeter of the room, and behind each one was a representative from one of the federal agencies and one damage control person. There were two documents available to read, one from the ATSDR titled *Public Health Assessment, Brick Township Investigation*, and one from the CDC titled *Prevalence of Autism in Brick Township, New Jersey, 1998: Community Report Centers for Disease Control and Prevention April 2000*. I grabbed a copy of each and started to say hello to friends and acquaintances in the audience.

Giacomo's dad, Giacomo Sr., tapped me on the shoulder. He gave me a big hug and a kiss, and said, "This is all you, you did it." At first I didn't recognize him, and was taken aback. I hadn't seen or heard from him since the DYFS investigation of the teacher who sat on his son. When I realized who he was, I grabbed him and hugged him harder. I wanted to know what had happened, where Giacomo was, what they were doing. I had so many questions. He told me they were offered an out-of-district placement at a private school for children with autism. He apologized for not contacting us and for not staying involved with the parent group. He went on to explain that his son got the placement with the stipulation that he be quiet and remove himself from Brick POSSE. I couldn't be mad at him. His son was getting the services he needed, and his priority at that moment had to be his child. We hugged again, this time with a complete understanding of why it had been so long since we last saw each other.

As I mingled with the different families and caught up on where everyone's children were, I saw that it was nearing eight o'clock. I went up to the front and asked, "When is the presentation going to begin? People are starting to leave." I was informed that there was no formal presentation. I could take this opportunity to read the two documents presented, and if I had any questions the federal representatives were there to answer them. I could not have been more confused by this presentation, or lack of presentation, of the information. They expected people to arrive between six and eight o'clock at night, read two long technical documents, and approach the federal representatives if they had questions? On the walls of the room were eight-by-eleven graphs to represent the findings, so small you had to stand right next to them to see them. Where was the projector? Where was the formal Q & A session? What were they doing?

They didn't even announce the format for the evening, you were only told about the plan if you asked. Many families were sitting in the audience waiting for the press conference to begin.

Some people began to line up at the tables. When someone would ask a question that was too explosive, the damage control team would take that person aside. One mother asked why she wasn't contacted. Her child was born in this town. She tried to contact Dr. Vago with questions, but never received a return call. She was removed from the line by a member of the damage control team. The next person in line got to ask his questions.

This format permitted them to control the information and keep the families from feeding off of each other's questions. It was crowd control and information control. By not allowing attendees to ask questions publicly, no one got to hear the concerns others had about the study.

I was approached by a reporter who had been at town hall since the afternoon presentation. She informed me that the information was presented to the media in the same format. Reporters who require the short and sweet approach for delivering the news were expected to read these documents and come up with questions for the professionals. She said this was "the oddest press conference" she had ever been to. She asked me a few questions, but I was at a loss for words and my mind was not on the interview. I was looking for Billy. I was trying to figure out what was going to happen next. I saw the people from the CDC and the ATSDR begin to pack up. They were leaving to catch a flight, they explained. I had so many questions, and they were gone.

The eight-by-eleven graphs were left on the walls. The government officials had left the room. It was over, and little did I know at the time just how over it was. Billy and I reviewed the publications, the graphs, and the numbers. The numbers did not match up with those discussed at our home. The documents given out at the press conference said the prevalence of autism in Brick was one in one hundred and sixty six, very different than the ratio of one in eighty-eight that we had been told. Something wasn't right. As we continued to read, we began to realize how little of an "investigation" was actually performed. I called Dr. Vago. I left messages for everyone we had contact information for. I never received a return call.

Billy and I were unaware of how little was actually investigated in a cluster "investigation." We had set our hopes high, very high, only to learn that very little got done. The ATSDR had a long and fancy name—the Agency for Toxic Substance and Disease Registry—but it did not conduct a single scientific analysis of water, soil, or air. They did not test the water we used in our homes. To put this into perspective, in the neighboring town dealing with the cancer cluster, not only was the water tested, but they took dust samples from attics of the affected families and conducted air quality studies. In Brick, they only collected data from the local water company. Data the water company collects on its own water supply and sends to the state. Data created by the very source that may have caused the problem. That was the data the ATSDR chose to analyze.

Although the data showed periods of time when our water supply had elevated levels of toxins known to cause harm, the researchers could not prove those toxins reached mothers during that five-day period of gestation. Therefore, the results were labeled *inconclusive.*

The CDC did not take a single sample of blood from any of the parents or children to see if the identified toxins were in our bodies. They said it was too late because it would have happened years ago. Besides, they only analyzed existing data, they didn't do testing. So that was the extent of the investigation. They evaluated the children to determine if they had autism, and they analyzed data provided to them by one of many possible sources under investigation. They barely scratched the surface of what needed to be done.

Seriously? All they had done was identify that Brick Township had a higher rate of children with autism than expected, with more cases of classic autism than typically seen in other studies. But we didn't get any answers to our questions. Were these toxins still in our bodies? Were they still in our water? If we drank them years ago, do they remain with us? Will they cause us to have more children with autism? What about the siblings when they want to have children? We would never get the answers to our questions.

Billy and I had put ourselves out there, hoped and prayed for answers, and all we ended up with was a report that stated the results were inconclusive. How can you say something is inconclusive when you haven't really looked for answers and narrowed the possibilities until it's impossible to find a cause? They tried to link the specific dates that toxins in the water were high to specific dates of gestation of the mothers in our town. But they wouldn't check whether those toxins were still in our bodies. They wouldn't show us the research about how long those toxins remain with a person.

We would later be contacted by an organization called Physicians for Social Responsibility. They sent us a booklet titled *INCONCLUSIVE BY DESIGN: Waste, Fraud and Abuse in Federal Environmental Health Research, An Investigative Study by the Environmental Health Network and the National Toxics Campaign Fund.* This interesting document explained how answers are never found in public investigations such as this; instead, there is usually an attempt to squash fear and reassure the public that all is well.

All was not well, and it was time for us to focus on the needs of our own.

Moving Forward?

April 2000 to September 2001

With the cluster study behind us, it was time for us to focus on our family. I had returned to school and needed to concentrate on my studies. Alanna was doing beautifully at the Wilson School, so well that there was discussion of what the next move might be for her. By this time, the small program that Alanna and Austin started in an old dorm room on the Wilson campus was beginning to look more like a classroom. The school opened another dorm room with two new students. One was Kevin Fryczynski, whose family also fought the Brick school district for appropriate services. As spots opened at the main school on the campus each year, the children from the little dorm room program would be considered. The school was always looking for the right fit to ensure a positive experience for all.

Kevin was eventually accepted to the main building and a new student filled his slot at the Outreach building with Alanna and Austin. At our next IEP meeting, everyone agreed that Alanna had outgrown the environment. She was requesting items, talking in sentences, and making strides in academics. But the big question was, where would we put her? The Brick school district didn't really have any options. She didn't meet the requirements of someone who could be fully included in general education classes, but she didn't need the intensity of a self-contained special education program.

We considered placing Alanna at Lakeside, the small private school Chelsea attended. At the start of the new school year in September, the second grade classroom was going to have only five children. Everyone agreed this might be an appropriate option. Alanna would have a small class size with typical peers, her own aide provided by the Wilson School, and the opportunity to learn in individual sessions when necessary. Although it sounded wonderful, our case manager Ellen Luminas wasn't sure if this could be arranged because there were so many regulations involved. I investigated further and found the NAPLES Act, legislation that permits placement of special education students in private schools.

So in September of 2000, Alanna started school as a second-grader at the Lakeside School in Sea Girt, New Jersey. She rode the same bus as Chelsea. Mr. Bill Wall, the principal, sent a letter home to all the parents in the school. Some might say this wasn't necessary, or that it singled out Alanna. I think he did the right thing. In his letter, Mr. Wall explained to the parents that the school had accepted a child with autism, and that their children may have some questions. He assured them that Alanna would have the support needed to be educated in the second-grade classroom. He explained that he felt this was a learning opportunity for all, and he hoped that Alanna would learn as much from the staff and students of the Lakeside School as he was sure they would all learn from her. His letter was so touching it brought tears to my eyes.

The attitude of the administration and the wonderful staff were major factors in Alanna's success at Lakeside. Joanie was asked to supervise the program and made regular visits. Jean Harper, a paraprofessional from the Wilson School, became Alanna's personal educational aide and was by her side every day. The other students in the classroom were incredibly accepting.

We worried if this would be detrimental to Chelsea. She had been attending Lakeside for several years, and now she was going to have her sister there with her. We weren't sure how this would impact her. Initially she received many questions from students and staff alike. Over time those questions subsided and Chelsea simply became the older sister, just like she would have been if they attended public school together.

As the months went on, any remaining hesitation about Alanna's placement at Lakeside dwindled. Alanna struggled with some of the textbook information, but she was a part of the class and at times she would surpass expectations. We learned she had phenomenal rote memorization skills. Alanna excelled when the class had to memorize the state capitals, so much so that the other students would wait to hear Alanna's answers when the test was administered. The teacher would ask, "What's the capital of Florida?" The students were supposed to write their answers on a piece of paper. Alanna would comply with the writing, but she also had a tendency to say the answer out loud, "Tallahassee." She did the same during spelling tests. Eventually, much to the other students' disappointment, Alanna was moved to the hallway during tests.

The classroom teacher, Mrs. Margaret O'Reilly, mentioned that the other students were impressed and sometimes challenged when Alanna knew more than them. I liked to think it helped them see that she was more than her disability. When they played sports outside during gym, Alanna was never one to volunteer; she needed coaching to get her to participate. The other students would not allow her to sit and hide. They pulled on her, encouraged her, and insisted she stay with them both physically and mentally.

During recess the girls in the class would always include Alanna, and her best friend Kayla taught her how to play "Miss Mary Mack." She was not successful in teaching Alanna to do a cartwheel, but she kept trying. Alanna went to birthday parties and had sleepovers. She was included and accepted as much as we could have ever hoped. A young man in the class, Corey, approached Chelsea and asked, "Will Alanna always have autism?" Chelsea responded, "Yes, but she will get better and talk more." The seven-year-old boy announced, "Ok, then I will marry her."

Austin was still going to school in the old dorm room across from the main school at Wilson. Now that Alanna was gone, her spot was filled with a new student, Tony. Tony was much younger, barely three years old. Another September had come and gone and Austin did not make it into any openings at the main school. Joanie was no longer the teacher, and we had gone through a few other staff changes.

Austin did not progress as quickly within the program as his sister had. I could see that he often did not understand what was being asked of him, and that he relied mainly on the visual cues in his world to interpret what was expected. For example, if you placed colored blocks on the table, he would immediately begin to stack them without waiting for instructions. But he could not sort the blocks by color. However, he could sort plastic teddy bears by color because he had been taught to do so. Because Austin was first taught to build with blocks and sort with bears, to him that was all those items could be used for. He was not able to follow verbal requests to switch it up. When staff attempted to step in and explain, he would become agitated.

There was considerable repetition in the presentation of his teaching materials. Staff were instructed to teach each lesson ten times in a row, also called mass trials. They asked Austin to complete the same task ten times consecutively, such as placing pictures on the desk and asking him to "touch the dog, touch the dog, touch the dog, etc." Regardless of whether his response was correct or incorrect, he would be asked again and again until the 10 trials were complete. Then the staff would calculate the number of correct answers. If he recognized the dog eight out of the ten times, he would get an eighty percent marked on his data sheet. In order for him to move beyond touching the picture of the dog, he would have to score at least ninety percent for three consecutive sessions. Eventually, we all agreed that this format was not effective. After watching videos of the teaching sessions we could see that he was right more often than not at the beginning of each session. This indicated that the repetition either caused him confusion or boredom and he just wasn't attending when he responded. The teacher instructed the staff to change the format and use less repetition.

No matter what we tried, Austin never progressed at a rate that seemed appropriate. I was told that he was a "slow learner," or given some other reason associated with his level of functioning. I simply didn't believe this was true. I always remembered my friend Claire saying, "You can see it in his eyes. They are so clear, you just know there is intelligence in there that we're not tapping." I believed that. Austin had figured out the PECS system to communicate, and he had moved on to an augmentative communication device called a Dynavox. He would touch a picture on the screen of the device and it would say the word for him, letting others know what he needed. He learned how to navigate through folders of pictures on the Dynavox to get his needs met. He could type and play computer games that involved spelling words.

But he wouldn't do the tasks we needed him to do. Somehow we were still not tapping into his learning style sufficiently. If we couldn't do that, how would he learn? What was it that *we* needed to learn?

The local POAC parent support group, run at that time by Bob Riccardi and Carrie Riley, had grown to provide trainings to parents and professionals. Fences had been mended between us. We were all on a mission to find better services for our children. Early in 2001, POAC held a conference at a local college with a speaker who brought some insight to the challenges we were facing with Austin. Dr. Vincent Slimetti, a Board Certified Behavior Analyst (BCBA), presented strategies to encourage verbal behavior or language from learners with autism. Dr. Slimetti was a small man who, from the scars on his face, looked to have suffered from acne as a teenager. He had a New Yorker's in-your-face approach to naysayers. He presented information in a charismatic manner that got people to listen, especially parents who were hungry for results for their children. Based on the videos he used during his presentations, he was getting those results.

After an initial workshop, Billy and I were convinced that the strategies discussed in the presentations held some answers for Austin. Dr. Slimetti talked about removing the use of repetition and how this could lead to behavioral challenges. He was speaking our language and we were soaking it all up. All the reasons why a child might struggle with a traditional approach to ABA teaching were being explained to us, and the solutions seemed easy.

It was nearing time for Austin's annual IEP, and he was passed over for an opening at the main building yet again. New students had been enrolled for the upcoming summer months in the Outreach program, and all of them were under the age of 5. Austin was 9 years old, and everyone was in agreement that he had surpassed what could be offered to him in this setting. Ellen Luminas asked if Lakeside would be an appropriate place for Austin, like it had been for Alanna. But Austin was so different from his sister. He would need more one-to-one sessions in a quiet area and less time in the classroom, but it was worth exploring.

Lakeside was willing to give us a chance. There was a small private room behind the nurse's office that could be used for the one-to-one sessions. The second grade classroom was slightly larger than the group Alanna had started out in, but everyone was flexible and up for the challenge. There were going to be some other changes as well. Jean Harper was now going to supervise Austin's program while still being the support person for Alanna. Alanna needed less moment-to-moment supports by now, and Jean could use some of the downtime to help Austin's paraprofessional, Heather Kaminski. When Jean first started with Alanna, she had a long history of working with both of our children at Wilson. Heather had not met Austin until her first day of work.

Over the summer months, Jean attended some of Dr. Slimetti's workshops with us. We really wanted everyone to be on the same page moving forward. Jean had been working at schools for children with autism for so long that switching gears to a new way of thinking was a challenge for her. The comments Dr. Slimetti made regarding how children had been taught in the past, and the manner in which he presented them, did not help professionals like Jean warm to his message. Jean also felt she was already being effective because she had a good track record. Why would she change? The professionals at Wilson were also challenging these new approaches, and Jean certainly needed to follow the advice of her supervisors. In retrospect, I don't think Billy and I had our eyes open to the number of discrepancies, and we were under the wrong impression that everyone was in agreement on how to move forward with our children's education.

In September 2001 Austin started at Lakeside School. All three children now took the same bus in the morning. I can still remember seeing Chelsea sitting with her brother and thinking to myself, "I never thought I'd see the day that all three of my children would be at the same school." I was so excited about this new adventure. I was almost finished with my bachelor's degree at Monmouth University. My children were all in the same school, soon I would get a job, and Billy would finally be able to be home more. In no time we were going to be as close to a "normal" family as we could be.

We were all moving forward, or so we thought.

November 2001 to May 2002

Billy and I continued to attend Dr. Slimetti's presentations whenever he was local. We wanted to learn all we could about teaching our children. In November 2001 we hired one of Dr. Slimetti's associates, Bethany Pratt. Bethany was a Board Certified Assistant Behavior Analyst who taught children with autism using the strategies Dr. Slimetti demonstrated in his presentations. We asked Bethany to come to the Lakeside School, review the programs designed for our children, and provide her opinion on what we could improve. But Billy and I did not think this plan through sufficiently. We were so focused on what Alanna and Austin needed that we did not see how this could be perceived as a threat to Jean, who had been teaching our children for the past three years, here at Lakeside and previously at Wilson. Bethany thought everyone was on board with making changes to the children's programs. Billy and I failed to consider whether Jean would actually want this input.

Prior to Bethany's consultation, Austin's teacher Heather had started to become afraid of him. He was biting his own hands up to fifty times a day, and the reason wasn't always known. He made a loud "eee, eee, eee," sound during the biting. When he was angry, he would bite his hands and move in the direction of the person he was angry with while making the sound. Heather was intimidated by this behavior. Austin was now also pinching and grabbing her when attempting to gain access to an item or get something out of her hands. Unfortunately, because of how she reacted following these aggressions, she inadvertently reinforced them.

For example, Austin often wanted to watch a VHS tape, regardless of the task at hand. He would physically try to reach the wall of tapes and Heather would attempt to block him, telling him he could watch one after he had completed the current task. He started to become aggressive toward Heather and caused much damage in the room, and out of fear she allowed him to choose a VHS tape. Eventually, Heather needed to avoid the room with the VHS tapes altogether to prevent aggressive behavior from Austin. But Austin knew where they were, and he would still attempt to access them. Because of Heather's attempts to avoid the room, his covert behaviors increased and he made increasingly aggressive attempts to get to those tapes.

Austin spent snack time with the second grade class. The children were wonderful to him. Two little girls would draw pictures for him and desperately wanted to interact with him. Heather had been instructed to convince Austin to share his snack with his classmates. This was not a good idea. Heather should have let Austin spend time with peers without having to give up a preferred food item, especially in exchange for someone else's snack. Austin did not understand the concept of sharing. He didn't see it as an even exchange, he saw it as giving up his favorite food to someone else. Austin began to engage in hand biting in this classroom as well, and eventually he attempted to get his cheese doodles back by pinching and grabbing Heather. Heather would quickly give them back to keep him from frightening the other children. There was some fear that Austin might hurt one of the children, and at the very least his self-injury was difficult for them to watch. So it was decided that he should remain in the small room where he received his one-to-one instruction.

The pattern grew: Heather blocked, Austin aggressed, Heather granted him access to preferred items or avoided situations altogether. All this shaped Austin's use of aggression to get what he wanted. He wanted to eat cheese doodles and watch VHS tapes away from everyone else.

Clearly, Austin was not doing well in his current program. We received reports of increasing rates of self-injurious behaviors. Within weeks he was biting himself more than three hundred times per day. He was spending more and more time in the small room behind the nurse's office, and much less outside of the room for fear of what he might do to himself or others with small children as witnesses. Heather was not equipped to know what to do without more supervision, and Jean was unable to divide her time as effectively as we had originally hoped. We thought bringing in a consultant would be helpful. As we watched Austin flounder, we became very insistent that Bethany's suggestions be followed immediately. But Heather did not have the training to understand how to implement the new guidance without more supervision.

Bethany also made some suggestions for changes to Alanna's program. We wanted to use the teaching strategies we learned at Dr. Slimetti's presentations to move Alanna away from rote memorization and try to teach her more information through concepts.

Dr. Slimetti stressed that to get a child to want to learn, you have to work with the child's motivation or desires. In the past, we had learned that getting a child's compliance was most important, because then we could drill them repetitively on the task we wished to teach. Dr. Slimetti showed us that if we could take advantage of Alanna's and Austin's motivations, we could get them to focus for longer periods during learning sessions. He also showed how information can be presented at a quicker pace and in a more varied manner to increase the child's interest while getting the same—if not better—learning results compared to repetitive drilling.

At home we were seeing positive results when we used some of these new teaching strategies. Alanna was learning more words and had more ways to describe what she saw. She was beginning to learn how to tell us about her day, something she had never done before. She began to speak in longer sentences, and most importantly, she was answering questions that didn't have a predetermined answer. In the past if you asked her, "What did you do today?" Alanna would answer, "Good," the rote response she had learned to the question, "How was your day?" After we started using strategies from Dr. Slimetti's workshops, she started to answer, "What did you do today?" with phrases like, "baseball, horses, writing," all activities she had engaged in during the day at school. They weren't full sentences, but they gave us some idea of the activities that made up Alanna's days.

Jean was not in agreement with changing the teaching style. She felt that Alanna best learned rotely. Billy and I agreed that she was able to memorize, but we were concerned that she was not able to use the information outside of the very specific situations where it was learned. Alanna could complete math worksheets at record speed because she saw the same worksheets every day. We wanted her to learn the concepts of math, not just memorize the problems on that worksheet.

Jean felt that an outside consultant was an intrusion, and her boss from Wilson, Mary Cooper, agreed. We tried to explain that we really wanted Bethany to help us train the staff. But Ms. Cooper put her foot down: her staff worked for Wilson, and Jean had attended the workshops by Dr. Slimetti at our request. Jean would implement Dr. Slimetti's strategies as she saw fit, but outside consultants would not be allowed to instruct her staff. Then, in February of 2002, Wilson pulled their staff for both of our children.

That was a very sad day for us. We had trusted our children to the professionals from Wilson for so many years, and now we had to look elsewhere for help. I quickly reached out to others in the field and found another company; Starbright Children's Center could supply us with a paraprofessional. It just so happened that a member of their staff had previously worked at Wilson with Alanna, so Jennifer Ruddy was able to pick up right where Jean had left off. But we had no one for Austin.

Austin remained at home while we continued our search. We provided him with ABA services, much like when he was two, but this time I was his only teacher. Bethany set up a schedule for me to follow and taught me how to use the strategies from Dr. Slimetti's workshops. We used pictures to show Austin what tasks he could expect on that day, and what we would do during a fun downtime activity. The schedule would show him that he was going to get dressed, eat breakfast, learn at the table, and swing outside. There was time set aside for him to request preferred items, which we called "manding," to help increase his use and understanding of language. Austin began to say words when choosing food items from his pictures, including chip, doodle, and Skittle. Billy and I were so excited that this was working. We had waited so long to hear Austin's adorable, squeaky voice.

During that period, we saw just how much Austin could learn. He began to make verbal requests on a regular basis and learned to label items. We would hold up a picture card and Austin would identify "juice" or "video." We felt like he was finally on the path to using language more effectively to get his needs met. He loved when we read Dr. Seuss books to him. One day when Billy was home, Austin lined up his books in front of our bedroom door. Billy sat on the floor with Austin and started to read *Dr. Seuss's ABC*. He got to the page with G on it. "Big G, little G, what begins with G?" Billy read. Austin filled in, "goat, girl, goo-goo goggles." Billy was nearly overwhelmed with excitement, but he had to control his reaction. Austin had a history of stopping what he was doing if we yelled in joy or otherwise revealed our emotions. I stood in the doorway and just listened; with each page Austin would fill in a word when Billy paused. Tears poured down my face. My son was speaking. It was a sound I hadn't been sure I would ever hear. He struggled to use words to make requests, but he tried. Those small glimpses of hope kept us going.

Weeks passed and there was no success in finding the staff that would allow Austin to return to Lakeside School. We contacted the school district and talked with Ellen. Dr. Slimetti had been consulting in the local school district and everyone felt the best decision would be to put Austin in the Verbal Behavior Pilot Classroom that Dr. Slimetti had helped the district to develop. We were excited for this next move. Austin would be in a program where everyone would be following the recommendations of Dr. Slimetti. The staff would have support and training. We thought all our troubles with the school district could be put behind us, and Austin would be able to get the programming he needed.

We attempted to prepare everyone for the transition. By this time, Bethany had left Dr. Slimetti's consulting firm and started her own business. Dr. Slimetti sent out letters letting families know that Bethany was leaving and asked us to transition to one of his other employees, but we opted to keep Bethany. She knew our children and we felt that Austin had been through enough transitions. He needed some consistency, especially because we were seeing progress for the first time in a long time. We asked the district if Bethany could visit the school and help the staff to better understand Austin. But Austin's new teacher Kelly Leeman and others from the district did not feel that they needed Bethany's presence on the first day. They were confident that they would be able to get Austin settled into the new program. I was optimistic, but not convinced this was the best decision. I had visited the program a few days earlier, and unfortunately my confidence in this program, especially the staff, was not strong. But on May 7th 2002, I brought Austin into class for his first day.

We were naïve to let them go it alone.

Mrs. Leeman sent home a note to let me know that Austin's first day had not gone well. The next day, Austin exhibited a few challenging behaviors. He was non-compliant on the playground and wanted to go inside. The staff attempted to keep him in the area with the rest of the class. Austin also bit another child, Bob Riccardi's son Tony. Tony wasn't hurt because he was wearing a large sweatshirt and Austin only got a mouthful of cloth. Following the incident, Austin was brought back into the classroom and allowed to watch a video to calm him down.

Later in the day, Austin began biting his own hands and it was described as "out of the blue." The staff did not understand why he was biting himself. To distract Austin from the self-injury, the staff brought him out into the hallway and took him for a ride around the school in a wagon. Mrs. Leeman said he really enjoyed the rides and they seemed to calm him. However, transitioning him out of the wagon and back into the classroom was difficult and often resulted in him biting himself again. I could not understand how the staff didn't see that their actions only reinforced Austin's challenging behaviors, and that over time the behaviors would inevitably increase. The behaviors became Austin's way of communicating that he wanted to continue the wagon ride or get back to the video. This was becoming a repetitive pattern in Austin's education. This time, I thought the staff would be different. I thought they understood that challenging behaviors would be reinforced if they were followed with a preferred activity.

Everything we had achieved at home came undone in just a few short days. Austin's challenging behaviors at home had been at near zero levels. He had a few hand bites, but mostly when alone and enjoying a movie. It was hard for us to figure out why he would still bite his hand when having all of his desires met. He'd have a Muppet video on his TV, juice in a cup, and a bowl of chips, but he would still bite his own hands. But for the most part he was doing great. He displayed no aggressive behaviors at home, and he was talking to us. The behavior Mrs. Leeman was describing sounded similar to Austin's actions at Lakeside.

The next day Bethany was scheduled to come to our home. After a discussion with the district, it was decided that she should visit the school instead because they needed her help with Austin. Upon her arrival, a paraprofessional asked, "What type of restraints do you use?" Bethany was floored by the question; she had never needed to restrain Austin.

Bethany tried to help the staff implement some of Austin's home programs at the school. Mrs. Leeman explained that she did not use picture schedules or visual prompts in her classroom. She had been taught that to get a child to use language, the use of pictures should be limited. She wasn't using Austin's PECS book, which contained all the pictures he had learned to use to request items, and she wouldn't use a schedule to show him what was coming next. Bethany tried to explain that Austin had these items in previous programs, and that if they were going to be removed they should be faded out gradually. The sudden removal of the tools Austin had become familiar with could have caused the behavior challenges. If he didn't know how to communicate to the staff, he was going to communicate in some other way. For him this included pinching or biting. Mrs. Leeman told Bethany, "Dr. Slimetti said to remove pictures or any augmentative devices from the children's programs and get them to use their own voices."

The class went swimming in the afternoon. Bethany went along to help the staff in this setting. Austin had some difficulty getting into the pool with a staff member, so Bethany carried him in on her hip and he was happy. Once in the pool, he enjoyed the activity. Later, back in the classroom, Bethany gave the staff specific instructions to not give Austin reinforcement, such as walks or videos, after behavioral episodes of hand-biting. She asked them to use his PECS book to allow him to make requests, but they said they couldn't do that. Instead, they promised to have plenty of the items on hand that Austin could say verbally. By the time Bethany left the classroom she felt the staff was better able to handle Austin. He did well while she was there.

Reports from the classroom varied over the next few days. Some days went by with no challenging behaviors, but then a few brought many challenges including pinching and biting. On May 15th Jenna Vecchio, one of Dr. Slimetti's associates, was hired by the district to visit the class. She worked directly with Austin and his paraprofessional at the district's request. Ellen watched Jenna interact with Austin. She later reported that Jenna had worked with Austin continuously, with no breaks or let-up of demands. Ellen was concerned by this approach because Austin had just returned to the school environment and this was a crucial time of transitioning him back into a classroom setting. Ellen had been told that this should be a time to make the classroom fun and decrease expectations as Austin learned the new routine and tasks. But Jenna continued to push Austin in this work session to the point where Ellen had to ask, "Are you *trying* to get him to bite you?"

Austin did eventually bite Jenna. I received a phone call asking me to come to the school and meet with Jenna and the teacher. But Austin was mistakenly placed on the bus that afternoon, so while I was driving to the school, Austin was heading home. Luckily, the school staff contacted the bus company and Austin was returned to school during our meeting. Once inside and seated at one of the children's tables, I was scolded for not warning anyone about Austin's behaviors. Jenna went on to claim that my son was uncontrollable and that he had attacked her. Even after she discontinued working with him he kept trying to reach her, requiring multiple people to block and restrain him. I explained to Jenna that everyone involved was aware of Austin's history, and that we were back in the district precisely due to similar difficulties at his previous placement.

But we had agreed to place Austin in this program because we were told the staff were trained in the same way that Bethany had been. It was our understanding that the same strategies we had learned at Dr. Slimetti's workshops would be implemented here. When Bethany and I were teaching Austin at home, his behaviors had decreased to nearly zero. He didn't bite or attack anyone.

Jenna would not believe anything I said and was quite vocal in her disdain for me, insisting that we had not been forthcoming about Austin's difficulties. I tried to explain that these behaviors didn't happen in our home. I did not have any bruises or marks, my husband didn't, and neither did our daughters. Bethany worked with Austin at home and school without difficulty. Jenna left the room in the middle of my plea.

Austin had a history of self-injurious behaviors and some aggression, but nothing like what they were describing. Jenna and the teachers claimed he was attacking others and seeking out aggressive interactions. This was the first we heard of Austin reacting this way. He almost always bit himself when he was upset and often pinched others to make them stop doing something he didn't want, but biting others was a rare occurrence. Jenna requested that the district reduce the time Austin was in school to just two hours per day. I knew then he wouldn't last in that class.

I wrote our case manager trying to find some answer to all of this. Dr. Slimetti would be in the school district the following week, so I asked Ellen to please place Austin on Dr. Slimetti's list of children to observe. In addition, I offered to come into the classroom during Austin's two hours of study and help the staff find ways to work with him. I wanted Ellen to be aware that Billy and I were willing to do whatever it took for Austin to progress both behaviorally and academically in the program.

The weekend passed and we sent Austin in to school on Monday morning. At 10:20 am I received a call from Ellen. She told me to come pick up Austin, the bus would not be bringing him home. I didn't know if Dr. Slimetti had seen Austin or not. Ellen met me at the office and she had Austin with her. She was obviously distraught and said that she would call me later. She acknowledged that Dr. Slimetti had seen Austin, but from her reaction I could tell it hadn't gone well.

Ellen called late that evening. She wanted me to know that a meeting had been held at the end of the school day, and that she fought as hard as she could on Austin's behalf. Dr. Slimetti, Jenna, assistant superintendent Marianne Sampras, director of special services Anthony Asinello, Mrs. Leeman, and Ellen had all met to discuss Austin's situation. No matter how hard Ellen tried to convince everyone present, the district decided to place Austin on home instruction and remove Ellen as his case manager. There was nothing she could do. Although they knew they were not following legal procedure for removing a child from a program, they were taking the advice of their expert, Dr. Slimetti, and placing Austin on home instruction. Marianne or Anthony would contact us regarding our next steps.

At this point, all we could do was wait. We had no other options.

The next day, Austin celebrated his tenth birthday. Because Austin had started going back to school we no longer had staff to provide programming, except for me. Bethany came to the house and we set up a plan to keep Austin engaged throughout the day like we had done before. I did my best to keep him occupied, but I was overwhelmed. Certainly, I could work and play with my son, but I needed help. I couldn't keep up the level of teaching that he needed to make real progress.

The district informed us that they would arrange staff to implement a home program. It would be a collaborative effort between the Brick school district, Bob Riccardi of POAC, Tom Folgen of the Behavior Network, and Dr. Slimetti. They would work together to train staff, conduct a functional behavior assessment, and develop a behavior intervention plan. Dr. Slimetti would act as the lead. He asked that Billy and I sign a consent form to allow all parties to be involved in Austin's educational program, and to give permission for video recording of the sessions to be used for case study and/or professional and parent training. Anthony Asinello explained that Austin was going to be "the poster child for verbal behavior programming." He would become an example of how Dr. Slimetti's strategies worked for children with autism.

We believed that having Dr. Slimetti himself on Austin's case would catapult us back on track. With all these eyes on Austin and so much support from all angles, I was sure he would be back at school by September. I was hopeful that we finally had all the right people in place to help Austin. I could not have been more wrong.

Poster Child

June 2002 to July 2002

We were ready to embrace this new chapter in our lives. We had a behavior plan and someone who was ready and willing to work with Austin. Diane Salazar, a local speech therapist who was interested in learning more about how to teach children with autism, joined our team. She worked for the Behavior Network run by Tom Folgen. Our consultant, Bethany, helped train her on how to implement the behavior plan designed by Dr. Slimetti and Jenna Vecchio. The excitement was palpable. Bethany was confident that we could show our new team the Austin she knew, the Austin who liked to learn, and learned quickly.

Diane arrived truly ready to get started. She was thrilled to be a part of this new adventure. Billy and I thought it odd that Austin's behavior plan had been crafted over the summer without any input from us and without anyone coming to see Austin in his home, but we respected Dr. Slimetti's reputation and we were on board. According to the plan, Dr. Slimetti, Jenna, Bethany, and Diane would work together to implement a program for Austin. Jenna, who was also a Board Certified Assistant Behavior Analyst like Bethany, was in charge of designing the program. Bethany would help demonstrate techniques to Diane, and Diane would be the person actually delivering the program four hours per day five days per week. Dr. Slimetti would be available to Jenna as a consultant to address questions and concerns.

Although Diane had worked with children with autism in her practice as a speech therapist, she had only recently taken an interest in verbal behavior and ABA. She had no background in these areas. She attended her first workshop the week she began working with Austin. We saw this as both a positive and a negative. On one hand, she needed to be taught each step. On the other, our last experience at Lakeside illustrated that getting someone to change from what they already knew was difficult. Starting with an eager and enthusiastic blank slate would hopefully be a smoother path to success.

On the first day of home instruction, Bethany came to show Diane how to run the steps spelled out in the behavior plan. First up were compliance trials. Simply put, we were to allow Austin to engage in preferred activities, then interrupt him and ask him to perform a very simple task. Once he complied he received reinforcement via a preferred item like a Skittle, and then was permitted to return to his activity.

Bethany reviewed the plan with Diane and confirmed that she was ready. We all went outside where Austin was already on his swing set. Bethany placed a small plastic chair in the area and told Austin to come sit down. Austin engaged in some attempts of aggressive behaviors of pinching, grabbing, and biting his own hands, but eventually he complied. Bethany was satisfied with her success and asked Diane if she was ready to try. I could almost smell her fear. By this time, Austin had returned to the swing and the stage was set. Diane approached him and asked him to sit down. Austin jumped off the swing set and came toward Diane biting his hands, making his accompanying "eee, eee, eee," sounds as he attempted to grab her. Diane ran away from Austin and dumped the chair to stop him instead of standing her ground and blocking him as she had been trained. I could already tell this was going to be too much for her. She was not accustomed to this level of intensely challenging behaviors. That night she called Jenna to report what had happened. Without coming to see the plan in action, Jenna changed the plan based only on the information provided by Diane.

Jenna instructed Diane to remove the compliance trials and only run the portion of the program where she gave Austin reinforcing items. She was to "pair" with Austin, and develop a relationship as someone fun. Bethany had concerns about the behavior plan from the start based on her nine-month history with Austin. But once the compliance trials were removed she became even more worried that this was a huge step backwards. Bethany was especially concerned that we had all been instructed to engage in planned ignoring of Austin if he engaged in any self-injurious behaviors. Jenna's plan stated that if he bit himself we should stop all interactions with him until he was calm for at least twenty seconds, and if he attempted to approach us we should walk away until he was calm. This procedure would prove to be disastrous.

Diane was told to establish herself as a fun person in Austin's eyes. She was to deliver fifteen reinforcing items, like Skittles, or complete an action for him, like turning on the DVD player. She was told to present the Skittles one at a time with brief pauses between each, or press play on the DVD player and then hit pause to set up a new opportunity to push play again. Austin was not required to do anything more than take the candy or watch the video. Only after getting fifteen Skittles or having the DVD player started fifteen times would he be asked to make a request verbally. He only had to say one word, such as "Skittle," or "play." That was the only demand to be placed on him during this initial phase of the plan. Fifteen free Skittles before having to request one Skittle. The person writing this plan obviously thought our son could not withstand much in the way of demands. Austin was also required to show zero challenging behaviors while accepting those fifteen Skittles or other items. If he engaged in any challenging behaviors, Diane was to start over at one again. Dr. Slimetti wanted Austin to have a long history of receiving positive items from Diane, with few demands and little effort on Austin's part. This was supposedly going to build a relationship between them.

This process was to be repeated a total of fifty times without Austin engaging in any challenging behaviors. Fifteen Skittles, fifty times, before phase two would be implemented. That was a lot of Skittles without a single challenging behavior before we could move forward. The next phase would require Diane to ask Austin to complete a simple task. She would then reinstate the compliance drills. I could see that this was going to be impossible. Austin's self-injurious behaviors occurred even when he was happy and all his needs were being met. Had Jenna or Dr. Slimetti come to our home to observe him, they would have realized how unrealistic their plan was.

So, after only one day of programming, a new plan was in place. This time there was no one to help Diane interpret it. She was told that no demands were to be placed on Austin, including no denial and no stopping him from potentially dangerous situations. All Diane was to do was hand our son reinforcing items fifteen times in a row, then request that he ask for one reinforcing item. She was to get Austin to come to her, and she was not to approach him.

Diane stood in the living room like a human Pez dispenser, placing one Skittle at a time in her open palm and waiting for Austin to pass by and take it. This was their idea of pairing, or building a relationship. When I questioned Jenna about it, she said, "your son is so severe that he needs to learn to tolerate people being near him." I wondered exactly what child she was talking about. My son lived in a house full of people, and he didn't hurt any of us. Austin listened when we asked him to get dressed and put away his toys. He would work at the table and label pictures or sort colors. He liked when people played with him, read books to him, or jumped on the trampoline and sent him high into the air with a bounce. He loved being pushed on the swing and watching others write letters on paper.

I set the video camera up in the living room and went about my usual chores. As I came back toward the living room, I could see that the front door was open. I heard Diane ask Chelsea, "Where does he usually go?" *Usually go*? I thought, *He doesn't usually go anywhere. How did he get out of the house?* Diane explained that she wasn't supposed to tell Austin "no," so she had allowed him to leave the house alone. We all ran outside and found him inside my van. We tried to get him to come back inside, but he wouldn't. Diane's time with us was nearly up and she had to leave before we could get Austin out of the van. Once she was gone, Austin was willing to come back into the house.

That night I watched the videotape. The playback showed Austin sitting on the couch next to Diane as she held the DVD player. Austin pulled her arm to get her to stand up, and she stood while holding the DVD player. Austin then tried to pull her to get her to move. She didn't budge and looked frightened about what might happen next. He began pushing her toward the front door, but she didn't go. He grabbed a chair and climbed on it to unlock the chain on the front door. Diane sat on the couch and did nothing but watch. The calmness with which she watched our son leave the house was frightening. We did not allow Austin in the front yard without supervision. I wrote to Jenna that night and asked if she or Dr. Slimetti could come see this plan in action. She said no, but she would talk to Diane about what happened.

The next day, Diane confirmed that she and Jenna had discussed the events. They felt that Austin's desire to get Diane to leave the room was actually a request for wanting to be with me. Diane, Jenna, and Dr. Slimetti decided that nothing they could offer Austin would compete with my presence. According to them, Austin was aggressing toward Diane to get to me. Perhaps I should have felt honored, but come on, who can't compete with a chubby 40-year-old woman whose energy has been zapped? A few minutes on the trampoline and Diane would have had him in the palm of her hand. I was instructed to give Austin the impression that I was not available, but I was also not permitted to leave the grounds. So now when Diane arrived I left through the side door of our home, walked around outside of the house, climbed through my bedroom window, and remained there. I locked my bedroom door and was told to not come out until the session was over. This was how Austin would learn to go to Diane to get his needs met, and they could build trust and a relationship. I had to spend four hours in my bedroom while Diane and Austin bonded. I caught up on a lot of daytime television court dramas and folded a great deal of laundry.

Near the end of the session, I could hear Austin's "eee, eee, eee" that always accompanied the biting of his hand or fingers, but I couldn't hear anything else. The sounds were loud and excessive. I pressed my ear up against the door as hard as I could, and heard him cry, screech, and bite himself for twenty-five minutes. I couldn't hear anything from Diane. I finally reached a point where I couldn't take it anymore. I had no idea what was going on with my son, and no way to contact Diane without opening the door. The awful sounds continued. I didn't hear anything changing, and I needed to know why he was so upset. I opened my bedroom door and walked out into the living room. The couch cushions were on the floor, Austin was completely naked, sweaty, and crying with tears pouring down his face. Diane was nowhere to be seen. He was biting a throw pillow so hard he had ripped the corner off. I could see the base of the couch was wet, and I knew it was urine. He was in such a state of distress that even my presence didn't interrupt his behavior.

I walked through the living room in search of Diane. I passed through the dining room and the kitchen, and still no Diane. I found her in the pantry, sitting on the steps behind the kitchen looking as if she'd just witnessed a car crash and was sitting on a curb wondering what to do next. "Oh, thank God you came out, I didn't know what to do. It's twelve-thirty and I have to go," she said, with obvious relief that her time here was over. I was dumbfounded. "What do you mean you have to leave? What happened?" I asked. She said she had no time to talk, she had clients back at her office that she had to get to. She was so afraid that she had been unable to get up the courage to walk through the living room and knock on my bedroom door to find me. Instead she chose to sit on the steps and wait.

Diane didn't come to our home the following day. Bethany worked with Austin instead. She got Austin to the work table and, while he did have a few episodes of hand-biting, he had a great day. Billy and I could see that this was all about who worked with Austin. He needed to develop a sense of trust and understand the person's role in his life. For the next few days we were on our own, and I welcomed the lack of visitors.

After the weekend passed, we returned to the home program with Diane. Monday started off with a bang. I was on the computer and attempting to avoid interaction with Austin and Diane, as I had been instructed to do. Austin went into his bedroom, stripped off his clothes, and urinated on the floor. Because Diane was not permitted to give any instructions or place any demands, I went into the room and had him clean up. The rest of the week would be filled with similar interactions. Austin learned that urinating or having bowel movements in his pants would get Mom to come out of hiding and interact with him. This new plan was creating behaviors that were unbearable. Watching the videos of the day's events would leave me in tears.

While swimming outside one day, Austin tried to drop a brick into the pool. Diane came outside at that exact moment. Austin must have perceived her as someone who was going to make him stop. He moved toward her, making his "eee" sounds. She ran back into the house. Austin was bullying her and she was taking it.

Another session looked like an episode of Tom and Jerry. Austin and Diane were on the couch watching a video on the DVD player. He pinched her to stop her from pressing pause. She stood up, and he managed to get the DVD player away from her. When she sat back down, he thought she was going to take the player from him so he grabbed her. She tried to get away from him. The video captured her running back and forth between the kitchen side door and the sunroom back door in an attempt to get out, but she was unable to unlock the doors quickly enough. Meanwhile, Austin chased her and tried to bite her. I was sitting outside, hiding as usual, and when I saw her come to the side door I could see that he was pushing her. I opened the door and she leaped out. Once she was outside, Austin walked calmly back to the couch to watch his video.

Soon we began to see Austin use these types of behaviors with everyone. He was learning to gain access to items by biting himself. In Dr. Slimetti's plan, when Austin bit himself or aggressed to get something, we were to turn our heads away, count to five, and repeat the counting until he was calm. We were then supposed to have him request the item. This was described as "count and mand."

If Austin reached the level of aggressing in his attempt to gain access to something, we were to walk away and ignore him until he was calm. Then we were to have him appropriately ask for the item. I was told specifically that, due to his strength, I should place myself behind a door and wait to hear him calm. I explained that if I was behind a door, he would go for one of his sisters. I was told to bring the girls into the room with me. "So let me get this straight," I confirmed. "If Austin engages in any of these behaviors, I am to gather up his sisters and go hide behind a door until he is calm?" Jenna responded, "Yes, he has to learn that he must ask for things appropriately. This is a 'walk and peel' procedure, and when he is calm, he needs to ask appropriately for the item before access is allowed." So that is was what I did. It made no sense, but I did it. "Walk and peel" meant that if Austin wanted something but attempted to get it through biting himself or aggression, I was to walk away from him and peel him off of me if he grabbed a hold.

Poor Alanna would be calmly working on a puzzle at the dining room table and Austin would come into the room and bite himself or pinch me. I would then take Alanna away from her puzzle and lock the two of us in my room while Austin attempted to open the door. Alanna would cry because she just wanted her puzzle back, and I would wait to hear the silence. I felt like I was waiting for an intruder to leave. I would open my bedroom door, and there he would be: naked, on the floor, playing in a puddle of urine. I couldn't take this. What were they doing to my son? I would later be scolded by Jenna, who told me I was reinforcing the urinating because I opened the door. *You told me to wait for quiet, and I did. How was I to know that he was quiet because he was playing in his own piss? I can't see through doors.* What I did know was what the situation had become absurd. We couldn't live like that any longer.

Austin was out of control. He regressed to urinating anywhere in the house, including on the furniture. He was having bowel movements in his pants and smearing it on the walls of his bedroom, the sliding glass doors, and in the pool. During episodes of rage, he would bite the door jams hard enough to remove the paint with his teeth. Finally, the aggressive behaviors that were once strictly used with people who instructed him began to be exhibited toward all of us.

If I tried to interrupt these rages or prevent him from hurting his sisters or destroying our home, he would pinch and grab me, leaving scratches and bruises on my hands and arms. I was no longer exempt from his attacks. I wore Kevlar sleeves on a daily basis to prevent him from scratching my skin, but somehow he would find the one place where skin was exposed and grab me there. If I insisted that he complete any task he didn't want to, he would charge at me and a fight would ensue. I found myself afraid to approach him unless Billy was home because I never knew what his response would be to something as simple as "get off the swing, it's time to come inside."

He started to aggress toward his sisters. Chelsea would just leave the room. Actually, we rarely saw Chelsea anymore, she mostly stayed in her bedroom. She was safer there. Alanna began to anticipate having to leave the room when she heard Austin's sounds. Austin began to learn that Alanna was the key to getting to Mommy. One day while they watched a movie together in the living room, Alanna on one couch, and Austin on another, he went over to her and scratched her arm. She cried and I appeared from around the corner. Soon, Alanna would just offer her arm sacrificially when Austin cried out "eee eee eee," to begin the process of my coming to her rescue. I was at a loss and had no idea where to turn for help.

Earlier that year I had graduated from Monmouth University. Billy and I planned a graduation party. Although we were going through so many difficulties with Austin, we were adamant about continuing with the party. We were trying to keep some sense of normalcy in our lives, or maybe it was simply an attempt to feel that we were in control of something.

Billy went overboard in preparation for the party. He spent every spare moment doing something to make the yard look good. We got a new fence, new shrubs and flowers, and he painted the swing set; nothing had been left untouched. I suppose it is human nature to do what you can to find something to control when the rest of your life is in chaos. Personally, I wondered what the point was when everything was such a mess. But we found tasks to fill our days to help us avoid the problems we found too difficult to tackle.

Inside the house we lived with a terrible secret, a stark contrast to the pristine exterior Billy was creating for our guests. We were losing our son.

The Gallaghers, who were known for fighting for their children and getting only the best, had the worst child in the district. A stranger lurked inside our home. Each day I wondered when he would appear and what the damage would be.

This was supposed to be a happy time in my life. At the age of 39, I had completed all of my courses and was the first in my family to graduate college. But all the tasks leading up to the party were tainted by the effects of Austin's behaviors. When picking out my dress for the party, I was not looking for the wow factor that a Belle of the ball might want for her big day. Instead, I was just trying to find something that would cover the bruises. With the party being held at the end of June, finding such an outfit would prove to be a difficult task.

Each time I went to the mall, the grocery story, or the bank, I noticed the disdainful glances from others. I looked like a battered woman, and it always felt as if their stares were intended to make me feel ashamed. With all the awareness around domestic violence, I thought there might have been more empathy. But not one person who saw the marks ever asked if I needed help.

Visually I was the epitome of a battered woman, but my bruises had not come from my husband's hands. The emotions were similar: if I could just make him happy, he would stop. When it is your son who beats you, you have to stick it out. There is no divorce, no leaving him to get away from the situation. I loved my son, but at that time I did not like him. Each morning when his bedroom door opened I would briefly close my eyes and hope I had only imagined the clicking of the doorknob. But the squeak of hinges always followed and I knew he was awake. I would think, "FUCK, he's up." And so my day would begin.

As we were prepping for the party, Austin let himself out of the house. I ran outside to find him. How on earth was I going to enjoy a party while constantly worrying whether he would get out of the house? I found him at the side of the yard, near the street. He fought me as I tried to get him back into the house. During the struggle, he scratched my arm and left me bleeding. I wanted to have a nice day, just one nice day with my family, was that too much to ask? Billy and I decided to place a TV in Austin's room with his favorite DVDs in hopes that he would stay in his room and not require much of our attention.

The caterer arrived and the house wasn't even close to being ready for guests. Austin wanted juice and my hands were full of dirty clothes I was trying to stash in the laundry room. I asked Austin to wait a minute in a tone that I'm sure expressed my stress. It was the wrong answer. Austin immediately came at me. First he bit his own hands and grabbed my arm, trying to make me return to the kitchen. But once I started on my way to the laundry room I couldn't stop. I had to commit to what I said and put the dirty clothes away first to avoid reinforcing his behavior.

Austin grabbed my arms. They already ached from all the previous encounters that left bruises and scratches earlier that day. I just wanted him to stop touching me, I could not stand a single moment more. I kept thinking, *please not today.* He pinched and squeezed, and then he attempted to bite me. I finally had enough.

I backed him into the bottom of the stairway, shoved him into the side door, and thrust his hand into his own mouth, yelling, "You want something to bite? Here, bite this." From the corner of my eye I saw someone watching, and I turned to see the waitress hired for the party frozen in shock. A wave of complete embarrassment rolled over me. I let Austin go and I ran to my bedroom hysterically crying.

Although we had asked our guests not to bring their children, some did. This only heightened my nervousness and made it impossible to enjoy the event, because I needed to know where everyone was at every moment.

Each time someone went into the house I would follow to ensure that Austin did not aggress toward them. His bedroom was right next to the bathroom, and sometimes people would wait outside the door for it to become vacant. I just knew he would not want them there, or that he would eventually need something they wouldn't be able to understand. If any of the children wanted to touch his things, he would hurt them.

For the rest of the day it was all I could do to control my emotions and pretend everything was okay. The bruises and scratches were impossible to ignore, but my family knew why they were there and the others must have been too embarrassed to ask. The next morning, I wrote an email to Jenna and Dr. Slimetti begging them to come to our home. They refused.

After that weekend, I cried every day as soon as I woke up. I cried over my coffee. I cried while setting up the video camera to capture this train wreck of a program. With each passing day, Austin got worse. I have to admit that he did learn something. He learned how hurting himself got people to leave him alone, even if only for a brief moment. He learned that if he aggressed toward his sister, someone would come to her rescue and he could then try to get what he wanted. He learned that if he was left alone but wanted something, playing in his urine or smearing his feces would get someone to appear. He learned that hurting others got them out of his way, and he could then access preferred items unsupervised. Austin learned that aggression and self-injury would get his needs met.

A few weeks later, Chelsea asked if our neighbor Cassie could sleep over. The next morning, they came downstairs to the kitchen just when Austin was making his "eee, eee, eee" sounds. Diane had left him in the living room and was sitting at the dining room table. I snapped at Chelsea and told her to get back upstairs, I didn't want Cassie to get hurt. I also didn't want her to see anything if this escalated. As Chelsea turned around and started back up the steps, I heard her mutter, "well happy birthday to me." My heart sank. I had completely forgotten that Chelsea turned thirteen that day. I felt like I was failing at being a mom in every way possible.

The next day I received an email from Bob Riccardi of POAC. Dr. Slimetti and Jenna had talked to him about Austin and he wanted me to know that they were aware of what was happening. But why would they talk to Bob instead of me? How could they know anything when they refused to come to my home and see it?

I was at a loss for how we could get Austin back. Each day brought new challenges, new ways that Austin discovered to up the ante and ensure that Diane left him alone. By this time Diane was also wearing Kevlar sleeves to protect her arms. One day, while Austin was in the pool, Diane sat outside with him and wrote some of his favorite words with sidewalk chalk on the cement. Austin bit the side of the pool, so Diane stopped writing, turned her back to him, and waited for the mandatory twenty seconds of calm. When Diane turned to resume her writing, Austin had stripped off his bathing suit and was once again biting the side of the pool. Diane moved away from him. When she thought she could return to the pool area because he appeared calm, Austin jumped out of the pool and chased her to the other side of the yard. She ran around the trampoline in an attempt to avoid getting hurt. She tried to get to the door of the sunroom. She made it inside and locked the sliding glass door behind her. Diane stood on one side, and my naked son was on the other trying to get in. I was supposed to just stay put and not intervene.

Austin went back in the pool and had a bowel movement. Now she needed me because he was sitting in a pool of water with feces floating in it. It was up to me to get him out of the pool and put him in the shower. I went back outside and hooked up the hose to drain the pool. I completed each step robotically, completely numb. I was just going through the motions as Diane tried to explain what had happened. I didn't care what had happened. All I cared about was making this insanity stop.

July 17, 2002

The day started just like any other. I woke up. I had coffee. I cringed when Austin's bedroom door opened. Bethany had come to help Diane, but a few moments before Diane was supposed to arrive, the phone rang. "After talking with Jenna and Dr. Slimetti last night, they decided that Austin should come to my office for programming," Diane explained. They had determined that Austin was still trying to gain access to me, and Diane simply couldn't compete with that. She would be able to gain more of Austin's trust in a controlled environment free of the history of all that had happened. Although I disagreed that the behaviors occurred because he wanted me, I was willing to try anything.

I packed a bag for Austin, including a change of clothes just in case. I had to bring Chelsea with me because she wasn't in school and I couldn't get a sitter on such short notice. At least Alanna was at school. I packed the video camera and tripod and got both kids in the car. Bethany followed us.

When we arrived at Diane's office she showed us the room where she would work with Austin. There was a one-way mirror in an adjacent the room, and I set up the camera in that area. Bethany, Chelsea, and I went into the viewing room while Diane brought Austin into the therapy room. We could see and hear what was happening, but Austin couldn't see us. The room was filled with toys and books, and Diane had set up a TV with a Sesame Street video cued up.

Besides a large vinyl-covered bench, there was little other furniture in the room. Diane sat on the bench and opened a bag of Doritos. Austin wandered around the room and examined all the new things. Most importantly, he tried to figure out how the VCR worked. About five minutes passed before Austin went over to Diane and pinched her. She ignored him and stayed seated. She began to count out loud. Then we heard her ask Austin, "Chip?" He returned to her and took a Dorito. A few more minutes passed and Austin bit his stuffed animal, a puppy. Again Diane remained seated and was counting. Austin put his hand in the chip bag and Diane tried to count to twenty before letting him have one. Austin bit his puppy and pinched Diane. I was sure that Austin was confused about why Diane was not leaving the room when he bit or pinched, as she had done every time at our home.

Austin grabbed Diane's elbow and pulled her toward the door. She did not open it and was not permitted to tell him no. She just ignored his request for her to open the door and returned to her seat on the bench.

Diane started to play with some toys she had hoped Austin would show an interest in. He listened to the music from one toy and watched the Sesame Street video in fast forward. Diane had the remote to the VCR, and she pushed the play button. Austin went to her and grabbed her hand, pulling her in an effort to get her to stand up, which she did. He brought her to the door and placed her hands on the doorknob. Diane tried to go back to the bench, but Austin kept leading her back to the door. She ignored all of his gentle requests for her to leave the room.

Diane tried to bring out a new toy to interest him, a train set. We let her know through an intercom system that he was not interested in trains. She went to get another item and searched through the books on one of the shelves. Austin grabbed her more forcefully and took her to the door. She tried to get to the bench to sit down. Austin pinched her and bit her arm. Luckily she had the Kevlar sleeves on, and the only thing he got a mouthful of was fabric.

Austin grabbed Diane by the back of her shoulders and pulled her toward him with every intention of biting her on the face. I could not believe my eyes. I gasped in horror, and then heard Chelsea gasp too. Why had I brought Chelsea? It all happened so quickly after that.

Diane stood up to avoid the bite, Austin reached the door and was trying to get out, but a child-proof protector on the knob prevented him from opening it. He shoved his puppy in his mouth and cried out in a constant wail of "eee, eee, eee." He grabbed Diane and pulled her toward the door. She just stood there, not saying or doing anything. He kept placing her hands on the door, but she wouldn't open it. Austin grabbed her hands, pulled her down, and bit her shoulder.

He again brought her to the door. I explained to Bethany that without a clear "No" from Diane, Austin couldn't understand why she wouldn't leave. Austin had a hold of Diane's arm and tried to bite her again. He got hold of the Kevlar sleeve and wouldn't let go. With his teeth locked onto the sleeve, he spun Diane away from the door. He tried to pull her to the ground and ripped off the sleeves. He bit her exposed skin and she winced in pain. This couldn't continue. Bethany told her to get out of the room.

I was sobbing hysterically. I had never seen my son so violent, acting with such intent to cause harm. Chelsea was crying too, fearfully asking, "Are they going to take him away?" We left the observation room in tears and met Diane in a small office outside of the therapy room. She was obviously shaken by the events and just sat quietly for a while. Bethany tried to figure out how it had all come to this.

We all agreed that Diane could not continue to work with Austin in this way. We needed Jenna and Dr. Slimetti to see this and change the plan. Austin had calmed down and Diane was feeling a bit better, so Bethany suggested that Diane try to do something positive with Austin to end the session on a better note and maybe help set the stage for next time. They decided to leave the door to the therapy room open so Diane wouldn't be trapped inside with Austin. Diane brought in a large therapy ball for Austin to bounce on. She gave him a few Doritos, and shortly after we decided to end it while it was going well.

Later we reviewed the horrific scenes on the video playback. We could see that Austin simply wanted Diane to leave the room. He had a history of getting her to leave, so he was determined to ensure that happened. As soon as she was out of the room, he went to the VCR, turned it on, and starting watching Elmo. He was perfectly content to remain in the room, and eventually he began to look around and notice himself in the mirror. He wasn't looking for me as Jenna had suggested, he was trying to gain access to his preferred items without someone interrupting him. And he had been successful.

The next day we waited to hear what would happen next. Would Austin continue to be taught in our home? Would we return to Diane's office instead? Diane called to let us know that Jenna and Dr. Slimetti had instructed her to discontinue all programming until everyone involved could meet. When I asked when that would be, she couldn't tell me. The school district was supposed to arrange something.

I contacted Ms. Sampras, the assistant superintendent, and asked when our meeting could be held. Austin could not go without services. But the first date that Dr. Slimetti and Jenna were available was August 14th, a month away. "What do we do for the next month?" I asked. She explained that she or Mr. Asinello would get back to me if the meeting could be scheduled sooner. That was the last I heard from the school district until I received a letter confirming that we would meet on August 14th.

I was alone with my son every day for the next month.

July 2002 to September 2002

I stood in line at the grocery store oblivious to everything happening around me. Suddenly, Austin started crying out, "eee, eee, eee." Someone in the background was trying to get my attention, but their voice seemed very far away.

"Excuse me?"

"Eee, eee, eee..."

"Miss?"

Suddenly I was startled by a tap on my shoulder from a woman asking, "Is he okay?" The checkout person pointed to my 10-year-old son, who was sitting inside the shopping cart, biting his own hand, and making that awful sound. "He's fine," I answered mechanically, without even registering the look of horror on her face. I continued to write out the check for the groceries and moved through the transaction on automatic pilot. Then I realized that I had not only learned to ignore the sounds and behaviors of my own son, but of most everyone with whom I came in contact.

On my way back to the van I broke down. My tears began to fall, and Austin continued to be upset. I kept him in the large part of the cart to make sure I could get in and out of the grocery store as quickly as possible. I would only buy a few essential items that would fit in the front section. I also put him there because I could keep some distance between us in case he decided to reach out and hurt me. I had hit a low point I was not sure I could recover from. I knew what had gotten us here, but I didn't know how or when we would be able to resume what little normalcy we had once known.

Desperate thoughts often ran through my head. I just wanted out of this situation. Austin was known to occasionally leave the house or yard, maybe one day he wouldn't come back. Maybe, next time, I wouldn't look for him. Billy would be out on the boat; he would never know. I would take my time and wait to call the police. Of course I never did that, but I thought about it. I dreamed of scenarios that would make my life easier, and there were times when being without Austin seemed like the only answer.

Austin's self-injury had escalated to over a thousand incidents per day, causing his hands and fingers to split. His aggressions were well-documented in the data kept by Dr. Slimetti's team and the marks left on my arms. He urinated everywhere and played in the puddles he made. He smeared his feces on his bedroom wall and the sliding glass door. Attempts to have him complete a task as simple as getting dressed were now met with refusal and aggression toward himself or me. He couldn't be left alone with his sisters for fear of what he would do to them. We arranged our home and routines to keep everyone safe.

Billy and I prepared for the upcoming meeting by gathering all the videos and data collected over the thirty days that Diane had worked with Austin. We also brought videos and data from before this program was implemented. We wanted them to see the child we knew prior to all of this so they could realize the magnitude of his regression and understand why we were asking them to come to our home.

At the meeting there was a clear division at the table. Dr. Slimetti, Jenna, and Diane sat on one side. Billy, Bethany, and I were on the other. Ms. Sampras and Mr. Asinello sat together at one end. There was a television set up with a VCR connected. We thought we were going to have a chance to tell them about our son and discuss what the next moves would be. We were expecting to review the videos and have everyone collaborate to establish what Austin needed. Billy and I felt that once they saw the entire picture, they would realize we needed their help. We were wrong.

This was the first time that Bethany saw Dr. Slimetti since leaving his practice. The red blotches on her skin revealed her nervousness. Mr. Asinello asked for a brief update, but when Bethany began to describe what she had witnessed she was quickly interrupted by Dr. Slimetti. He asked her why she didn't tell him how bad Austin really was. He blamed her for everything that had happened. Bethany tried to counter by describing her work with Austin from his time at Lakeside until now.

Billy and I could see this was going in the wrong direction. I asked Dr. Slimetti if we could show him the videos…the videos we had been told to take for him.

But the videos weren't going to reveal the miraculous change he had been hoping for in this "poster child" for his work. So he refused to look at them. He said he talked with Diane and he didn't need to see any videos. Billy tried to explain that Diane was new to this, and that she couldn't have all the answers. We didn't understand why he was relying so heavily on someone who had just begun her career in the field of ABA. He didn't ask us a single question, and Diane certainly wasn't willing to discuss any part she might have played in Austin's decline.

Dr. Slimetti felt that I was the problem because I didn't believe in him. He said if I wanted to listen to what Bethany had to say, then I should just work with Bethany. He and his team were pulling out of our case. I was enraged. I didn't believe in him? I did everything he told me to do, even things I knew weren't right. I listened to every word, and when they told me it would get worse before it got better, I hung onto those words and waited for the better. Better never came. I believed in him so strongly that I removed my children from the care of professionals I held dear and burned bridges under the premise that I had to do what I did for my children's sake.

Dr. Slimetti, Diane, and Jenna left the meeting together. Through the window I could see them chuckling as they left. They smiled as though they had just put someone in their place, arrogant and full of themselves. They were proud of having abandoned Austin. We had done all they asked of us. We begged for their help throughout the process. They destroyed a little boy, and in the end they laughed as they exited his life.

Ms. Sampras and Mr. Asinello turned to us both, and in a sudden 180 the district offered us as much of Bethany's time as she could provide. They would pay her to conduct the day-to-day teaching and help us get Austin back into a program in the district. Bethany looked at her calendar and her limited schedule. She started writing Austin's name in every blank space she could. She broke down in tears, unable to understand how Dr. Slimetti could just leave a child. She worried that her involvement in our case might have caused some of the animosity. We assured her that she was the reason we knew what Austin was capable of, and together we would all move forward.

Bethany and I became Austin's teachers once again. We created a schedule and worked hard to get his behaviors under control. We set up the video camera every day to document what we knew was going to be a successful program. Austin did well. He began to learn a few more words and we started to teach him to read. We always knew he had a love for letters, so we tried to use this to our advantage. We put words on everything in the house, and we would have him match a word card in his hand to the object: the word "chair" had to be placed on a chair. He loved this and thought it was a game. Still, whenever he didn't want to complete a task his immediate reaction was aggression. We needed to find some way to teach him to stop hurting others.

Mr. Asinello offered additional help. He had a teacher who was starting in September, and she was available to work with us if we wanted to include her in the home program until then. I was hesitant, but Bethany suggested we give it a try. Melanie Kerwin was a young teacher with a lot of enthusiasm. She had been through many of Dr. Slimetti's trainings in the district. She came to our home to observe the sessions. She didn't have a degree in special education; her experience came from a third grade classroom in the district. I had nothing against her, but I just couldn't put my child in the hands of another person who had no experience. She asked a lot of questions, and we learned that she had not worked with children with autism before. We asked that she only come to the house on days that Bethany could also be present.

In September, the district offered to put Austin in the classroom that Ms. Kerwin was starting. Bethany and I decided to observe the class first. There was only one other child in the room: Timmy, the boy who banged his head to get the catalog in Mrs. Ramirez's class. Ms. Kerwin had been provided a large classroom with lots of supplies. Timmy's program was being supervised by Jenna. My heart sank. If we placed Austin in this classroom, we would inevitably come in contact with Jenna at some point. I didn't want her near my son.

We watched Ms. Kerwin work with Timmy. He had grown quite a bit since I last saw him, and he looked like a young man now. Timmy was in a manding session, a scheduled time in his day when he asked for items he wanted. Timmy only wanted two items, a set of small plastic dinosaurs, and wooden beads that he would string. Over and over he would alternate between asking for these two items using sign language. He never developed the ability to speak verbally while in the district program, so he was now being taught sign language for the first time at the age of eleven. Like all the children in Dr. Slimetti's school district program, Timmy was not allowed to use pictures, augmentative devices, or other forms of communication.

Billy and I wanted Austin to get back into a program, but we wanted his teacher to have experience with autism and an understanding of Austin in particular. We asked the district if they would allow Bethany to work with Austin in this room, and they agreed. Austin's initial success in that room varied, but we were hopeful.

The district called an IEP meeting in an attempt to confirm this classroom as Austin's permanent placement. We were not ready to do this. We wanted Austin to have a longer history of success before we would transition him to the district's staff. He had been through so much. At the meeting, Ms. Kerwin asked us to give her a chance. I had already given enough chances. Austin was not the district's guinea pig, he was my son. I needed to start demanding what Austin needed without worrying if people's feelings were hurt.

Although the district agreed to let Bethany continue in the classroom, they wanted a plan that indicated we would eventually transition the teaching to Ms. Kerwin. They sent Ryan McDuff to our home to work with Austin after school as part of the transaction. Mr. Asinello wanted to have Bethany train Ryan to work with Austin so that he in turn could train the school staff. What they really wanted was to keep Bethany out of the district. I was sure Dr. Slimetti played a part in this decision. We quickly began to see a repetition of Diane's first days in our home. Ryan was frightened by Austin's behavior, so he started to give in to him to keep him happy. When Bethany wasn't present, Ryan would opt to run the programs he saw fit instead of doing as he was instructed. Austin's self-injurious behaviors were increasing and was once again stripping his clothes off. Eventually he aggressed toward Ryan.

It seemed as though unless the entire world was set to his exact conditions, Austin would bite himself or aggress. I couldn't maintain a perfect scenario for him throughout the rest of his life, and there was certainly no way I could get the rest of the world on board. We needed to get him some real help. Every encounter outside of our home was a challenge. The physical effort and mental energy required to keep Austin happy was unhealthy and exhausting. We weren't helping our son if we couldn't teach him how to handle the real world.

One day I had to take Austin to an appointment at the local hospital. In an attempt to find out if anything physiological might be contributing to these behaviors, Austin's neurologist Dr. Weyman ordered an MRI and an EEG. I had to take him to Shore Medical Center early in the morning for the procedures. Because he would be sedated, he could not have any food or drink. I waited until the last second before waking him up and managed to get him dressed and into the car before he could get into the cabinets.

Austin was hesitant but followed me as we entered the hospital. We sat in the pre-op area and provided the usual medical information. A nurse came over to take Austin's temperature with a regular thermometer. "You'll never get him to use that," I warned. She informed me, "he has to or we can't do the procedures, will he hold it under his arm?" I snapped at her. "You're kidding me. This hospital doesn't have one of the ear ones?" She could hear my annoyance. "They aren't accurate, he has to use this one. Can you just hold it under his arm?" I realized this was destined to be yet another misadventure due to the medical profession's lack of familiarity with autism.

"Let's give it a shot," I told her, all the while knowing he would never comply with this. As she moved toward him, he verbally protested with, "eee, eee, eee," and the accompanying finger bites. The nurse then handed the device to me and I attempted to show him by using it on myself first. But as I lifted his shirt out of the way he grabbed my arm and let me know he did not approve. I finally got it under his arm, but he gripped my arm with his nails and dug into the skin. I was used to it by now; I continued to hold the thermometer in an attempt to get the job done. Austin would not hold still and I couldn't keep the thermometer in place long enough to get a reading. Austin flopped to the floor to escape the situation. The nurse continued to insist that he had to have his temperature taken before we could continue. So I put him back in his seat, handed her the thermometer, and told her, "Then you do it." She left in a huff.

The nurse returned to let me know that the doctor had waived the need for the "mandatory" temperature measurement. She then asked me to dress Austin in the gown and put him on the stretcher. "Are we ready to go up?" I asked. "No, not yet, but soon," she replied. "I'll put it on when we're ready," I explained. "He is going to protest and I'm trying to keep him as calm as possible before all this." She grumbled something under her breath before leaving us alone, unhappy with my unwillingness to follow the rules. Was it really necessary for me to battle everyone just to try to keep my son calm?

We were finally called to go for the procedure. They wanted Austin on the stretcher to be brought up to the next floor, but he refused. I realized that they thought I could not control my own child, and maybe they were right. But I was trying to avoid what I knew would happen: Austin was going to hurt someone. "He has not been sedated, would it be okay if we just let him walk?" I asked. They allowed us to leave the triage area and head upstairs, with the orderly pushing an empty bed and Austin and I walking beside him. Austin didn't want to enter the elevator. He got away from me and I had to stop the elevator doors from closing or he would have been left on the floor alone. I told the orderly to go without us and asked if there were stairs. He pointed to the door behind me.

With some effort, I finally got Austin up the stairs. When the staffer behind the desk saw that Austin didn't have a gown on and wasn't riding on the stretcher, she greeted us with, "Well, that's a first." I was told that Austin would be injected with a sedative before he was placed on the stretcher and fitted with the sedation mask. I attempted to hold him on my lap for the shot. He was fine until the nurse came near. I was unable to hold him, he squirmed to the ground. We all agreed that if the goal was to get him on the stretcher with the sedation mask on, we should just do that instead of trying to get the needle in his arm. Either way we were going to have a fight, so we needed to limit our efforts to just one fight.

Four professionals surrounded Austin. Two nurses, an anesthesiologist, and a doctor all attempted to pick him up off the floor and place him on a stretcher. The struggle was intense as he was grabbed and pulled by strangers in scrubs. One nurse was bit on her neck and several people were scratched and bruised. They finally got him onto the stretcher and I held his head and shoulders. Austin fought the sedation for more than 3 minutes. His body eventually relaxed and we could tell he was out. However, as I looked at his face, through the clear mask I could see he was still clenching his teeth. My heart was breaking for him and I began to cry. I was trying so hard to help him and he didn't understand that. All he knew was that his mom was letting these people hurt him and I was sure he wanted to know why. How could I have ever explained all this to him?

After more than two hours of struggling to prep him, the actual procedure took all of thirty minutes. When he woke in the post-op room, I took him home and prayed that the sedation would keep him calm just a bit longer. I needed the quiet. As I drove I wondered how I could ever teach him that his aggressive behaviors had to stop. How could I undo what had been done to him?

On the Right Path?

October 2002 to January 2003

We began to investigate other options for Austin. We didn't want to continue down the wrong path, and we weren't going to put him in Ms. Kerwin's class. We needed expert help. A few months earlier I had attended a conference by Dr. Richard Smith, an expert in the field of aggressive and self-injurious behaviors. The conference gave me eye-opening insights about how behaviors were reinforced and what it took to get them under control. At lunch, I approached Dr. Smith's table and sat myself right next to him. I asked him questions about Austin to get his opinion of what we could do. He quickly realized that I was going to be relentless, and that my story would take more of his attention than he could offer at that time. He gave me his email address.

I immediately wrote to him. I shared all that we had been through and provided him with as much documentation as he would accept from a woman from New Jersey who wasn't paying him. I gave him a detailed history and inquired about the behavioral plan implemented by Dr. Slimetti. Dr. Smith's response was, "something doesn't sound right." He explained that the behavior plan as it was designed would actually increase challenging behaviors in a child like Austin. We asked if we could hire him to help us. Dr. Smith explained that he had limited availability and that I might want to reach out to the Kennedy Krieger Institute, a facility located in Baltimore, Maryland. Some of the doctors there were previous students of his, and he was sure they could give us the help we needed.

Austin couldn't stay at home forever and he needed to learn from others, but first we needed to get him to a state where he could learn. We were done giving people a chance with our son. He was ten years old and weighed only eighty pounds, I didn't want to imagine the damage he would be able to do at sixteen. We would do whatever it took to get him the best help available. Based on what Dr. Smith told us, it sounded like Kennedy Krieger Institute (KKI) was the best.

We were so grateful to Dr. Smith for referring us to KKI. Had it not been for him we would not have known such a place even existed. We were desperate for help from anyone at all, and he was the only one who gave us direction. After reviewing the website for KKI I felt confident this was our answer. I contacted the office at KKI and submitted all the documentation. We were scheduled for intake on January 30th.

We traveled over three hours to see what the facility had to offer. Dr. Irene O'Connor met us at the door and led us upstairs to begin the process. Austin waited less than patiently as we filled out paperwork in a small hallway. Billy paced the floor, reading all the bulletins on the walls. After the paperwork was done we were brought into a fully padded room with a one-way mirror and a few chairs. Here Dr. O'Connor asked us about Austin and his behaviors.

Once the interview was over it was clear that Austin met the criteria for their services. And it just so happened that there was a possible opening in one week. I can't say we were thrilled; none of this made us happy. Relieved was a much better word. We were offered a tour of the facility. We would have to go separately because one of us had to watch Austin, so I went first while Billy, Austin, and Dr. O'Connor waited in the lobby.

One Flew Over the Cuckoo's Nest had nothing on this place.

I had to be buzzed in to enter. Nurse Faith Rigby greeted me and began the tour at the North Tower. She informed me that her husband was ill and she was waiting for an important phone call that she would have to take should it come during the tour.

Most hospitals are cold in their décor. This one did not disappoint. It was not just unwelcoming and sterile, but hard. The walls were painted in drab shades of grayish white and blue; it took me a moment to notice that every corner was padded. The tables were set up cafeteria-style and the chairs were large blue plastic shapes without padding or fabric.

I immediately noticed the children in the room: a teenage girl with platinum hair and the palest skin I'd ever seen, a boy around Austin's age who appeared apathetic to all that was happening around him, and a large teenage boy playing with blocks.

Nurse Faith gave me brief run-down of what I was observing as the children worked with their staff, but none of what she was saying penetrated my ears. In fact, nothing seemed to make any sense at all. We left the North Tower and passed the observation/clinical rooms where most of the assessments were conducted. I began to tune her out entirely. I couldn't bear one more word. How could I bring my son this far from home and leave him with strangers?

She showed me the sleeping arrangements. There were four beds per room, and each room had a one-way mirror. Two staff members were always on hand to observe during sleeping hours. The beds looked like large cribs with strong metal bars. Nurse Faith informed me that these were not to keep the children in, but instead to protect them should one wake in the middle of the night and aggress toward one of the others. By now I knew this wasn't the place for Austin, so I just vacantly nodded each time she spoke.

The main area was furnished with TVs, dining tables, and furniture padded with blue vinyl. At the back of the space were more observation rooms. I saw a very large boy, over three hundred pounds. He was so heavy that even his forehead showed it, causing his sunken eyes to look like he was squinting. His hair was dark blonde and his face appeared to hold a permanent smile. Barney was playing on the television as the boy was being fed thickened Diet Sprite. He started to shriek, "yeeeeeeee." Over and over his sounds echoed off the cold and sterile walls, "yeeeeeeee, yeeeeeeeee, yeeeeeeeee." He seemed happy, but I was unable to tell.

Screams of profanity erupted from the main area of the South Tower. I quickly turned to see two staff members, each on either side of a large boy, moving him into a bedroom as he yelled at them. Then Nurse Faith received the phone call about her husband that she had been waiting for. She left me alone. Without my guide there to explain, I tried to figure out what I was seeing as I stood in the doorway of the South Tower. Now that the screaming boy had been removed, the space was calm in comparison to the other room. A small girl was eating her lunch while a staff member talked sweetly to her. What an amazing contradiction to the rest of this place, I thought. A second nurse came to find me and showed me out. Once I was on the other side of the door my thoughts spun quickly, like watching a movie in fast forward and then trying to recap it. Just as quickly, I made my decision. My son would not be treated here.

I did all I could do to hold back the tears; I didn't want Billy to see me cry. I went down to the lobby to join him, Austin, and Dr. O'Connor. We quickly acknowledged each other and then Billy and the doctor were off. I was left in the lobby with Austin, unable to continue to control my emotions. My entire face was soaking wet within a split second of the closing of the elevator door that took Billy up to that horrendous place. I turned to see Austin sitting in the chair, slightly upset that we weren't leaving and beginning to bite on his fingers. I sat next to him and told him that everything was okay. Daddy would be back soon and we'd get some fries.

Completely overwhelmed, I stared blankly as I waited. Absolutely nothing was able to penetrate my mind. Billy and Dr. O'Connor came back down and we discussed the possible opening next week. I pulled myself together and just yessed her as quickly as possible in an attempt to get out of there faster.

One of the requirements for Austin's admittance would be blood work. KKI was offering to do it that day to avoid any delays. Billy quickly agreed that would be best. I was floored. He was just up there; didn't he see the horror? There was no way Austin was going here. Billy took Austin into a small room off to the side and let them draw blood. I was numb; I just sat in the waiting area wondering why we were going through with this. Austin was not going to this place. The screams that came from the examining room were all too familiar to me, they reminded me of every other doctor or dentist appointment for Austin. I dealt with my own pain by tuning out. This would all soon be over and Austin and I would be home. I would apologize to him for even thinking about putting him in this place.

The valet brought our van around. I've never been so happy to see that big green monster. Once Austin was in and settled and we began to drive away, again my tears came flooding out. I wanted to put as much distance as possible between us and that horrible place. We drove without speaking for a while. At a stoplight, a man came to our window asking for money. Billy actually spoke with him and offered him a few dollars. I am always amazed at his naivety in certain situations, his lack of street smarts. Or maybe Billy just tends to see the good in everyone until they prove him wrong. We continued down the street, pausing at more red lights, stop signs, and left-turning vehicles than seemed possible. It felt like an eternity had passed since we got into our van, I was still panicked and needed to get father away. It was only then that I realized where we were. We were in the inner city, the extremely poor and forgotten part of Baltimore. Not the Baltimore Harbor area so many visitors recognized, with its wonderful aquarium, nightlife, and food. We were surrounded by run-down buildings, dirty streets, hard-looking people to whom life had been unkind, and the effects of drug abuse everywhere.

We finally made it to Interstate 95; we could finally speed away from all of this at 75mph. I turned to Billy and blurted, "He's not going there." Billy's questioning eyes said it all; he had every intention of admitting Austin into KKI. What was he thinking? As I described my experience with Nurse Faith he continued to look puzzled. His impression, based on what Dr. O'Connor had shown him, was nothing like what I had seen. He saw a well-organized floor, with activities and procedures that were clearly established and run by professionals. "He doesn't belong there, did you see those people?" I mumbled through my tears.

"I'm not going to come home to a wife that cries every day. He has to go there, it's our only option," Billy insisted.

Billy was right.

We couldn't continue to live as we were. The answers we needed were not just going to walk through our front door. KKI was the best program available, and that's what we wanted for Austin. Yet again, we had to trust our son's life to others. It wasn't the first time I wondered how one little boy could need so much help.

That evening Billy wrote this poem for Austin:

For Austin

How do we each prepare
For the day that lies ahead
How do we stay composed
On that day we both will dread
How do we get to sleep
That first night when you're not here
How do we come to grips
With all the questions that we fear

How do we tell ourselves
It's a step toward normalcy
How do we mediate
A heart and head that don't agree
How do we find the comfort in
It's the right thing to do
How do we go a day
Without hearing and seeing you

How do we tell our heart
That letting go is not good-bye
How do we tell our eyes
To keep the faith and not to cry
How do we find the trust
To pray that others will be kind
How do we drive away
When part of us is left behind

January 2003 to February 2003

After we got home from KKI we began to prepare ourselves for the next step. We made a list of things Austin would need for his three-month stay away from home. I purchased extra underwear, pajamas, t-shirts, and pants to make sure he would have enough clothing. Tears welled up in my eyes as I packed them. I couldn't believe I was preparing my ten-year-old son to live anywhere but with us.

We packed his suitcase with all the new items a few days before he was scheduled to leave. It was too difficult to do all at once. In our hearts we knew we had to do this; KKI was a place that held some promise of change, even though we harbored a lot of fear that there would be no change at all. The day before we were to leave we received a phone call.

"Mrs. Gallagher?" the caller asked.

"Yes?"

"This is Georgia, from Kennedy Krieger Institute. There has been a problem with your insurance," she continued.

"What kind of problem?" I asked.

"The insurance company won't pay for Austin's stay at Kennedy Krieger because it is an out-of-state facility," she proceeded to explain. I began to panic.

"We're sorry, we've never had a problem before with patients from New Jersey, but Austin is on a different plan than the one we generally deal with, and we didn't know it would cause a problem until today. Here is the number to call. You can talk with the case manager there," she said in an apologetic tone. We said our goodbyes and I hung up the phone.

I would be lying if I said I wasn't relieved, but the feeling was brief before the tears came again. I couldn't take this. The thought of what might happen if he didn't go was even more frightening than the idea of sending him away. I didn't know how I would be able to live without him, but more than that, I didn't know how I could continue to live with him.

We spent the entire day making calls. We asked for referrals from doctors to help us appeal the insurance company's decision. We talked with heads of departments at the insurance company and the Division of Developmental Disabilities. We contacted Congressman Smith's office. I could only muster up a "Hello..." and then Billy had to take the phone. The tears took over again. I couldn't beg one more person to understand our crisis.

I wanted to believe this was a sign from God that he shouldn't go there. Somehow, this meant we were supposed to find something else, something better, something that didn't require packing his belongings and sending him so far from home. But we had exhausted all the options. KKI was our only choice. Four o'clock had come around and all the offices we had been calling were closing for the day. Everyone was going home to their safe, normal environments. We were left completely confused, worrying that Austin's slot at KKI would be given away to the next deserving child and we would have to wait for another opening.

The next morning my eyes were swollen from all my crying the night before. I was at a loss for what we could do next. I moved through my routine slowly and quietly, hoping Austin stayed asleep while I got my coffee, carefully avoiding clinking mugs and clattering spoons. Chelsea and Alanna went off to school. Billy was at the dining room table making a list of people to contact. I had resigned myself to the fact that Austin wasn't going, and my head was full of worries about what would happen to him. At nine o'clock the phone rang.

"Mrs. Gallagher?"

"Yes?"

"This is Georgia from KKI. I don't know what you did, but he's in. You can bring Austin in at noon today."

I couldn't breathe. With my first inhale and exhale came a stream of tears, a pain in my heart, and a whirl of confusion. "I haven't even taken a shower yet, and we didn't finish packing his bag. And it takes us three hours to get to you…"

"Okay, but try and get here by 1:00 if you can, they will be waiting for you in the lobby."

I hung up the phone.

I cried with each sock, shirt, and pair of underwear I placed in the suitcase. I watched Austin sleep. He was unaware of what was about to happen, and unable to be told even if he was awake. How could I ever explain to him what we were doing and why? We got all of his things together, his toys and paper and a pen to write his words for him. But when it was time to get him ready I was unable to move. I stood frozen, gripping his dresser, paralyzed with grief. Billy had to help me. As we packed up his puppy I realized that he really was leaving, his room would be empty and I would have no idea what was happening to him. I truly believed I could have died from the pain in that moment. My knees were weak. I couldn't catch my breath. I couldn't move.

Silence was punctuated by sniffles as we put Austin into the van. He had no idea what awaited him. Riding in the van was an activity I would often use to make him happy. He sat in the back of the van, smiling, enjoying the view, and playing with his stuffed puppy. He probably thought he was getting French fries from McDonald's. I felt as though I had conned him into thinking he was going somewhere he would enjoy, and worried that when we got there he would know we had tricked him.

There was no way to explain the situation to Austin, and even if I could he would have obviously protested. I was in such a fragile state that any protest from Austin would have reinforced my unwillingness to leave him and nothing ever would have changed. Conversation between Billy and I on the ride down was forced and awkward. We couldn't talk about what we were actually doing. We would never have completed a sentence without sobbing.

We pulled up to the front doors of KKI and the valet came to take our van. Austin recognized where we were and began to protest. I was sure he was remembering his last experience, which ended with a needle in his arm to draw blood. Thankfully he got out of the van and followed us in. We signed in at the reception desk and were swiftly surrounded by a team of three people, all introducing themselves, shaking our hands, and trying to help us with our bags. I had no idea what they said, who they were, where we were going, or what the procedures were. I looked down and noticed Austin had wet his pants, something he hadn't done in a long time. "Is he afraid? Maybe it's just because of the long ride?" they began to question us. "I don't know. I don't know why. He doesn't usually have accidents," I started to explain. He might play in a puddle he purposefully created, but he didn't have accidents.

We were brought up to the unit and told we would have several meetings with different staffers and supervisors. Austin was handed over to a clinical assistant (CA). We had our first meeting with Brian Konik, a doctoral student who was assigned to Austin. On that first day they asked us to complete a questionnaire about our expectations for Austin's stay. We would take it again at the end as part of a research project on parental expectations. Brian explained that Dr. Louis Hagopian typically would have joined us, but because of our delay in getting to Baltimore he was unable to be with us due to another meeting.

We met with social worker Louise Heck and several other professionals. We spoke about Austin's abilities, his deficits, his habits, everything imaginable. During breaks between meetings we were permitted to see Austin. We were buzzed in to the Neurobehavioral Unit and the CA showed us the bedroom Austin would be staying in. She had already put all of Austin's belongings in the drawers designated for him. We noticed that the walls were bare and asked about putting up posters or pictures. The CA explained that wasn't allowed because some of the children's behaviors included ripping things off of the walls. They wanted us to bring Austin's stuffed puppy home with us in case it got damaged or lost, but we couldn't take that away from him. If it got lost, at least he would be with staff who were trained to handle the behaviors that would result from the loss. I couldn't intentionally leave him without Puppy.

The beds were the same large metal cribs that I remembered. "For Austin's protection," I had been told. I couldn't stay in the room any longer. Seeing his clothes in the drawers and not being permitted to personalize the space was making me too sad. I didn't want to cry.

We finished the meetings and went back to the unit to see Austin. Billy read Dr. Seuss books and I wrote words for him. Dinner trays arrived and the CA explained that Austin would be eating in the South Tower. We went into the room and saw several of the patients seated at the table with their staff. Some were more cooperative than others. Julie, one of the patients, needed her arm restraints removed so she could eat. The moment the splints came off she began punching herself in the face. The dining behaviors of the children varied from quiet and cooperative to throwing and spitting food at the staff. Austin would only eat the bread and drink the juice. It was hospital food, and he wanted nothing to do with it.

After the meal was finished one young boy sat on a large mat in the corner of the room looking for someone to play with. Derrick had some verbal skills, and Billy attempted to engage him by tossing a ball back and forth. I stayed with Austin. The staff put a video on the TV and Austin remained at the dining table while it played. Seven o'clock was craft time. The floor had a set schedule of activities; the patients didn't have to participate, but there was something for them to do each hour or so. Austin was not going to participate in a craft, so we left the South Tower and went to the main area to watch Barney.

A nurse informed us that we would have to leave before the bath-time routines started at eight o'clock. Billy and I had been having a hard time finding a moment when we could say goodbye. We would have slept there if they let us. Having someone else set an end time for our visit was a relief.

We discussed how we would leave, and the staff told us they would bring Austin to the door to say goodbye. We weren't sure this was the best idea. Kadesha Prickett, the staff person assigned to Austin, explained that they did not want to hide the fact that we were leaving. Austin had to learn that we would leave and come back. As I walked down the hall I could feel my eyes well up and my knees get weak. The closer we got to the door, the more I wished we had made a different choice for Austin.

We tried to hold it together for Austin's sake. We said goodbye and I exited through the main door first. I made the mistake of looking back. Through the tall rectangular window, I could see Austin attacking Kadesha, pinching, grabbing, and trying to bite her. He was making his awful "eee, eee, eee," sound and attempting to knock her off her feet by dragging her down. Billy told me to just keep going. We turned the corner and pushed the button for the elevator.

I couldn't hold my tears back any longer. As my next breath rushed into my lungs, I cried out like a wounded animal. Tears and snot ran down my face, and I didn't care that I was using my shirt to wipe them away. We had already trusted others so many times, and they had failed us. Why should I believe that this time would be different? I heard Billy break down with a loud "aaahhhh" from deep inside as his tears started to flow. He sniffled and tried to hold it in, trying to be strong for me. He had been a rock all day, paying close attention to words and details when it took all I had just to physically be in the room. It was finally impossible for him to stay strong any longer. His outburst had no words, just a sound of unbearable internal pain that echoed in the elevator. Seeing Billy break down was more than I could take. My heart and stomach hurt, my throat felt like it was closing, and there was a weight on my chest so heavy that I couldn't catch my breath. I would have done anything to trade places with Austin. He didn't deserve this. So many had failed him, and now he was paying the price.

The valet brought our van around to the front entrance. We cried all the way to the Ronald McDonald house, where we would be staying until Sunday. We needed to sign in and get our bags to our room. Billy left to get some food; we hadn't eaten since lunch. I sat on the bed and tried to compose myself. I needed to call my Dad. I started talking to myself, "Just breathe. Stop crying. Blow your nose." When I thought I had it under control and would be able to speak, I called. "Dad, I'm in Baltimore," (as the lump rose in my throat) "I really need your help. We had to bring Austin here..." (the sniffling and runny nose began). The tears started flowing and I was barely able to get the rest out without taking a breath between each word. "We'll be back Sunday night. Please call me and let me know you got this message. I don't know what to do."

I hung up the phone and wept.

February 2003 to May 2003

The next day we met Dr. Hagopian, the director of the Neurobehavioral Unit at KKI and the leader of Austin's treatment team. Dr. Hagopian was a quiet man, with a gentle face and a comforting manner. He immediately asked us to call him Louis, and he tried to put us at ease. He explained the process and what his role would be in supporting Brian and the rest of the staff. In addition to Brian and Louis, Austin was assigned two graduate students, Kate Litman and Allie Bonner, who would conduct much of the data collection and interventions during Austin's stay. With his quiet confidence, Louis reassured us that they were going to help Austin. There was no egotistical presentation, no videos of children he had helped, just a calm explanation of what needed to happen next. He let his years of research and experience speak for his abilities. He was a stark contrast to Dr. Slimetti.

We had completed most of the meetings and paperwork on our first day, so on Friday we got to spend more time with Austin. We met Kate and Allie and observed some of what their work entailed. They each carried a laptop as they engaged Austin in different settings and jotted down his every move, but mostly they looked to document his challenging behaviors. Austin would be with his team everyday from nine o'clock to four o'clock, except weekends. I'd thought it many times before, but I couldn't stop wondering: how could one little boy need so much help?

We started to become a bit more convinced that we had made the right decision. This place was going to give us positive results; Austin was going to get better. Leaving that second night was a little easier both because we had seen the team in action and because we knew we would be back the next day.

Weekends at KKI were starkly different than weekdays. There were far fewer staff people, and no one walked around with laptops. Austin was assigned a CA for each shift so that he could be constantly supervised in this sterile environment. He could walk from the North Tower to the South Tower, watch videos, or go into his bedroom to escape the noises of the other patients. These activities were repeated over and over to fill the hours.

Although the day seemed to drag with so little to do, our time with Austin was still passing too quickly. I knew it would be eight o'clock soon, and we would have our last moments together before we had to go back to New Jersey to be with the girls. The very thought brought me to tears, though I tried to hold them in and stay strong until I reached the van. I could feel the clock moving. I wanted to hold on to those last minutes and make them count. But the day had to end, and we had to leave. We couldn't explain to Austin that it would be days before he saw us again, unlike the last three days where he saw us for breakfast each morning. We said goodbye and asked the staff to leave him in the South Tower instead of bringing him to the door. We needed the peaceful exit. I couldn't bear the sight of him hurting someone, not understanding why his parents were leaving him there. My heart broke with each step toward the door.

As we drove home we each broke out in alternating bouts of tears, but we held onto the hope that this was the right decision. We convinced ourselves that with all the supervision there, no one could hurt Austin. The closer we got to New Jersey the more real it became that our home would be missing one person when we returned. Tomorrow morning would mark the first time that I wouldn't hear the squeak of the hinges on Austin's door. Funny how a sound I learned to hate could become one I would miss.

When we arrived home, Billy's mom and dad were at the house with my dad and stepmother. They were sitting at the dining room table looking at photo albums with Chelsea. I was so happy to see my family, but when I saw the albums I broke down. There were pictures of Austin that I just didn't want to see, pictures of his smile and of him enjoying life at home. I couldn't bear to look. I went straight into the kitchen and began to cry.

Everyone left Billy and I alone with the girls. We tried to wrap our minds around what we would need to do over the next few months. We started with a plan to get Austin more food, because he wouldn't eat anything from the hospital. Billy made a list of items that I could bring down with me when I returned to KKI on Wednesday. As the girls completed their nighttime routines, Billy and I laid down on the bed. He held me while I cried, something that happened often in the days that followed. Chelsea came in, sat at the end of our bed, and floored me with her words.

Through tears she asked, "Why did you take my brother away from me?"

"Oh my God honey, we didn't take him away from you," I said as I reached for her. "We had to bring him somewhere he could get help." Chelsea was upset with us. She wanted us to make other people do the right thing for Austin, and she couldn't understand why we couldn't make that happen here in Brick. We never thought she would be angry about our decision. Honestly, we hadn't thought much about what she would think. We were so focused on Austin we didn't even discuss this with her; somehow we assumed she would be relieved. She had spent so much time in her bedroom avoiding him that we thought she would welcome the peaceful change in the house.

Many might think that we would relish the newfound quiet of our home. We didn't. It is impossible to explain how much it hurts to not have your child with you, how painful it is to know that you had to send him away. Our guilt was tremendous. We had allowed him to be a guinea pig for Dr. Slimetti's work in Brick. That poor decision made us question our current choice to place him at KKI. We had to be right this time. We couldn't survive another decline.

And there was no enjoying the quiet of the house when there was work to be done. I spent every Tuesday preparing food for Austin. I would make long shell pasta and mix it with olive oil, garlic, and parmesan cheese. I packed it into multiple Tupperware containers and made sure I also had plenty of Stouffer's Macaroni and Cheese, bagels, and Welch's 100% White Grape Peach Juice. On Wednesday mornings I would make the trek down to Baltimore after putting the girls on the bus. One of our family members would get the girls off the bus, feed them dinner, and stay until I got home, usually around ten or eleven o'clock at night.

I went down to KKI during the week not only to bring Austin food, but also to ensure that I got to meet with Brian, Kate, and Allie. I wanted to be aware of everything that was happening. I needed this treatment plan to be a success. During each visit I got to spend just a few brief moments with Austin. I would get to see him for lunch or during a break, and then I had to wait for four o'clock when his team left and the night shift took over. Several weeks passed before Brian and the team allowed me to see Austin throughout the day and let me spend sessions with them.

In fifteen-minute increments, staff observed and interacted with Austin in different settings. Sometimes he would be placed in a small padded room while his team performed functional analysis of his behaviors. Two team members observed the session through the one-way mirror as the third spent time in the room with Austin. I got to watch a few times. Functional analysis is a very detailed experiment in the field of ABA. When conducting it, the team would manipulate Austin's environment to determine the function, or reason, behind his behaviors. Once the function was identified, they could design a behavior intervention plan.

During one visit, I watched from the observation room with Brian and Allie as Kate sat in the room with Austin. Kate was supposed to provide attention to Austin if he engaged in any self-injurious behaviors, including biting his hand or fingers. All other behaviors were to be ignored, and she was to remain as stoic as possible throughout. Shortly into the session, Austin tried to convince Kate to open the door. He grabbed her hand and placed it on the doorknob. She didn't open it for him. Instead of becoming more insistent, he stripped off all of his clothes. The next thing we knew, he was jumping up and down making joyful sounds. His penis was bouncing as he lept around, and we all began to chuckle when it looked like he caught onto the cause and effect of his actions. Kate had to remain unfazed.

Austin grabbed his socks from the floor and started to swing them, still bouncing his penis and laughing. Those of us behind the observation mirror got quite the show, and we futilely tried to remain professional. Austin moved closer to Kate and rubbed his penis against her leg like a Chippendale dancer as he swung a sock in each hand. I was hysterical, and Brian and Allie could barely hold it together. Kate held her ground, focusing on a spot on the wall and doing her best to get through the remaining minutes with a straight face. The fifteen-minute timer finally went off, and Kate opened the observation room door. "You guys suck!" she blurted, "I could hear you laughing!" Everyone broke out in uncontrollable giggles.

Those were not typical interactions for Austin, so it was nice to have a little chuckle. More often, the staff wore padded football-style arm protectors during sessions and Austin would sink his teeth deep into the foam. He had episodes of rage that reminded me of the events at Diane's office. These sessions were held every weekday until all the functions of all Austin's challenging behaviors had been identified.

Austin also challenged staff outside of the education and observation rooms. One day I waited in the main living space while Austin was in a session. Behind me was a young man who worked as a CA. He had on short-sleeved scrubs, and his arms were wrapped in gauze in multiple areas. Another CA asked him what happened. He attempted to shield me from his answer by mouthing it silently, but I turned around just in time to see him respond, "Austin." I felt awful. I apologized to him. He reassured me that he really enjoyed when he got a shift with Austin, saying, "He's so smart!" When I asked what happened, he explained that he had been trying to give Austin a bath. He didn't know that Austin didn't like to have his hair washed, and once he put shampoo in Austin's hair he had to wash it out. Because the CA's skin was wet Austin had been able to scratch him pretty badly, and his arms needed to be wrapped. As he turned away, I saw more marks on the side of his face and neck.

Weekends were the worst. The staff made many attempts to fill the long days, but Austin had no interest in their activities. Instead, they spent hours on end reading Dr. Seuss books, writing words for him, and watching videos.

Because of Austin's behavioral challenges, it would be weeks before I could sign him out for activities off the floor. We were permitted to take walks around the floor below us, which was empty on weekends. We couldn't go outside, so we had to settle for excursions one flight down.

Finally, the day came when Austin was able to leave KKI for brief trips. We had to sign a document stating that we understood the risks and that we promised to return him to the floor within four hours from the time we took him. Having to ask permission to take your child and signing him out like a rental car was strange. At first I was fearful of signing Austin out alone, so Billy made an effort to get more weekends off from the boat so we could spend time with him together. We took him to the local playground and let him swing, or brought him back to the Ronald McDonald house so he could use the playground equipment there.

Austin loved the Baltimore Aquarium, especially the stingray pool. We would stretch our four hours to the very last second. Austin would get upset when we had to return and start to bite himself. Ending the day like that took away much of the joy we would feel when he was out. So many times I wished we could just keep driving back to New Jersey and let him sleep in his own bed with all his favorite things.

Every week was the same: cook and prep on Tuesday, make sure I had all the things I needed. Drive down alone on Wednesday. Meet with the team. Watch Austin challenge everyone around him. Spend dinner with him. Leave crying. I spent Fridays packing enough food to get Austin through to the following Wednesday when I could get down to Baltimore again. Every time we visited KKI and signed Austin out we tried to make his world a little bit better. Then we would bring him back under protest and wish he could just understand why this was happening.

When we brought the girls we would try to make an outing of it, even though their presence made things a bit more challenging. We tried to entertain them, but also have them realize that it wasn't a vacation. We just wanted Austin to see them regularly. At first it was hard for Chelsea to understand why we had to do this, why Billy and I couldn't fix Austin ourselves. But after she got to meet some of the other patients at KKI, she grew to understand that she wasn't the only one who had someone she loved "taken away."

During one visit we got to meet the parents of some of the other children and the hospital served us all dinner in the cafeteria. Billy and I went first when the time came for introductions. We explained some of the reasons why we were there, including how we had started the admission process in November and how Austin arrived at KKI in February. We didn't know how lucky we were. One family had waited years. Many of the other families waited between nine and twelve months. Not all the families could come for visits. Many never saw their children.

There was little turnover in the children during our time at KKI. We learned so much about them all, and it was comforting to share the similarities about how our families ended up here. A common factor was professionals working outside their scope of practice, people whose egos would not let them say, "This child needs more than I can provide," and direct parents to seek advice elsewhere. Instead, they often blamed any decline on the child or others. It was certainly a familiar story for us.

Finally, we were creeping up on the three-month mark and were getting excited to bring Austin home. But, heartbreakingly, we were told we'd have to wait a few more weeks; Austin's plan was not ready yet, and they needed to implement it within KKI for a while to make sure it was effective before using it to train Austin's school and home staff. We were distraught that Austin couldn't come home yet, but the staff explained that it was rare for a patient to leave on their original discharge date. I think if someone had told me this up front, I might not have gone through with it.

The commute was taking a heavy toll on me. It was draining to have every day consumed with making food, packing items, planning sitters for the girls, and still running a household. Watching all the other children at KKI, learning the circumstances that brought them there, and knowing the limited resources many would have when they left was sobering. Who would be there for them when they left KKI? How can we ensure that our children will be safe when they return home? What about the ones that can't go home? The constant reminder that we needed to rely on others to help us with our children even after we brought them back home was depressing. When we were told Austin wasn't coming home as planned, that he needed even more help, I was defeated. How did I let him get this bad? How did I let others do what they did? As far as I was concerned, Austin was this way because I failed him.

My part in Austin's challenges haunted me. I could not forgive myself for each and every time I knew we were headed in the wrong direction but still blindly followed the recommendations of the "experts." My guilt was overwhelming. I reached the point where I tried to plan my exit, my death. I would constantly imagine ways that I could end all this. I wanted it to happen in a way that wouldn't make me look weak. Each time I left KKI,

I got into my car and exited the well-protected parking lot. The guards always acknowledged me. What they didn't know was that I left my van unlocked, and I wished someone sinister was hiding inside it without my knowing. Then maybe they could help me put an end to all that was happening by putting an end to me.

One night on the way home I made it to the entrance of 495 before I broke down, shaking, crying, and unfocused while driving at 85 mph, a deadly combination. An accident would be an easy way out. I took my usual breaks along the way, coffee at the rest stop before Delaware, a bathroom break when I reached New Jersey. Each time I entered a rest area, I did so with my music blasting louder than would be expected for a woman my age. I wanted to draw attention to my vehicle. I drove a large green Chevy conversion van that would be easy for anyone with bad intentions to hide inside. I never locked the doors when I got out. I was trying to make myself an easy target.

Each time I returned to my car, thoughts of what I would do if someone were in my van played in my mind. In these scenarios I was not the hero, but an apathetic participant in my imaginary thriller. I told myself I would ensure the worst possible ending by not obeying any of the requests the intruder would bark at me. I would intentionally do the opposite to make him so furious he would do away with me within the first few minutes. My fear and torture would be my well-earned punishment for what I'd allowed others to do to Austin.

Or, maybe I would pretend to do as they wished and then put my foot to the floor, speeding away. I would reach terrifying speeds before crashing into the largest solid object I could find, smashing and exploding my tank-sized vehicle into rubble. I fantasized about how much easier my family's lives would be if the outcome were my death. I imagined the headlines: MOM OF TWO AUTISTIC CHILDREN DIES HORRIFIC DEATH. Not only would my misery end, but people in our immediate social circle and the autism community would reach out to support my husband and children. They would be fine without me.

Death seemed to be my best option, but I was too much of a coward to take my own life so I prayed someone else would do it for me. If I committed suicide, my family would hate me. Billy would curse me. Chelsea would never forgive me because I would have robbed her of having a mom there through dating, college, and her future dreams. Alanna would probably survive it the best, as long as her routine wasn't interrupted. Every day I hoped that someone else would end my life for me and let me off the hook.

Peace. I just wanted a moment of peace. Death held the promise of ultimate, permanent peace.

I hated when I sunk into exhaustion and depression. I had no right to think like this. The only person my death would truly benefit was me. I was so deep inside the hole I had dug myself that I couldn't see any light.

Soon Austin would turn eleven. He would spend his birthday in an institution, surrounded by people paid to supervise or research him and not by those who loved him. He would not be allowed to ask for anything special to eat because it was his birthday. There wouldn't be any extra hours before bedtime to watch a favorite TV show, or a night out at a movie with a few friends. There wouldn't be any surprises, no indication that it was a special day. It would be business as usual, the same as every other day since he entered KKI on February 6th.

Austin's birthday fell on a Wednesday that year, so I didn't get to him until after noon. I had to get the girls on the school bus before I could leave. He woke up in the morning to a CA. His routine was the same as that established for him on his first day. He was taken to the bathroom, had his teeth brushed, and was made to change out of his pajamas. He took a trip to the nurse's office where he was given his medication and had his blood pressure taken. Finally, he made his way to the South Tower carrying a food tray with a hospital breakfast on it that he didn't want. After breakfast he was taken into an observation room and more research was done to develop a possible behavior plan. This was all there was for Austin. But this was the best place for him to be. In 2003, this was the best we could expect.

I had reached a point where I questioned not only my existence, but also the existence of any higher power because of the state my life was in. I was questioning life itself. I had been told that everything happens for a reason. Bull! There was no reason for this except human error and egos, and through it all Austin was a casualty who no one wanted to help.

But Austin and all the other children at KKI were also what kept me going. If they could wake up every day and start again, so could I. I needed to make sure Austin had the best life we could give him. I needed to make it right, to let him know I wouldn't listen to others again. All of the people who claimed to be looking out for his best interests but failed him would eventually find out just how amazing he was. We knew they had done him wrong. Austin Gallagher deserved a mom who was a fighter. The children at KKI needed someone who would make a difference in their lives. I decided to go back to school and be a part of that change by becoming a BCBA and help as many children as I could. I would start with my own. Austin Gallagher deserved to be given back his life as he once knew it.

I was going to make sure that happened, and I wouldn't stop until I did.

Anywhere in the United States of America, Just Not Here

June 2003 to October 2003

An IEP meeting was held on June 6th while Austin was still in KKI. At the meeting were Mr. Asinello, Austin's new case manager Lillian Papageorge, the proposed new teacher Kim Gonclaves, the assistant principal of the school, Billy, and me. Brian joined us via telephone conference. We also asked Robyn Catagnus, a BCBA, to attend, because Bethany was no longer confident that she had the expertise to treat a child who had been to KKI. I also think being involved with the Brick school district and having to face Dr. Slimetti and his team again was too much for her to handle. She needed to move on.

The district was supposed to find an appropriate replacement BCBA for us, but claimed it was very difficult. We found Robyn after posting on a listserv about Austin's needs; a colleague of hers from Temple University responded within a day of our request. We were confident Robyn would be able to help Austin, and she looked forward to the experience and the opportunity to work with an expert like Dr. Louis Hagopian.

Everyone at this IEP meeting agreed that Austin would return to school in Ms. Gonclaves' classroom, and that he would get services at home as well. Robyn would oversee both settings to ensure continuity. We were excited for the next phase, but we had been optimistic before. Robyn went to KKI along with another member of her staff to be trained in the behavior intervention plan designed by KKI. I met her there, and I was thrilled that she was so excited about this opportunity to learn and to train others.

Ms. Gonclaves also went to KKI to receive direct training from Brian on how to implement the plan. Brian had videotaped the sessions and was happy that he did, because at one point Austin engaged in what was called "extreme agitated behavior," or EAB. We used to call these the "buggies" at home, because it looked as though Austin had bugs crawling on him. He would start crying, scratching at the back of his neck and then up and down his entire body. These episodes could last minutes or hours, but Brian's video captured their first occurrence at KKI. Fortunately, they were able to add an intervention for it to the plan before he came home.

Just days before Austin was to come home, the district called another IEP meeting under the premise of discussing Ms. Gonclaves' visit to KKI. Because of the short notice we could not coordinate all the people who needed to attend. Mr. Asinello, Ms. Papageorge, Ms. Gonclaves, the assistant principal, Billy, and I were able to participate. Brian could not dial in for a teleconference, and Robyn couldn't join us either. At this meeting, Mr. Asinello told us that, based on Ms. Gonclaves' visit to KKI, she had decided Austin would not be a good fit for her program. The district was not going to permit Austin to return to school.

Billy and I were at a loss. One of the conditions for Austin's acceptance at KKI was confirmation of a placement for him when he returned back home. There had to be a team ready to receive the child upon exit. Mr. Asinello explained that the Brick school district child study team had decided that it would be best for Austin to instead be placed in a residential facility upon leaving KKI. After he had spent some time in the residential placement, they would reconsider bringing him back into the school district. Billy and I could not believe what we were hearing.

I had no idea what Ms. Gonclaves saw, but Brian indicated it was not an unusual day. Robyn and her team were confident that Austin's return to the district would be successful. How could Mr. Asinello think that Austin wasn't ready?

We reminded them that everyone had agreed Austin was ready at our last meeting, but Mr. Asinello held strong with little explanation other than "the team has decided." Billy turned directly toward Mr. Asinello, put his finger in his face, and let him know, "I will be unpacking my son's bags when he comes home, and I will not be packing them again. He deserves that." Mr. Asinello explained that, based on the input of Ms. Gonclaves and the team, Austin would not be welcome back to the Brick school district and that we should begin looking for other placements.

My face burned red and my heart pounded as I pleaded. We needed the district to accept him. We had nowhere else for him to go. He was coming home in three days. We didn't go through all of this to leave our son in a residential facility. Mr. Asinello looked at me and emphatically said, "He can go anywhere in the United States of America, Mrs. Gallagher, just not here."

Just not here. Those words stuck. Not your son, lady, he can't come here. He doesn't deserve a chance here. I couldn't help but wonder whether Dr. Slimetti had played a part in this decision. Perhaps he didn't want others to see that Austin was a success without his help.

With or without a placement, Austin was coming home on June 26th. Billy and I had been through multiple trainings at KKI, and we met the ninety percent accuracy requirement for Austin to come home with us. KKI had to ensure that all the progress that had been made would not be undone once Austin returned home. Their training gave our family the tools we needed to be successful, especially in the initial days back home.

I was overwhelmingly excited to have Austin back in his home. The district couldn't dampen my joy. My baby boy was going to wake up in his own bed. I would get to see him on his trampoline and swing set. His skin was so pale after four and a half months of hospital life without any real time outside. There wasn't a hint of pink to his coloring. But now it was summertime at the Jersey shore. Austin had a date with some sunshine.

After we picked up Austin, Brian followed us home. We turned off 195 at exit 31A and made our way off the highway ramp. As we reached the first light at the corner of Herbertsville Road, Austin realized we were in familiar territory. His wonderful, beautiful, soft smile with its incredible dimples lit up his face, along with an obvious understanding that he knew where he was. He sat up just a bit and began to absorb the view from his window with much more attention. He knew this wasn't just another four-hour outing.

When we arrived we exchanged excited greetings with our family who were watching the house, but all our focus was on Austin's reaction. He immediately went out to the backyard to jump on the trampoline. Brian and I followed him. His screeching of delight was bittersweet. He was so happy, but it also made me realize how deprived he was of the things that brought him joy in the past five months. Our neighbor Cynthia had come outside, and she told me, "The neighborhood has been too quiet without him." It made me happy to know that even our neighbors could appreciate those screeches of happiness.

Brian quickly had me engage with Austin using the behavior protocols designed for him at KKI. It was probably the best thing Brian could have done; old habits die hard, and it would have been easy to start giving in to Austin's desires. I had to tell Austin to come off the trampoline. I showed him the "My Way" card, a visual representation to warn him that a demand was coming. I told him, "It's my way, come here." The finger biting began. He then aggressed, so next I had to block him and keep moving him away from the trampoline. There was no great fight on Austin's part, and soon he fell right into the routine. He understood that I would allow him to play again if he would just comply for a moment. He had to learn that the protocols from KKI were going to be implemented here at home.

Austin's behavior plan had several components. KKI had determined that the function or cause of Austin's behavior was denied access to preferred activity, and his preferred activity was often to be left alone. That is, Austin was aggressing toward other people to get them to leave his environment. Sometimes this was just because he would rather be left alone, other times it might be because he wanted to continue an activity or was trying to do something he perceived would not be permitted, like throwing a brick in the pool.

If a task was presented while Austin was in one of his preferred settings, he had to decide whether he was willing to give up his current situation and comply with the demand. He usually chose to stay put. KKI developed a visual system to let him know when demands would be placed on him: a blue circle with the words "My Way," meaning that things had to be done the instructor's way. Demands were always followed by reinforcers, such as watching a DVD, access to preferred items, or time alone.

Once the demands were completed, Austin was given another visual signal: a green triangle with the words "Free Time" to let him know he was permitted to engage in activities of his choosing. Austin also had a competing reinforcer component. This part of the plan was designed to make sure that he always had something in his hands. The staff at KKI determined that if Austin held an item in his hand, often his puppy, he had fewer hand and finger bites. He would instead bite the object.

Billy called me inside; Brian chose to stay outside and observe Austin in his downtime activities. That was something he never got to see in Baltimore. Billy handed me an envelope from the district and went out to the deck to be with Brian and Austin; he knew I was not going to be happy. The district had sent an IEP they claimed to have developed after our meeting on June 23rd. I flipped through it quickly and turned to the page describing the placement—RESIDENTIAL—it stood out so harshly. Home instruction would be provided by the district until a residential facility could be found. Residential, were they insane? Our son was only eleven years old. Prisoners got more leniency than this.

I knew this meant there would be another fight. I was so tired, physically, mentally, and emotionally. We had put all our energy into getting Austin back home, back to being an incredibly loving child with a great smile and a constantly happy demeanor. The district wanted us to send him away from home again. We would never pack his bags again, I promised him that. Billy promised him that. Never again.

I immediately dialed our attorney Herb Hinkle. Fortunately he was in, and the secretary put me right through. I briefly described what had happened. We had touched base once or twice during this whole ordeal, but now I really needed him. As always, Herb listened closely and brought great reasoning to the conversation. He knew what needed to be done. We had to file for emergent relief. We needed a judge to say that we could keep our son out of a residential facility while we settled the disagreement with the school district. It sounded so simple, as if Austin was just a piece of furniture that needed to be divided during a divorce. But it made so little sense. We needed to fight our school district to keep our son, when we had only just gotten him back from KKI.

Herb was sympathetic, but he had so many cases on his plate that he had to refer us to one of his associates, Paul Prior. "Paul has a brother with autism," Herb explained. "He'll be able to help you with this case. I'll have him call you later." My anger turned into fear. Was it possible that the school district would be allowed to do this? How could these people possibly have that much power? Through tears, with my voice quivering, I begged, "Herb, don't let them take my son away from me."

Due to the urgency of our situation Paul filed for emergent relief immediately, a procedure that requested a quick decision in front of a judge while the two parties moved to either mediation or litigation. The judge saw us on July 2, 2003, just a few short days after Austin arrived home from KKI.

Not much was accomplished at this hearing. Judge Victoria Gracias ordered that the school district place Austin in the summer program with Ms. Gonclaves and have Robyn oversee both the home and school settings. The judge insisted that the district provide programming throughout the summer months. When the district's programs closed at the end of the summer, they were to use staff from Clarity Behavioral Consulting, Robyn's company, to provide a full-day program in our home. At this court meeting we discovered Ms. Gonclaves had given her notice and the district was claiming no other staff would be appropriate for Austin. In light of that change, Judge Gracias ordered that the district put effort into finding staff for Austin in order to have a program ready for him in September in the Brick schools.

Based on the judge's decision, Austin started at the Drum Point School in July for four hours each day. He was the only student in the classroom with Ms. Gonclaves and an aide. They placed him in a room that was used for storage for the other classes, and sometimes served as a makeshift related services room during the summer months. I drove him each day, and the school permitted me to stay with him in the beginning to show the teaching staff how I worked with him. The teacher and the aide assigned to him were less than enthused and merely appeased me. When I asked them to demonstrate a component of Austin's plan that I had showed them, they refused and instead said they knew how to do what I was doing.

Ms. Gonclaves was on her way out, and I am sure she had no desire to be in this room. The students she had worked with all year were in another building, and she had to spend her last days with Austin instead of them. The weeks that followed were inconsistent. Robyn was able to get into the classroom a few times, but commitment from the district staff was lacking and there was only so much she could do if they didn't want to learn. Ms. Gonclaves and her staff had been trained by Dr. Slimetti, and many of the components of Austin's new plan went against what they had learned.

After the summer program ended, Austin received all of his services in our home from Clarity staff. There was still no plan from the district to return him to any other classroom. In early September we were back in court to see what the district would propose. The judge inquired about the progress made on finding staff or placements for Austin. During the summer, the district had proposed alternate placements outside of Brick Township schools. However, they opted to take us on tours of these locations during August, when they were closed. They tried to tell the judge that I was being uncooperative because I wouldn't take the tours. I explained that I didn't need to see empty buildings, I needed to see teaching in action.

The judge was not happy and asked the district to produce proof at our next meeting that they had made an effort to find staff for an in-district placement, and that they had scheduled observations of other placements at times when the students were present.

Prior to the court date, Lillian, Austin's newest case manager, announced that she was also leaving the district to take a position at another school as a consultant under Dr. Slimetti. We all agreed to have her speak in court to preserve her testimony in case the dispute could not be resolved and we moved forward with litigation. The judge explained that once Lillian's testimony was completed, we would discuss what the next steps would be for Austin.

After the usual formalities and swearing in, Lillian took the stand. She explained that she had drafted the June 23rd IEP that stated Austin's placement would be residential. Under direct questioning from Thom Natale, the district's attorney, Lillian explained why she felt this was the right decision. She had observed Austin at KKI and saw some of his challenges. Additionally, during the time Austin was in KKI, the district had placed other children in the classroom that was supposed to be his. One of the other children had outbursts, and she testified there was a "procedure in place where if this child was having that type of tantrum, we would evacuate the room. I'm not sure that Austin would be able to handle the interruption. And I also thought that another child in the room who yells and screams would affect Austin's programming."

My son couldn't go to school because the district decided to place more children in the classroom they had originally designated for him. More children who had behavioral challenges that Austin allegedly wouldn't be able to handle. Why didn't those children need to find a new place to be educated? Why did my son, who had already been through so much, have to be the one who was turned away?

When it was Paul's turn to cross-examine Lillian, he immediately asked her about the IEP dated June 5th, which placed Austin in the district classroom with additional home programming. He asked her if everyone who attended the June 5th meeting agreed with the IEP. Lillian stated, "At the end of the meeting, we were going forward with that plan." Paul asked a simple question that would later prove crucial in our litigation: "This was an IEP meeting, right?" Lillian answered, "Yes."

When asked why the plan had changed, Lillian repeatedly responded that after seeing Austin at KKI, she felt the need to change her recommendation. I needed to speak with Paul. I know he didn't like me interrupting, but I had to tell him when she had actually been down to visit. He asked for a brief recess and we stepped outside of the room to talk. When we returned to the courtroom and went back on the record, Paul asked, "Ms. Papageorge, when did you initially go down to Kennedy Krieger and perform your observation of Austin?" She responded curtly, "Do you want an exact date?" as she looked my way. I could tell, she knew that I knew. She then resigned to admit, "It was before June 5th." The IEP of June 5th was written *after* she had been to KKI. She had been lying to the court, lying under oath; she saw nothing new that caused her to make such a drastic change. Someone else ordered had this.

To replace Lillian, the district had to assign Austin yet another case manager, Mike Green. Mike called me the day before our next scheduled court date to let me know that he had been talking with Mr. Asinello about the case. "Anthony said we're going to court on Monday," he said, "and we need to show the judge that we've reached out to your family. That's why I'm calling you." He was being completely clear that this was only a formality. When the judge asked if the district had contacted us, they could honestly say they had.

By the end of September, we were back in court for the third time. It should have gotten easier, but instead it became harder to remain calm. Each time a court date was set, we thought a final decision would be reached. And as each court date drew near, anxiety about the outcome grew with each passing day.

I arrived in court before anyone else. After passing through the metal detector and signing in, I went directly to the assigned courtroom. I sat in the courtroom alone, knowing any second *they* would come walking in.

They wanted to put my son away in a place where he could be forgotten, except for the mandatory annual visit they would need to be legally able to write the reports that would keep him in whatever hell hole they had chosen.

My heart pounded so hard I could feel it echoing in my chest. I was sure that my shirt was moving with its force. My hands shook, partly due to nerves and partly from not having been able to eat beforehand. There were so many things to be done before I could leave the house in order to ensure Austin's day ran smoothly and his therapists were well-prepared. Because the district had not yet provided any staff, Austin was still being taught in our home.

Paul arrived smiling and confident, always carrying a cocky lawyer's attitude that assured us we had nothing to worry about. He looked every inch the attorney in his tailored green suit with matching shirt and tie. I knew he was on our side and I knew he wanted to win more than anything. But I didn't know whether he truly understood our decision and the reasons why we were fighting to keep Austin home. He had made it clear to us that he thought we should take the offer of a residential placement. He knew how hard it would be to later find a place for Austin when he became an adult. I couldn't accept that was our only choice. Paul explained that other parents who had gone down similar roads often had to fight their districts to get residential placements at this young age. I told him that our decision was for our son to live with us.

Mr. Natale walked in wearing a nervous smile as he prepared to represent the school district. An obvious air of discomfort surrounded him. His small talk seemed rehearsed. He looked like a short-bearded Santa Claus, and he appeared not to have been in a courtroom in quite some time. He wore a tan corduroy sports coat with buttons that had not met the buttonholes in years. He didn't look like a man of his age or stature, and certainly not like the partner of a law firm.

The attorneys greeted each other with the courtesy expected among professionals. After some chit-chat about a recent vacation Mr. Natale had taken to France, they set off to see the judge in her chambers. An even stronger wave of nervousness washed over me. Had I told Paul everything he needed to know? Did I express myself well enough to ensure that Austin would get what he needed? Would the district fight us again?

As I waited for their return, I wondered if having a female judge was a positive or a negative. I had no idea whether she was a mom or not. Would that even matter? Does being a female in a male-dominated world make you colder than the men in order to prove your strength? I desperately hoped she would see why we couldn't be content with the way things were, and I hoped she'd have the strength to force the district to do right by Austin.

An hour later Paul walked in and tossed the file on the table with disgust. While in discussion, the district's attorney stated they would not offer a teacher and an aide, only either an out-of-district day placement or a residential placement. Nothing had changed since July. The district's argument was that I was actually hindering their efforts to establish a day placement by refusing to return phone calls and make necessary arrangements. That was a lie. First, we never received any phone calls from the district except when Mike called the Friday before court. Second, I had most certainly made appointments to visit schools. Why on earth wouldn't I? If I could find a placement that didn't involve these people, my life would be so much easier. None of the places they were offering even had a history of working with children with autism, never mind one with severe behavior challenges.

Mike came into the courtroom where Paul and I sat. He and Mr. Asinello had also been in the meeting with the judge and the attorneys. I couldn't understand why they all got to explain their sides, but I had to wait in an empty courtroom. Mike told us that he was excusing himself from our case. What Mr. Asinello didn't know was that Mike had known Billy and me since we were kids. During the summer months when he wasn't working in the schools, Mike ran an umbrella rental business on the beach in Asbury Park. The town was a small one, and everyone knew the locals. Mike saw Billy and me throughout our teenage years and often threw a football around with Billy during slow days. He was no longer comfortable being a part of whatever Mr. Asinello was planning, and he didn't want to stay on as case manager.

The district refused to allow Austin back when school reopened in September, and they continued to hold that stance. The judge ordered that we continue to visit out-of-district placements. She also ordered that the district continue to provide Austin with programming at home during this time, using Robyn and her staff from Clarity Behavioral. The district was to find a new case manager for Austin, and they would contact me with a list of possible placements to tour.

The new case manager was Dave Massey, not a district employee, but a private marriage counselor who the district hired specifically for our case. He had no experience with autism, but he had worked for a school district as a case manager in the past. He was going to research some schools in the area and schedule appointments for us to visit. Over the next few weeks we went to many schools; several had no experience with children with autism, and others had no openings. He kept bringing me to places that simply couldn't help Austin. But I had to go so they could show the judge the laundry list of schools we had refused. Some of the schools told us they wouldn't take a child with Austin's level of challenging behaviors, and that we should come back if the situation changed. Why didn't Mr. Massey accurately describe Austin prior to scheduling the visit and save everyone's time? There were few places for a child like Austin, and those schools that could handle him had no openings. This reinforced why we needed the district to open a classroom for us, but they still refused.

Austin's progress in our home program didn't seem to matter, he was still shut out of his home district. "Anywhere in the United States of America…just not here," they had said, and they were sticking to it. They refused to let him be a part of his community. We would hear from others that the administration described Austin as a "monster." If that's what they thought, then he was a monster they had created. He was an amazing boy who was making incredible progress despite all the obstacles set before him. He was no monster. This boy was a superhero.

November 2003 to November 2005

The next two years of our lives played out in two parallel worlds. We would return to court regularly to inform the judge of any updates. However, we often would arrive with little or nothing to tell her, because the district refused to follow her order to find staff to work with Austin. This was just a waste of time and an attempt to exhaust our financial resources.

Regardless of the judge's orders for the district to provide proof of their efforts to find staff, there appeared to be no repercussions for their lack of effort. The judge asked for copies of the newspaper ads showing that the district was trying to recruit staff. They would claim they didn't have them. Mr. Asinello would state that he reviewed the district's substitute roster, but couldn't find any candidates capable. With each visit to the courthouse our legal fees soared. By this time we had surpassed fifty thousand dollars. At one meeting, Mr. Natale asked Paul, "How is a fisherman paying for all this?" Paul told him that he didn't know and didn't care.

School districts use financial drain as a way to wear families down. I am sure that the district felt that by then Billy and I should have run out of money. I couldn't work because I was overseeing the staff in my home all day, and Billy was a commercial fisherman. He had a good job, but we weren't rolling in extra dollars. We mortgaged, borrowed, used credit cards, and just made it work by any means we could. Money was not going to be the reason Austin didn't get what he needed. Still the district continued to drag out the case in hopes of siphoning all they could out of us.

The world playing out in our home was a happier one. Austin was flourishing. Robyn's team and I went through a four-month online training course from the STARS School run by Dr. James W. Partington and Dr. Mark Sundberg. The techniques we learned about teaching language to Austin were exactly what we needed. STARS staff showed us what had been missing from Dr. Slimetti's set of strategies. There was so much more to teaching verbal language to a child like Austin. The more he learned to talk, the fewer challenging behaviors he had. Austin's vocabulary went from ten, to thirty, to fifty words in a very short time. Making materials to keep up with his progress was a welcomed challenge.

Before KKI he asked for only a few items, and only when he saw them. If he saw a bag of Doritos, he would say, "chip." Then one day as I was having a pillow fight and tickling fest on my bed with all three kids, Austin said, "cookie." This was the first time in his life that he used a word without having the object in sight. I jumped up from the bed, hit my head on the ceiling fan, lept to the floor, and ran to the kitchen. I found a bag of Oreo cookies and ripped it open. I ran back into the bedroom and handed one to him. I was overjoyed. He was learning that words would get him what he wanted.

Chelsea looked at me and said, "soda?" We both laughed. She knew I wasn't going to get a soda for her, but she did make her point. There was an obvious discrepancy between what was expected from her and what was expected of her brother and sister. I jumped through hoops to get her brother a cookie, but she was expected to be independent. We would often have talks about why things were different for her. I made it a point to designate one night per week as our "special night." Chelsea needed a time when she could have me all to herself. We would get a movie and popcorn and lock ourselves in her bedroom while Billy watched Alanna and Austin. Now, at fourteen, this was even more important for her as she was about to face all of the challenges of being a teenager. Chelsea had started high school that year. She was experiencing all the joys and sorrows of growing up.

We would often talk about her sister and brother, and sometimes she certainly felt that life was unfair. Billy and I tried to explain that, in many ways, we had to be two different types of parents. We needed to raise her to successfully deal with the world outside of our home. We needed to raise her sister and brother with different goals. It wasn't always fair. Chelsea understood the importance of our work for Austin, and she knew this all needed to happen to get our family back to some sense of normalcy. She also had a lot of strong women role models to look up to as she watched Robyn's team work day after day. These experiences would shape her future.

Alanna moved to a new school. We loved the staff at Lakeside and wished we didn't have to leave. But there came a time when we realized that we could only modify Alanna's work so much to make it worth her learning. Did she really need to know that Clara Barton founded the Red Cross when she wasn't able to make a simple sandwich for lunch? It was time for us to focus on what she would need to be more independent as an adult. Alanna left Lakeside for the School for Children just a few miles away. The facility specialized in educating children with disabilities, and here she would be taught a combination of academics and daily living skills. All of our children were moving forward.

Then it finally happened. At the age of eleven, Austin called me "Mommy." The joy that one word brought carried me through whole days each time I heard it. It was slow and deliberate, "mmaaammeee," and it was beautiful. He said "chip," "doodle," and "cookie" before he learned to call me by name. This was the one word I had waited for all those years. It's still nearly impossible to describe the feeling. It didn't just bring me joy; it gave me validation. He could say "Mommy," and I felt more like a mom than I ever had in the past. He was defining me, giving me my title, letting me know I had earned it.

Austin loved to place his face on the inside of my forearm and against the back of my hands. He learned the word "hand," and then one day said, "Mommy hand." My heart melted, and I would have let him rest his cheeks on my hands for hours if he wanted. My baby boy was talking to me.

He began to talk in sentences and asked for DVDs by their titles, "I want Alice in Wonderland." I had waited too long to hear his sweet little-boy voice. He learned to be very specific about his desires by asking for "red Skittle," or "blue Dorito chips," and one of my favorites, "bye-bye in Mommy's red car." I was elated, and the dark shadow that followed me through the difficult times began to fall away.

But in the litigation part of our world, the district persisted in their opinion that Austin should be placed residentially even though we were making such progress. Our data showed that his aggressive behaviors were minimal, and he often went weeks without an episode. The district requested permission to have Austin evaluated by their experts. Of course, we had to allow this, and then have our own experts provide a counter evaluation. This legal battle was a ridiculous game in which we constantly tried to one-up each other. All the while, we were spending tens of thousands of dollars.

The district brought in outside people to conduct the evaluations instead of using their own child study team. Dr. Dennis Garner, a psychologist, observed Austin in our home. Dr. Garner had no background in working with individuals with autism. He asked me to complete a questionnaire that was geared toward children with ADHD, and had many questions about Austin's social interactions. I answered everything, but kept explaining how this didn't really apply to Austin. Dr. Garner stressed that he felt Austin needed friends. I wasn't sure that Dr. Garner understood autism, and he certainly didn't understand Austin. What Austin needed first was to learn. Friendship would be wonderful, but Austin didn't know how to be a friend. Simply placing him with other children and hoping he made a connection was not realistic. Who would Austin make friends with? By now he was twelve years old, and he had the vocabulary of a two-year-old child.

Weeks later the district sent Ms. Irene White, a learning disabilities teacher consultant, to perform an educational evaluation. Like Dr. Garner, she was also a private consultant with no prior knowledge of autism. Ms. White sat in Austin's makeshift classroom in our home and watched him from a distance. Austin didn't like when new people came into his space. He especially didn't like when they just sat and stared at him. It's hard to tell what Austin was thinking but I'm sure he wanted to know what her purpose was, like anyone would. Austin approached her, reached out, and squeezed her, as if checking to see whether she was real. This frightened her, so she moved into the dining room to ask me some questions and then quickly left. Her report would later give many details about the materials in the room and the space, but it stated that Austin was "untestable," a classic response from many "experts" who don't understand autism.

We then hired our own expert, Dr. David Holmes, to evaluate Austin. Dr. Holmes was an expert in autism who started the Eden School in Princeton, New Jersey, had conducted many of these types of evaluations, and was experienced in providing testimony in court. He came to our home just like the other evaluators. He observed Austin and asked many of the same questions. He approached Austin, put his hands on Austin's shoulders, and let him know he was interested in what he was working on. He also asked one question that no one else did: "What do you want for Austin?" Technically, parents are members of the IEP team, and their opinion is supposed to be considered when decisions are made for their children. We told him that we wanted Austin to have the trained staff necessary to keep his progress going, and we never wanted to return to the behavioral state he had been in before.

All the evaluations and reports were completed and we returned to the courthouse, but I knew by now we would accomplish nothing. The district's own experts didn't think Austin required a residential placement, and now the district was trying to force us to take an out-of-district placement at a private school that didn't specialize in autism or behavioral challenges. They used the argument from Dr. Garner that Austin needed to be in a classroom because he needed to have friends. But they wouldn't allow that classroom to be in the Brick school district. They continued to refuse to open up a space for Austin.

For a long time, we went back and forth between school visits, evaluations, and time in court. Finally, in March of 2005, we thought we had a settlement agreement. We all agreed that Austin would have a classroom of his own in a school not far from our home. He would have staff from Clarity, with Robyn's team initially implementing the program, and eventually the school would provide staff to be trained. Our case was going to settle; the judge put it in the records. We would be reimbursed fifty thousand dollars in legal and expert fees if we agreed to drop our compensatory education claim. All that was left was for the Brick Township Board of Education to give its formal approval.

Robyn played an important part in helping our case move forward. The judge was very impressed with her efforts and her creative thinking. Robyn had been consulting in a nearby private school for children with autism. She explained to the administration that all we really needed was an empty room. The director of that program offered an empty occupational therapy room, and everyone agreed that Austin's programming could be implemented there for part of the day. The rest could take place in our home. We set up the classroom space similarly to how our home was arranged. This was the closest to a school program Austin had experienced in years; it was the perfect scenario for getting him out of the house during the day.

Mr. Asinello insisted that, to ensure that Austin went to this program, Mr. Massey would come to our home every day to make sure Austin got on the van they provided and went to the school. Mr. Massey would drive up to our home, park his car on our lawn, and idle with the air conditioner running. The heat from his exhaust burnt up the grass. Once Austin was on the van, Mr. Massey would follow him to the school and watch him there for a few hours. We had no idea why the district insisted on paying for a babysitter for this project when all they had to do was call the van company to confirm that Austin was going to school.

The necessary documents were not completed in time for the March school board meeting, and we had to wait for the next one. But the April board meeting came and went, and the board didn't approve the settlement. We never did find out why. All we knew was we were somehow back to the drawing board. The judge was not pleased when we returned to the courthouse; she thought this drawn-out case had been settled. Mr. Asinello reported that the board would not agree to the terms and instead wanted Austin to be placed in the school as a student in one of the existing classrooms, even though all of the experts said such a transition was too drastic at this point.

The new school year was starting. Austin was now thirteen. His language had come along, and he was learning to read and do other academics as well as chores. We would go to the grocery store and allow him to purchase his own preferred items. This was a stark contrast to the pre-KKI days when we couldn't take him out at all. I remember the first day the staff decided we should take him to Walmart and let him choose his own reinforcers. My stomach ached, my knees were weak, and I began to shake.

The last time we went to Walmart, it had not been a positive experience. Bethany had come with us. We made it most of the way through, getting our items and checking out. But as we were about to reach the parking lot, Austin turned around and ran back toward the store. He grabbed a woman, scratching her hand. He went into the building alone through the exit door, which happened to be open. I ran after him, with no time to address the woman who had been injured as she screamed at me, "What the hell?!" The automatic doors shut and Austin was on the other side. I had to run around to the entrance doors to get in. I found him in front of the rows of shopping carts, biting himself and knocking over anything in his way. Bethany left the cart in the parking lot and caught up with us. The two of us tried to physically block any harm he might cause to others. A manager was headed our way, and I just wanted out. We finally got Austin calm enough for us to hold onto him, and we headed toward the van to find the injured woman parked right next to us. I avoided eye contact as I got Austin into the van.

Austin's new staff took on the challenge of ensuring Austin would always be able to be in the community. The first time we went back to Walmart, I think the staff was there more for me than for Austin. Jetty Becker, one of the therapists, provided the encouragement I needed to keep moving. I was panicking, remembering the last time. But she kept me in the present and reminded me of how awesome Austin was doing. One step at a time, we did it! We made it up and down the aisles, we bought chips and Skittles, and waited to check out. Austin helped put the items on the belt and bagged them while I paid. He was a champ, and we all did it together. His success was a team effort. Austin was ready. We needed the district to let our amazing team of professionals transition him back into school.

Chelsea was now a junior at the Marine Academy of Technology and Environmental Sciences, and she was doing well. The small school gave her a close-knit community and lots of attention from the teachers. She enjoyed the usual traditions with high school friends, such as proms and other events, but with a smaller class of only twenty-seven students. We weren't as involved as we should have been, and I never realized how fast the time was going. I kept thinking that once Austin was settled we could be more involved with the girls. Getting settled just took longer than we ever expected.

We transitioned Alanna back to the Wilson School because she wasn't making progress at The School for Children. She didn't do poorly; she just didn't do anything. Being a quiet child, she spent much of her time completing worksheets and just sitting. A reassessment showed that she was at the same level as when she left Lakeside two years earlier. Wilson had an opening for her in their adolescent program, and it was a little like coming home with our tails between our legs. We knew they would do right by her, but we also knew that we hadn't handled the relationship properly in the past. The staff made no issue at all, and they were happy to have her.

I headed back to court for Austin, the one child who still needed to find his place. The usual non-updates were given, and the general jabs were made about who was or wasn't cooperating. The judge asked about the district's efforts to find staff and space, and they told her there was nothing available. By now it was hard for them to maintain the stance that Austin still needed a residential placement. But changing their recommendation would mean a loss for them, so they stuck to it. We left the courthouse with no resolution yet again, and a new date was scheduled for November.

Paul called me the night before that date. He knew Billy and I had reached the end of our rope. We wanted to move forward with litigating this case. It was his job to be sure we fully understood all the possible outcomes. This wasn't television, and the good guys didn't always win. You couldn't always tell how a judge would lean. This was going to get expensive. Very expensive. In addition to the attorney costs, we would have to pay our experts on the days they testified, plus any time they spent prepping for the case. He wanted us to know what we were getting into, and that it might not go our way. As an alternative, he told us that if we agreed to place Austin in one of the day programs that had been offered he was confident he could get us back much of what we had already spent, a similar agreement to what we had reached back in March.

I was not comfortable with this decision. The thought of chancing Austin's future by placing him somewhere without all the supports he needed brought on panic-stricken visions of needing to return to KKI. However, the thought of moving forward with litigation and draining our financial resources was also anxiety-inducing. I wasn't sure we could keep going at this pace. I began to cry in disbelief that this was all there was for Austin when he deserved so much more. Austin was a fighter, and he had fought back from an awful place. But did we have the money and the emotional resilience to withstand the drain of a court case? Parents should not be forced to make such decisions. Why did we need to choose between money and what was right for our children?

As I spoke with Paul, I made sure Billy was near so he could hear the conversation. When he saw me begin to cry, he asked for the phone. "We're done. We are done playing games with these people," Billy told Paul. "It's time to take this one to the mat," he demanded, using one of his sports analogies that he is known for.

The next morning we were on our way to court.

Taking it to The Mat

November 2005 to December 2005

We arrived at court ready to begin the next battle in our lives. First, the judge requested to see both attorneys in her chambers. Paul came out of that meeting and explained that the judge wanted all parties to give it one more chance and have a discussion about settling this case. I could feel Billy start to rise out of his seat. Paul warned him that it would not be wise to go against the judge's wishes, and that it could possibly hurt any chances we had.

Of course the other side wanted another meeting. The longer they dragged this out, the more money Mr. Natale made and the more they got us to spend, all while not having to put Austin in their school. Keeping the "monster" out of the school system helped to solidify the district's position that Austin was too difficult for a public school program. But Billy was adamant. "This is it; we're done with meetings. It's time for you to start lawyering and her to start judging," he told Paul. Paul was on board. "Okay, let's do this."

Paul explained to the judge that we wanted to move forward with litigation. The judge notified the recording room that we were going on the record and asked Mr. Natale to present his first witness. Mr. Asinello took the stand and was sworn in. After more than two years of meetings, delays, and waiting, this was it. We had moved on to the big leagues.

Mr. Natale was obviously not prepared to start presenting his case that day. The announcement that he had to present a witness threw him. He had no documents or previous exhibits to refer to. Paul handed both Mr. Natale and the judge a four-inch-thick binder filled with documents that our side would be entering into evidence, along with the items already submitted during Ms. Papageorge's testimony two years prior, all neatly arranged and marked with tabs. Billy looked at me, licked his index finger and drew a line in the air, silently signaling, "one for our team."

Mr. Asinello's testimony began with some standard information about his education and background. He had spent twenty-six of his twenty-nine years in special education as an administrator. I couldn't help but wonder whether he had been quickly bumped up to an administrator because he had been ineffective as a teacher. He neglected to mention that the last district he worked in had kicked him out. According to the local papers, a million-dollar class action lawsuit was won against the district due to child study team decisions that he supervised.

Mr. Natale showed Mr. Asinello the IEP that recommended a residential placement for Austin and asked if he still felt that this was an appropriate plan. Mr. Asinello answered, "Yes." Regardless of how much time had passed, they had to hold fast to their original argument that Austin needed to be placed in a residential facility. If they changed their stance, they lost the case. It was another example of ego preventing progress.

How could anyone think that Austin needed a residential placement now? He was an amazing boy, now a teenager, who had proved himself time and time again. Mr. Asinello explained that he still felt Austin would require a restricted environment, because in the last two years he had been taught in isolated environments where he was the only child in the room.

He argued that although Austin had made progress, he would need a residential placement to incorporate him back into environments with multiple people before being permitted to come to the school district.

His argument was far-reaching, but he needed to offer some justification as to why they were sticking with the recommendation of a residential facility. But Austin was already in a school building where there were other people. He spent time on a playground where there were other children. The room he was in always had two staff people, and a receptionist right outside. Austin lived in a house with two parents and two sisters. He was in no way isolated.

Mr. Natale had Mr. Asinello review Austin's history of placements. I took notes and cringed as I listened to his version of our story. As Paul often reminded me, I tried not to let my feelings show. I had to remain calm and unaffected. But that was nearly impossible when Mr. Asinello claimed that Austin wasn't progressing in his current program and should go into a residential setting or maybe even back to KKI again.

Every morning I opened Austin's bedroom door. I no longer waited for him to wake. I stood next to his bed and gently woke him with "Good morning, buddy." Austin was always completely covered by blankets, head and all. He would get one hand loose and stretch it out while saying, "Mommy hands." I'd reach for him and he would gently rub the top of my wrinkled, veiny hands. It was a moment I looked forward to each day. One day Chelsea tried to trick him and snuck in with me. She handed him her hand instead, and he quickly said, "No, Mommy hands." It was nice to know he knew the difference, and that I was his choice.

So I had no idea what child Mr. Asinello was talking about, because my boy was leaps and bounds beyond where he was before KKI. "Isolated" became a catch-phrase throughout the district's testimony. They wanted the judge to believe that we had placed our son in a bubble, and that was why his behaviors had decreased.

That first day went quickly and little was accomplished because we had started the testimony after lunch. The judge ordered our next court date for early December.

After some requests to identify documents into evidence—a tedious task not seen in any television court dramas—it was Paul's turn to cross-examine Mr. Asinello. Paul reviewed each IEP the district had written for Austin since 1999, as well as the placements he was in during those years. Paul made the point that Austin had a history of being in placements with very few children, for years with only one other child—his sister, and that the district had no objections to those settings at those times. Now, all these years later, they claimed that being in such a small class was "isolating" and that the only way to transition him back into society was to remove him from all he knew and send him to live in a residential facility.

As the testimony moved to the more recent IEPs, Paul questioned Mr. Asinello about the district's decision to change its recommendation from a school and home combination program on June 5th to a residential placement on June 23rd. Mr. Asinello explained that after the team saw Austin they had concerns.

Paul: "Who on the team?"
Mr. Asinello: "Ms. Gonclaves, Ms. Papageorge, and Ms. Catagnus."
Paul: "But Ms. Papageorge and Ms. Catagnus had seen Austin prior to June 5th, correct?"
Mr. Asinello: "That's correct."
Paul: "Ms. Gonclaves then brought back the 'new information' about Austin's behaviors at Kennedy Krieger, and she in large measure was the source of that information which resulted in the

district changing its view about the appropriateness of Austin's placement?"
Mr. Asinello: "I don't know if she was 'in large measure.' Other people also traveled to Kennedy Krieger."
Paul: "But those people all went down before June 5th. Ms. Gonclaves is the only one that went after June 5th."
Mr. Asinello: "Right."
Paul: "And she brought back concerns?"
Mr. Asinello: "Right."
Paul: "Turn to page 28. About three-quarters of the way down it says: "'After Ms. Gonclaves' visit to KKI she had the following concerns about Austin's projected placement in district.'" You see where I'm reading?"
Mr. Asinello: "Yes."
Paul: "And there's about eight enumerated items."
Mr. Asinello: "That is correct."

Paul then proceeded to address each one of the district's concerns. "The first one is that Austin is not made to wear his shoes unless going on a walk," Paul read. Mr. Asinello responded, "Yes."

"Is that a reason to put somebody in a residential placement, because he won't keep his shoes on?" Paul asked. Mr. Asinello attempted to evade, stating that this was only one of the teacher's concerns. Paul pushed him to answer the question, "Is that a reason to put somebody in a residential placement, because they won't wear their shoes?" Mr. Natale objected, saying that Paul was being argumentative and stating the obvious. It was in the report; did it really need to be discussed? Judge Gracias responded, "Overruled. I'll allow the question."

Paul repeated himself once again: "Is the inability of a student to wear shoes, or refusal of a student to wear shoes, a reason to send him to an institutional placement?" I don't think any of us expected Mr. Asinello's response. "It may be when you consider the scope of the Oberti decision," he said. "If that's going to interfere with the benefit of all the other children in that class and it's going to cause a harmful effect, it could be a reason because the child is no longer able to fit—even with accommodation that could be made—into the class in question. Because not only do you have to consider the child coming in…"

Paul interrupted, "Mr. Asinello, is it your testimony…" but the judge stopped him. "Hold on. Please don't interrupt the answer."

My heart pounded, I was perched on the edge of my seat and furiously scribbling notes. I tried to take down every single word this idiot was spewing. When the judge told him to continue, I was petrified. Was she buying this line of crap? Was this making sense to her? Mr. Asinello went on to explain the Oberti decision and how it applied to our case. According to Oberti, the district needed to consider the other children in the room and whether Austin would make it difficult for them to be educated.

Paul held fast to his line of questioning. "Is it your testimony that Austin not wearing his shoes in class would have a harmful effect on the other students?" Mr. Asinello responded, "It may." Paul repeated incredulously, "It may, because he won't wear his shoes." Mr Asinello replied smugly, "That is correct."

Paul moved on to the other concerns that came about after Ms. Gonclaves' visit. "He cannot participate on class trips? Is that harmful to the other students, if he doesn't participate in the class trips? Is it your testimony that it is harmful to himself or other students?" Paul questioned. Mr. Asinello began to look as though he was outsmarting us by using his knowledge of the law to back these ridiculous concerns. "It may be harmful to himself," he stated. To make it clear, Paul specifically asked, "Because he won't go to the zoo on a class trip?" Mr. Asinello confirmed, "That is correct."

Paul moved on to the third reason Austin needed a residential placement. "How about, 'Requiring a different schedule from the other students?' Isn't it common, or at least not unheard of, for schedule accommodations or modifications to be made for students with disabilities?" Mr. Asinello simply agreed that it was common in special education classrooms for students to have different schedules.

"Number four," Paul continued, "During extended school year Ms. Gonclaves is the only staff member trained in VB (verbal behavior)/ABA. Is that somehow harmful to other students if she is the only other teacher who's trained in VB/ABA?" Mr. Asinello was becoming pompous. "It may be harmful to this student." Mr. Natale was uncomfortable with the questioning and attempted another objection, saying that these were a package of concerns and not meant to be examined individually. But the judge overruled the objection, "The witness has been handling the responses to these questions very well. You may continue. We were discussing VB/ABA, is it harmful to other students?"

I feared that Mr. Asinello was making sense to her, that she was buying into this. Mr. Asinello went on to explain that Ms. Gonclaves was the only teacher trained in the strategies used with Austin, and there was no backup for her if she left the district. Instead of discussing training others, this was listed as a reason that Austin should be placed away from his home.

The fifth reason had to do with the other child the district chose to place in the classroom originally designated for Austin, and how Austin might not be able to tolerate that child's behavioral challenges. My head was spinning. My son had to be placed in a residential facility because another child—whose behaviors were so difficult that he cleared out a room—was going to be permitted to stay in the classroom.

"Number six is very interesting," Paul continued. "He cannot tolerate loud noises. There is a student in the class who will scream and speak in a high-pitched voice," he read. "Now you're talking about the Oberti decision, removing a student from a class based on his harmful effects on other students. Here you are talking about a student who will have a harmful effect on Austin. So is it your testimony that Austin should somehow be penalized because of the behavior of another student, or the tendencies of another student?" Mr. Asinello spewed out, "Well, I think they're trying to protect Austin on number six, saying they know there's going to be loud noises in that class." My blood was boiling. So they wanted to "protect" Austin by taking him away from his home?

Paul asked Mr. Asinello why the district couldn't just give Austin his own individual classroom, similar to his other private placement. Mr. Asinello again began to quote the Oberti decision. The interaction was getting heated, and the judge stepped in. She permitted Mr. Asinello to continue. He stated that the law required him to make reasonable accommodations to protect and service a child appropriately. His reasoning was that because Austin was intolerant of loud noises, the district might not be able to protect and service him.

When the topic of creating an individual classroom came up, the question of Austin being isolated reared its head again. "Nevertheless, you're recommending a residential placement in order to 'break the cycle of isolation,' is that correct?" Paul asked. Mr. Asinello confidently responded, "That is correct." Paul tried to reveal the ridiculousness of this argument by showing how much more isolating a residential placement would actually be.

> Paul: "A residential placement would be, depending on where it was located, potentially distant from his home."
> Mr. Asinello: "That's correct."
> Paul: "And away from his mother and father."
> Mr. Asinello: "True."
> Paul: "Away from his sisters, correct?"

Mr. Asinello: "Correct."
Paul: "And away from the community that he knows."
Mr. Asinello: "Correct."
Paul: "Twenty-four hours a day."
Mr. Asinello: "That is true."

All of the places the district had proposed were more than two hours away; two of them were out of state. This didn't seem to matter to anyone from the district. Mr. Asinello stepped down, seemingly satisfied with his testimony. Testimony that supported taking a young boy out of his home and away from his family. *Anywhere in the United States of America...just not here.*

December 2005 to January 2006

Robyn was the next witness to follow Mr. Asinello. She was listed as a witness for both parties because the district had hired her, but she was also the BCBA on Austin's case. Mr. Natale mentioned to the judge that, due to this, "she may have to be considered as an adverse witness to myself or Mr. Prior. As such, we would proceed accordingly." At first I didn't understand what he was trying to say. But when he opened his mouth it became obvious that he felt Robyn was an adversary.

He did not start the questioning with the usual niceties about her background and qualifications. Instead he immediately asked about the financial arrangement between Clarity Behavioral and the Brick Township school district. He had her confirm the amount of money paid monthly to Robyn and her staff. This was an odd way to begin proceedings. He put his witness on the defensive, and essentially accused of her wanting to avoid Austin's transition to a classroom because the delay would benefit her financially. None of us had anticipated that line of questioning.

Robyn held her own. She was paid a fair rate for the services she provided, commensurate with the level of education and training of her staff.

She employed three people to assist on Austin's case. The district's proposed plan would cost them three times what they paid Robyn.

Mr. Natale went on to scrutinize Robyn's history with our case, her visits to KKI, her training of the Clarify staff, and her role in Austin's progress. He had Robyn tediously outline for the judge the behavior plan, including how each component was implemented and how she trained staff. He questioned any staff turnover at Clarity and wanted to know the reasons. Finally, she was asked to explain graphs depicting rates of Austin's challenging behaviors.

After that intense session of questioning, we took a recess for lunch. Mr. Natale asked Robyn if she wanted to join his team, but she refused. We also asked her to lunch, but she declined, "I don't want to have lunch with anyone right now. I just want to be alone." I understood completely. She had just been attacked professionally. She wanted to show that she had no favoritism to either side, that she was there for Austin. Robyn's documentation spoke for itself. Austin was succeeding with her team. He was learning academics, doing chores, beginning to use a vending machine to get his rewards, and taking walks for exercise. He had learned more in the past two and a half years than he had learned in the eleven years prior. I wished we could tell her that now.

When it was Paul's turn to cross-examine Robyn, he validated her role in Austin's world and ensured that she knew her integrity was not in question. Robyn never faltered, remaining steadfastly professional throughout. She was well aware of the heightened attention to this case. If anything, she wanted to be the person who helped to get Austin back into the district, or at least into a program of some kind, because that would bolster her reputation as an effective behavior analyst. She was the one who came up with creative ideas on how to possibly make that happen. Given the space and opportunity, she could design a transition plan to help desensitize Austin to other environments and get him into a classroom. The court day came to an end, and Robyn was asked to return on our next court date, December 6th.

On that December court date, Paul started off the questioning. He reviewed with Robyn the progress that Austin had made under her supervision and presented graphs and data she had collected. They discussed Austin's continued challenges and Paul asked Robyn her vision for an appropriate program.

When Mr. Natale cross-examined her, he pointed out Austin's deficits in comparison to typical peers and highlighted how Austin's behavioral challenges could be dangerous to others. He attempted to create a verbal picture of the "monster." Robyn simply described Austin as he was, a child with a long history of challenges and a need for structure and trust in the professionals caring for him in order to move forward. Mr. Natale asked whether she thought we had made the right decision to send Austin to KKI. She responded, "Yes, from what Kennedy Krieger showed me."

He asked why it took so long to transition Austin into new environments. Robyn explained that we introduced Austin to new settings in fifteen-minute increments and we did not increase the time until we saw steady low rates of behavior. This worked to keep everyone, including Austin, safe.

Mr. Natale also asked Robyn about our cooperation with her. Did Billy and I answer phone calls and emails? Did we attend meetings? Of course, she answered yes. He then asked her something I think he may have later regretted: "Have you ever discussed their primary concerns for him? What their hope is in terms of his ultimate placement?" Robyn eloquently responded, "Their primary concern has been his happiness. Other concerns include that he be able to be with his family, he be able to communicate with other people, and that he not bite himself or hurt himself. I know this because they have been very interested in working on this curriculum. They were interested in these particular skills, things like talking and concept formation, understanding numbers, and basic skills for reading." She explained that we wanted him to be the best he could be while not hurting himself or anyone else. I think Mr. Natale thought she was going to name a place, a facility, or a building. Instead, Robyn explained that what we really wanted was for our son to meet his potential.

We returned to court the following week so more experts from the school district could testify. Dr. Garner was the first to take the stand. As Mr. Natale reviewed his background, we realized that many of the district's outside consultants hired to serve as Austin's child study team members were professors at Georgian Court College. Mr. Asinello also taught at the college. He must have recruited his own dream team made up of his colleagues. No other child in the district had a child study team made up entirely of non-district employees.

Dr. Garner reviewed for the court how he had evaluated Austin, mainly through observation and interviews with his staff and with me. He explained that Austin's disability hindered him from completing much standardized testing, so he required more direct observation. He felt that Austin "was one of the more difficult individuals to assess because of the nature of his disabilities." He went on to say that he felt Austin's social development was the most important part of the district's recommendation. He specifically wanted Austin to relate to at least one other person, apart from family members, and have at least one other person reasonably close to his chronological age with whom he could develop a relationship. Dr. Garner said he "expressed this in his report four or five times, as well as in numerous conversations with Mr. Asinello."

Dr. Garner continually testified that Austin needed to be socialized with peers, that he needed friends. He understood that the behaviors were challenging, but he felt Austin needed to learn to tolerate other children his age in his environment. I just couldn't understand what he was thinking.

Austin wasn't in complete isolation, he was surrounded by a loving staff of experienced professionals. He didn't understand differences in age, and to him these people were his friends. He lived in a home with siblings close to his age and we had neighbors who played in our yard all the time. If Austin was ever going to develop friendships, it would be with the people he had the most contact with. Simply placing Austin with other children wasn't going to form friendships, and it was irresponsible to assume that other children with autism who were also challenged socially would be able to foster deep long-term relationships with Austin. Dr. Garner simply did not understand Austin's type of autism.

Paul questioned Dr. Garner about his participation in Austin's programming and the meetings he had attended. In an attempt to level the playing field in the eyes of the judge, Paul echoed Mr. Natale's line of questioning to Robyn and asked Dr. Garner about his compensation for being on this case. As they added up the numbers, Dr. Garner estimated that he worked between five to ten hours per month at two hundred and fifty dollars an hour on our case as a private consultant on Austin's child study team. This was a position that, for any other case, would have been filled by a district employee.

When asked his opinion regarding residential placement, Dr. Garner had little to offer. He felt that Austin should stay in the building he was in, but that if a residential placement was open it could work too. He mostly kept reiterating that Austin needed a friend.

It was hard to remain stoic while the district called each of their witnesses to talk about our son. After a lunch break, Mr. Massey was next up on the stand. As our newest case manager, he followed Austin to the school building each day. He seemed like a sweet man, but never seemed to offer us much information. During his introduction to the court, we discovered that he had been a school psychologist and guidance counselor before starting his private practice as a marriage and family therapist.

When asked about his role as case manager, it was not surprising to hear him rattle off duties that included ensuring the program ran smoothly and communicating information to the staff, attorneys, and parents. He was basically hired to keep an eye on Austin. When asked what the purpose of his observations was, he again explained it was "to make sure things were running smoothly." As a case manager, Mr. Massey held no authority; he couldn't make any recommendations or help identify any solutions. He was simply hired to ensure that a set of eyes was on Austin and his team at all times. Our rectangular patch of dead lawn was just a bonus.

Mr. Natale probably wished he could have asked Mr. Massey to step off the stand seconds after swearing him in. The testimony did nothing to help the district. When Mr. Natale asked him why he observed Austin through a closed circuit television while he received programming in his classroom, he answered, "It didn't have a purpose that I could think of." I think at that moment our attorney's heart skipped a beat from sheer joy. Paul sat up a bit straighter in his seat to watch the train wreck.

I could see Mr. Asinello's body stiffen in his chair the longer Mr. Massey spoke. Mr. Asinello had a nervous habit of tapping all five finger tips together, but as our case manager talked, he began wringing his hands. Mr. Massey wasn't intentionally providing information to help us, he was just being honest about his role. In doing so, he showed that the district had hired him as a human camera to spy on the program. He described himself as only being superficially involved with the child study team, and not an essential member. Austin's own case manager wasn't even considered an essential member of the child study team.

When Paul objected to a line of questioning about whether Mr. Massey thought I would accept any of the school placements we had observed, Mr. Natale took it as a welcome opportunity to end his direct examination. He simply stated, "I'll withdraw the question," and ended his questioning altogether.

I'm sure Mr. Natale said a brief prayer in hopes that Paul would be short in his cross-examination. Mr. Massey was not helping the district's case. But Paul immediately asked him about visiting our home, watching Austin get on the bus, and following the bus to the school. Mr. Massey acknowledged that all this happened, but he had no real understanding why he was supposed to do it.

Paul asked Mr. Massey about his financial compensation to keep things fair since Robyn had been scrutinized. The Brick Township school district paid him between two thousand and thirty-five hundred dollars per month to watch Austin and to "be available," but to play no essential role on the child study team. Following a few brief questions about Mr. Massey's observations of Austin, Paul ended his cross-examination. Mr. Natale had no redirect. Part of the district's hand had been revealed. They had hired outsiders for no other purpose except to create a group of people they could easily manipulate. Luckily for us, Mr. Massey hadn't known how to play their game very well.

Court was adjourned for the day. We would be back in a few days. And I was up next.

January 6, 2006

It's said that everyone gets their day in court. January 6th, 2006 was mine. Billy came after he got the kids ready for the day; I needed the support. As I drove to the courthouse a Martina McBride song came on the radio, and the words stuck with me: "Let freedom ring, let the white dove sing, let the whole world know that today is a day of reckoning. Let the weak be strong, let the right be wrong, roll the stone away, let the guilty pay. It's Independence Day." It's a song that still brings back memories of driving down Route 195 toward the courthouse, and everything else that happened that day.

I sat in the witness chair. It was a very different perspective to have Mr. Natale and Mr. Asinello directly in front of me. Paul had me review some basic information to ease me into the questioning process. He asked about my relationship to Austin and if I had any other children. We discussed that the girls were now sixteen and fourteen, and that Alanna also had autism. We talked about my background. At this time, I had completed my bachelor's degree and was nearly finished with my master's in special education. While Austin went to KKI, I went back to school online. While he was being taught at home and we were fighting the district, I was taking courses and had just one semester left.

I had sat on the Governor's Council on Autism to review grant proposals, and more recently I was part of a task force organized by the State Department of Education which was responsible for developing the Autism Program Quality Indicators. Paul went on to ask about the history of Austin's education and his placements, being careful to highlight the small placements that Austin had attended and the limited number of students in each, as well as the times when his sister was one of the other students. We reviewed the home-bound instruction and the destruction of our son by Dr. Slimetti and his team, with Paul asking for painful details about Austin's decline.

Paul presented the IEP created for Austin prior to Dr. Slimetti's involvement. "Mrs. Gallagher, can you read for the court what is indicated under Target Behavior?" I read from the document, "No specific behavior identified. Austin's several mild challenging behaviors are addressed in the Wilson Outreach Goals section of this report." I went on to read the section that addressed Austin's goals, including "the reduction of challenging behaviors where he bit his hand, engaged in hand flapping, and was non-compliant."

Not long before all this all fell apart, the most we had to worry about was hand-biting, hand-flapping, and Austin's tendency to flop to the floor in protest. By the time Dr. Slimetti and his team were through, I had to send my son to KKI because he had become violent, aggressive, destructive toward property, and caused harm to himself and others on a daily basis. As I sat on the stand I remembered the sweet little boy I had known before, and my eyes welled up. I told myself to hold it together; I couldn't let them see me cry.

I recounted for the court all that had happened in the year prior to Austin going to KKI, including the attempts to bring him into a district program. I explained that we first asked Mr. Asinello to help us by finding us a BCBA, but he had said there were none available in the area. Despite his claim, we found Robyn after just one email sent to a Temple University professor. We hadn't wanted to place our son so far away, but we had no choice but to pursue treatment at KKI. We did what was necessary to help our son.

Paul asked me, "Was the placement at KKI an easy decision for you to make?" I felt the lump in my throat, but tried to hold myself together. "No," I answered, short and sweet. But Paul continued, "Why not?" I mustered up the words through the tears. "Because it's Austin. We had to put him somewhere, and I would do the same if he had any illness. That's how I had to look at it. We had to find the best hospital we could for what was wrong."

Paul pushed just a bit more. "And what did this hospital do for him after he got there?"

"They saved him," I responded.

We discussed the plan that was developed and how each procedure helped Austin to get better, as well as how KKI discovered other medical issues that contributed to Austin's behavioral challenges, like his heart rate being too high. The team of professionals at KKI brought Austin's behaviors down to ninety percent below what they were when he entered.

I explained that Louis remained in contact with us to this day and continued to review all the data that our staff sent to him, all these years after Austin was released.

Paul then asked me about the district's involvement with Austin after he entered KKI. I acknowledged that district staff visited him, and that correspondence between KKI and Ms. Papageorge reported, "Every effort has been made to educate the necessary behavioral therapists so transition back to the school setting would be possible in a productive manner." The district promised they would have a place for Austin when he returned. But here we were, nearly three years later, with nowhere for him to go.

The IEP of June 23rd was our next topic. Paul asked why I thought they called another meeting; I explained that I was told Ms. Gonclaves had more information to offer. "It was here that we learned the district had placed more children in her classroom and that they weren't going to take Austin," I said.

Paul asked, "What recommendation did the district offer at the time?"

"Mr. Asinello offered us, 'Any school in the United States of America, just not here'," I told the court.

"Not here meaning…"

"Not Brick Township," I answered.

Mr. Natale interrupted. "We ask if that's a direct quote?" I confirmed, "Yes, it's a direct quote," but the judge told him to take it up in his cross-examination. Paul drove his point home: "And by 'Any school in the United States of America, except here,' what did you conclude, if anything?" For me, this meant Austin had no place to go when he came home.

I explained that we had been told at intake that KKI doesn't accept children unless they have confirmed placements when they are discharged. KKI would not spend months working with a child to have them returned to an educational situation that lacked the necessary supports. Paul instructed me to read directly from the IEP: "Austin will be placed in home instruction while residential placement is investigated." In multiple places in the document it appeared again, "Austin will be placed on home instruction upon his return from Kennedy Krieger on July 1, 2003 while residential placement is investigated."

Paul asked, "What, if anything, did you conclude from that in terms of the district's contemplative long term placement?" I couldn't hold back the tears as I answered, "That they were going to put Austin in a residential facility, or at least attempt to."

I told the court about Austin's progress since coming home from KKI. We were now able to take him out in the community, and clerks in some of the stores had gotten used to seeing Austin and Billy, especially Prime Time Video. The store employees would allow Austin to line up VHS covers on the floor and put them back in their correct places on the shelves. Austin enjoyed visits to the store, and the staff even held videos for him that they thought he would like.

Then Paul asked me, "Why is it that you oppose the provision of services in a residential setting for Austin?" The tears continued but I fought through them. "Austin's our son. You don't give up on your son. He needs to be treated like a member of our family and not some patient or client somewhere else. Austin belongs in our house, not some institution or facility that somebody else thinks is appropriate for him. Austin deserves to be with the people who love him, his parents and his sisters. I'm never going to pack his bags. I'm not going to take him to some institution and drop him off. Austin needs to be with us, with people who love him, not people who are worried whether he's worth their salary. Every morning he should wake up to us, and every night he should go to bed knowing that we'll be there again in the morning. He shouldn't have to wake up to a complete stranger. He doesn't need to be part of a group in a home, he needs to be part of a family and he deserves it more than anybody, because he's worked so hard to get there. Nobody has worked harder than that little boy has to get to where he is today. Nobody. He doesn't belong away from his family." Although my tears flowed and my nose ran, I made sure I spoke directly to Mr. Asinello. He refused to look at me. The judge ordered a break for lunch.

When we returned it was Mr. Natale's turn to cross-examine me. Mr. Natale reviewed some of the case's background and attempted to focus on my allegedly uncooperative nature. He noted that I would not accept a placement at a school because the school could not provide Austin with the program outlined by KKI. He implied that I hindered any progress to have Austin placed in other schools, but I responded, "I would have been happy to place Austin in another school if the district would have provided one that had training in ABA and the other methods used to teach him. But instead, they showed us generic programs for children with disabilities."

He went on to note that I placed Austin at KKI without consulting the district, as though I had done something wrong. My son was attacking his family, ruining our home, playing in his own urine and feces, and was unable to be taken outside of the walls of our house. I should have consulted with the people who made him that way? I thought to myself, "You're damn right we took it upon ourselves to look for more for our son. It was clear no one else would."

January 2006

"Who goes to Kentucky for autism?"

—*Chelsea Gallagher*

When it was the district's turn to resume their case they called an expert they had hired, Dr. James Charles Roark from the Kentucky Training Center. His resume was impressive, and he had spent some time at KKI earlier in his career. After providing the details of Dr. Roark's background, Mr. Natale beat Paul to the punch by asking about compensation during his direct testimony. The district was paying Dr. Roark a thousand dollars a day.

One of Austin's therapists, Jetty, once let us know that she had been introduced to Dr. Roark on her way out of the building, but only in passing while putting Austin on the bus. That day he was with Mr. Asinello and Mr. Massey. They seemed surprised that Austin was leaving, and told Jetty they would be back the next day. We contacted Paul as soon as we heard the news, telling him we had no idea who this person was or why he was there. Billy and I agreed that Austin shouldn't go to school the next day. Dr. Roark had to reschedule his visit. We later learned he was driving from Kentucky to Connecticut and stopping to do this consult on his way. He had to plan another trip to New Jersey to see Austin.

At the time, I looked up Dr. Roark on the internet to figure out why he was going to see Austin. Reading from the computer screen, I called out to Billy, who was in the next room. "He's from Kentucky." I heard Chelsea pipe up, "Who goes to Kentucky for autism?" I had to laugh a bit, no offense to Kentucky. Chelsea was growing up in New Jersey at a time when the world was focusing on the rate of autism in Brick Township. She had heard all the stories about how families moved here because New Jersey had good schools and services. She was going on 17 years old, and she had done high school research projects on autism. She had been a big part of most of our awareness campaigns. So when Mr. Natale called Dr. Roark to the stand, I heard Chelsea's voice echo in my head, "Who goes to Kentucky for autism?"

Paul interrupted the testimony to remind the judge that Billy and I had never met this witness, nor did we provide permission for him to observe Austin. The district argued he was hired as a consultant for the entire district, not just for our case. According to the law, they were permitted to have district consultants observe students and review records. Paul took issue with this, as the district could not prove he had seen any other students or provided any other consultation services.

Dr. Roark's testimony focused on his observation of Austin. He testified that he saw Austin on two occasions. Although he reported that Austin was on task ninety-three percent of the time, he didn't see Austin in any "inclusion academics" and he felt that the program was "too structured." I wasn't sure what "inclusion academics" meant, but I suspect he was referring to the fact that Austin wasn't taught in a group setting. He said he witnessed some attempts to aggress, but few maladaptive behaviors. Based on his observation, he felt that Austin should attend the out-of-district program that the school district was suggesting. He went on to explain that typically when he consulted with parents he asked them, "What is your vision? What are your dreams for your child?" He said he tried to get families to focus on functional goals for students when they became adults and identify what would be necessary to achieve them.

Mr. Natale began to realize that this was not helping his case, because Dr. Roark was saying that the parent's dreams are important. Dr. Roark caught on to Mr. Natale's body language just in time, because he awkwardly changed the topic back to placing Austin in the proposed school and not bringing him back into the district. He must have remembered who was paying his tab.

Dr. Roark went on to critique the behavior intervention plan and gave his opinion on each section. He noted that we had made changes over time and questioned our reasons for doing so. Perhaps if Dr. Roark had ever interviewed us, he would have learned why procedures had to be changed. Robyn's team had done nothing halfway. Every change was driven by the data they collected. And when they saw the slightest increase in behavior challenges, they reached out to Louis at KKI.

For example, Louis helped our team design an interrupting stimulus assessment. Jetty ran the assessment and I videotaped it. The goal was to find something that Austin disliked enough to avoid, and which would make him discontinue or interrupt the behavior, but not so much that he wanted to grab it or the person using the item. When we were unsuccessful on our own, Louis came to New Jersey and helped us. How many people could say that they had an expert like Dr. Louis Hagopian in their backyard running an interrupting stimulus assessment? That was the kind of person that he was, and still is.

Dr. Roark could critique all he wanted. We had the best people in place to make sure Austin never regressed. As he continued with his critique, Dr. Roark noted that Austin had control issues, and explained that he would introduce control trials to give Austin more opportunities to choose activities. But at this time, Austin already planned his entire day. He chose the order of his day, the items he wanted to earn, and almost every other aspect in which we could allow him to have a choice. I think Dr. Roark was just making up stuff to sound more intelligent.

Paul cross-examined Dr. Roark about the two observations, asking him for dates and times. Dr. Roark didn't have his calendar but had some approximate time frames. He saw him on one day from around ten o'clock to one-thirty. The testimony continued:

Paul: "And the other time, how long was that?"
Dr. Roark: "Briefly."
Paul: "Define briefly."
Dr. Roark: "Ohhhh..." (as he looked skyward as if to help him remember)

Paul: "Two hours?"
Dr. Roark: "No."
Paul: "One hour?"
Dr. Roark: "No. Very briefly."
Paul: "Less than half an hour?"
Dr. Roark: "Five minutes."
Paul: "Five minutes?"
Dr. Roark: "We went over to see him and he was leaving."

Dr. Roark tried to claim passing our son in the parking lot as an observation. Paul asked Dr. Roark if any other observations had been conducted, either in the home or the community. Dr. Roark had to admit he had not seen Austin in any other location, even though his educational program was delivered in more than one environment, not just the room Dr. Roark observed. He also had to admit that he never interviewed Billy and me, even though this was common practice for him when involved in these types of situations in other districts.

Paul asked, "You testified that when planning, I think you used the phrase, 'longitudinally for a student with autism like Austin,' that you would find out from the family, from the parents in particular, what their hopes and dreams were for the child." Dr. Roark agreed that was his typical procedure. Paul kept pushing Dr. Roark about his lack of contact with us. He asked if Dr. Roark had contacted me. Or if he had contacted Billy. Or if he tried using a telephone at all.

Mr. Natale stood up. "Objection! How many times does he have to answer?" The judge agreed, but Paul argued his point and pushed a bit more, asking if this was a departure from Dr. Roark's usual manner. Dr. Roark told the court, "I would never develop a program without parental input," but explained that this situation was different because he was hired as an expert witness for the school district. Paul pounced. "So you were brought into this because it was a court case. You were brought into this as an expert witness." The district had claimed otherwise, but Dr. Roark had just admitted that he had only been hired for our court case. That meant the district had not complied with the law that required parents to be notified of observations.

At the end of Paul's cross-examination, Dr. Roark finally revealed why Billy and I weren't involved in his interview process. He had been told by Mr. Asinello to hold off "until we see where this goes."

The judge rarely stepped in to ask questions, but she wanted to delve deeper into a few topics with Dr. Roark. She asked him why replicating what Austin was currently receiving in the Brick school district wouldn't be beneficial. Dr. Roark felt that the main issue was Austin's difficulty with change. He claimed that moving him into a classroom offered at the current school campus that had no other ABA programs would be the most beneficial because it would involve the least environmental change.

It didn't make any sense. Removal of ABA plus a change of classroom and staff would be less of a change than continuing ABA with the same staff in a different classroom? I hoped the judge would understand how weak his argument was.

January 2006

"There *is no greater intelligence than kindness and empathy.*"

—*Bryant McGill, Voice of Reason*

When it was our turn to present our case and our experts, Louis was up first. He had been in the courtroom during Dr. Roark's testimony, and I imagined that Dr. Roark's critique of KKI's behavior plan had brought him some amusement.

Paul went through the standard review of Louis' background and curriculum vitae. Louis told the court that he was an Associate Professor in the Department of Psychiatry and Behavioral Sciences at Johns Hopkins University. He listed the research articles he authored and the federal grants he received to research autism. In addition to his educational background—he was a graduate of Virginia Tech's clinical child psychology program, deemed best in the country by the National Institutes of Health—he was at this time the Director of the Neurobehavioral Unit of KKI. He was also on the editorial board of the *Journal of Applied Behavior Analysis*, in addition to many other professional credentials.

Paul established for the court that Louis was an expert in ABA and the treatment of children with autism. Later, Mr. Natale would make a laughable attempt to find a flaw in Louis' credentials. He asked Louis about his history of working with public schools, because Mr. Natale didn't see it on his curriculum vitae. But Louis had worked with many public schools to help transition patients back into classroom settings.

Keeping with the theme of asking experts about their compensation, Paul asked Louis, "You're here today to testify as an expert witness. Are you being compensated for your time and your testimony here today?" Louis simply responded, "No, I am not." It's true, Dr. Louis Hagopian came to New Jersey and testified for our boy for free. We felt so blessed and grateful for his contribution not only to our son's behavioral success, but also to our legal case.

As Louis discussed the admission process and how severity of behaviors is a key consideration for KKI, I was reminded of just how far Austin had come. Louis also explained that KKI had a policy to ensure that a child had a program to return home to once they were discharged because they "learned a long time ago that an intervention developed in the context of a hospital setting but not applied in the child's natural environment is not worth much. The interventions need to be carried out over time, and we have learned that making that a condition of admission results in better outcomes."

Paul asked Louis to describe Austin upon his admission to KKI. The memories rushed back as Louis told the court of a young boy who had nearly one challenging behavior every minute when he began his stay at KKI. He listed Austin's aggressive behaviors: biting, pinching, and grabbing. He then discussed Austin's agitated state when over-aroused, including the self-injurious hand- and finger-biting and the open wounds it caused. He explained how observation and testing lead to the development of a behavior intervention plan that resulted in a ninety percent decrease in the target behaviors from the baseline data taken during Austin's initial weeks at KKI. Once this amazing achievement had been met, the process was to train Billy, me, and Austin's staff to ensure that everyone was proficient in the implementation before Austin's discharge.

Paul asked if Louis agreed with the district's stance that Austin should return to a neurobehavioral unit, and then a day program with a residential facility, before moving back into an in-district program. Louis explained that a neurobehavioral unit was absolutely not necessary and that a child at Austin's current behavioral level would not even be considered by KKI. He told the court he believed that a residential placement at this point would be detrimental.

"Why would it be detrimental?" Paul asked. Louis responded, "For a number of reasons. One of the reasons we've had such a good outcome with Austin is the dedication of his parents, and his family providing him with a good environment. That's probably the best thing he has going for him. Take that away, put him in a residential setting...not to say all residential settings are bad, but I think the level of dedication of his parents is something that just cannot be replaced by anyone else. They are both dedicated and highly skilled, as far as I'm concerned, in the programs and in understanding his behaviors. I think that's one major reason why it would be detrimental."

Louis had other reasons: the change in environment, the level of staff turnover at most residential placements, and the need to train each new person in Austin's behavior plan while still maintaining the integrity of the plan.

The judge reached over and moved her computer monitor, which blocked her view of the witness stand. She had not done that for any other witness. I hoped the gesture meant that, for the first time in this trial, someone was making sense to her. She was listening to the voice of reason and wanted to be sure she heard it clearly.

The testimony continued. Paul and Louis discussed Robyn's competency and Louis' confidence that she could run Austin's program successfully. They also touched on the district's desire to place Austin in a larger classroom at the school where he currently "rented" a private room with Robyn's staff. Louis explained that this arrangement would not benefit Austin at this time. He said the very fact that this school had contacted him to help improve their programming for students with autism—while admirable—was an indication that they were not ready for a student with Austin's needs. He reinforced the point that a successful program was more about the people involved and less about the building. He felt that Austin would be able to transition to a similar placement in the district as long as the staff remained consistent during the transition and the data was followed to identify when changes should be made.

When questioned about the district's perceived need for Austin to have friends, Louis explained that Austin was more comfortable with adults because he could predict their behavior and because they were more apt to arrange an environment to suit him. He admitted that it is always a goal to have children in more natural settings and to increase exposure to peers, but that the development of a friendship was not a priority for Austin at this time. When that goal did move to the forefront for Austin, staff would need to be careful to implement such interactions gradually, pick peers carefully, and drive increased time of these interactions based on the data. If Austin's challenging behaviors increased, changes would be necessary.

Louis disagreed with Dr. Roark's testimony that Austin's program was too structured. He noted that this might be an easy conclusion to arrive at for someone who didn't know Austin's history. Louis was pleased to hear that Austin was responding correctly ninety percent of the time, and explained that this was not typical of a child who had the types of behaviors that led to Austin's admission to KKI. "So in the context of where Austin has been to where he is now," he said, "I'm pretty happy with the outcome we have."

After a break for lunch, Mr. Natale cross-examined Louis. He first focused on Louis' disagreement with Dr. Roark regarding Austin's progress in the area of generalization. When asked to explain specifically how he disagreed, Louis told the court that Austin had arrived at KKI with a communication book—the PECS system—with which he used pictures to communicate his needs. Now he used words. "Austin no longer needs a communication book. He will indicate his needs verbally, unprompted, and in all settings." He also noted that Austin could now read.

Mr. Natale spent a considerable amount of time questioning Louis about his opinion of the school that housed Austin's current program, trying to convince him that keeping Austin there would be the best option. Louis was very diplomatic, but stressed that Austin needed an ABA program. The building wasn't important, but the training and competency of the staff was. And it was especially necessary that any changes to the program should be made systematically and based on data.

The judge asked a few questions to have Louis clarify some statements, particularly whether anyone from the district had expressed any concerns about bringing Austin back into the district at any time during Austin's stay at KKI. "No," Louis responded. "Ms. Papageorge sent correspondence to let us know that the district was moving forward. No one indicated any concerns when they came down for the training. I didn't hear anything until the day of discharge when the family arrived home."

Then Paul was back on redirect, so he brought up the question of whether transitioning Austin to an in-district program might lead to challenging behaviors due to the number of students in the building. The district's argument had been that an in-district placement would be too overwhelming for Austin because of all the class changes and students in the hallway. Paul asked Louis, "He goes on vacations with his family, right?" Louis smiled and nodded "Yes. I think I still have a picture that Mom sent of him in Disney World in front of a fountain with Mickey and some other characters. I would consider that highly stimulating, probably too stimulating for me. In the picture you can see Mom has some of his programming materials to help him in that environment."

Louis' testimony was finished, and as always he brought a welcome level of intelligence and calm to a contentious situation. We had one more date to return to court at the end of January.

Our final witness was Dr. David Holmes. He was bringing up the rear like the Grand Marshall of a parade. Grand Marshall was a good way to describe Dr. Holmes, or Dr. Dave, as he preferred to be called. He was a tall man with a commanding presence. His strong confidence was something to admire, and his analogies were great if you understood sports. He had founded one of the first schools for children with autism, the Eden School, in 1975. He had spent his lifetime working with individuals with autism, from babies to adults. He had authored a book, *Autism Through the Life Span*, that received several awards from agencies serving individuals with autism.

Dr. Dave had conducted an evaluation of Austin and prepared a report for the court. He visited Austin on three occasions and interviewed Billy and me. He saw Austin at home, at the school program, and at the local video store with Billy. At first Paul began to review all the placement options that had been suggested for Austin, but then he interrupted his own line of questioning. "I'm just going to jump right into the ultimate conclusion of this case. Do you believe that Austin is an individual who is in need of a residential placement?"

"No, I do not," Dr. Dave answered. So Paul asked him to explain why. "In all of my professional activities and evaluations of family situations, I can say without equivocation that I've observed a family who is committed solely to insuring that their son receives an appropriate educational experience, and that he does not have to leave his natural home to get those appropriate services. Many times families are just frustrated beyond description when they have a youngster as challenging as Austin can be, and the Gallagher family has impressed me as being level-headed and even-handed in their approach to working with their son. Not only are they successful with their son, they also have another child with autism as well. That is a huge burden on a family. The Gallagher family is remarkable, beyond any view that I've had of families in my thirty-five plus years of experience working in the field of autism. I don't use that term lightly."

It would be difficult for anyone to not beam with pride after hearing that. I have to admit I sat up a bit taller in my chair, and for the first time felt that I finally had a seat at the table with the big guns. After the way Louis and Dr. Dave had described Billy and me, I was hopeful that the judge could see why we had fought so hard.

Dr. Dave continued when Paul asked him how Austin would be affected by being placed in a residential facility, and he described it as having a "scarring effect" because of Austin's emotional attachment to his parents and siblings.

The testimony moved on to Austin's current placement in his own classroom, with his own staff, at a school that did not provide ABA. Paul asked Dr. Dave about the appropriateness of continuing in this setting.

Like Louis, Dr. Dave also disagreed with Dr. Roark. He felt that this would not be an appropriate placement because of the intensive level of ABA that Austin required.

When asked about Robyn, Dr. Dave said, "Clarity Behavioral Consulting Group really knows what it's doing. Once in a while I see something that impresses me. They're doing it the way it's supposed to be done. Not based upon how they *think* it should be done, but actually how it should be done." He continued to explain that Austin's program was all about who was doing the teaching, just like we had tried to explain to the school district. The location was irrelevant; it was the training of the staff that was critical.

The topic moved on to Austin's lack of social engagement, but Dr. Dave said that he saw a young man who was very much engaged with his instructors, his parents, and even the clerk at the video store. He described how he saw Austin interact with Billy and the store clerk, not requiring constant supervision, going up and down the aisles and bringing up videos to rent.

Paul brought the questioning full circle. "We have all heard about cases involving children with behaviors that are comparable to Austin's, and those individuals have been residentially placed. Why is this case different from those types of cases?" Dr. Dave answered, "The family. This is a remarkable family. You can't fake it and say, 'Let's really look good while Dr. Holmes is in the house.' I can see right through that. This family is connected to their children. They are dedicated to their children. It's amazing to me. The engagement is just absolutely heartwarming. It sounds like I'm a big mush here, but I tell you, I don't see this frequently. And it's very impressive. To even consider removing this child from his family would be a real miscarriage of justice."

Take that Mr. Asinello. I tried to see Mr. Asinello's face, but he wouldn't look up from his notes.

Mr. Natale had little to cross-examine. He asked Dr. Dave about placements more than anything. Dr. Dave again explained that this was about the people, not the place. Then Mr. Natale asked Dr. Dave if he still had any pull at the Eden School, and whether he could get Austin in.

The judge ordered a two-hour break and told the attorneys that she wanted oral summations when we returned.

Judgment Day

January 2006

I HAD LONGED for this day to come so that we could finally move forward. Now that it was here I was petrified, hoping we had done enough. There was no going back.

Mr. Natale presented from his seat. He acknowledged the length of our case and how emotional it had been. Reviewing the facts, he said the district's position was that the IEP of June 23, 2003 should be implemented and that the "draft" IEP created on June 5, 2003 was not an actual IEP. The June 23, 2003 IEP recommended that Austin continue home instruction until a residential placement could be found. But the June 5, 2003 IEP placed Austin in a Brick Township school district program for students with autism and provided additional home supports. It was the one we were fighting for.

Mr. Natale continued by asking that the court disregard the opinions of the experts regarding our desires, needs, and wants as Austin's parents. Certainly, he said, our preferences were important information, "But ultimately a parent does not have the right to select the educational program for the child. Emotionally, a parent is too tied to the situation. Every parent wants the best for their child. And there are times when that desire perhaps gets in the way of what independent people might think is best for that child. That is why the district has the authority and the ability to determine an educational course for a handicapped child."

He then reviewed the witness' testimony, highlighting one common thread: they all felt Austin needed to move on from where he was. The disagreement was about where that should be. The district's argument was that Austin needed more than their program could provide, and that it was not logical for the court to insist that the district continue to accommodate Austin in a classroom all his own.

Finally, he stated, "Based on everything that's in front of the court, I believe the only conclusion can be that the June 23rd IEP was, at that time, the appropriate IEP for Austin. Subsequent to that time, there has been no further agreement as to where he should go from here because of this litigation. But clearly, an out-of-district placement has already been met with success and should be continued during a transitionary period, for however long it takes, until this child is at a point where he can transition back to the district or transition into a life as a young adult. Hopefully we can get to that point by the time he's twenty-one. That's all I have, judge."

Paul stood up. " 'You can have any place in the United States of America, just not here.' That pretty much sums up this entire case, judge, and it's why we ended up here in the first place. 'You can have any place in the United States of America, just not here.' How would any of us feel if the chief executive for our local school district said that to us about our child? 'You can have any place, just not here'," Paul hammered home Mr. Asinello's words. It brought back the memory of the first time I heard them, and I held back the tears in an attempt to be strong.

Paul clarified that much of what needed to be decided involved just two documents. We, the petitioners in this case, believed that the June 5, 2003 IEP was the last IEP that all parties had agreed upon. I couldn't contain my tears when he went on to say, "in February of 2003 the Gallaghers packed their child's bag, drove him hundreds of miles away, and left him in the company of strangers because the district failed to do its job. How would that make any of us feel?"

He detailed that although this was a difficult decision, Austin was now better because Billy and I had made it. After four and a half months he was able to return home with a plan that was effective. "The district made a promise to the family that Austin would have the opportunity to be around other students, to engage in other activities. He would have the opportunity to go to his home school, like any other student," Paul said. "Unfortunately, only a few days later, the district ripped the rug out from underneath the Gallaghers, and most of all from underneath Austin."

Paul's presentation was polished as he explained, "On June 23, 2003, the district broke its promises to the family and broke the law. Without warning, without notice, without reason, without evaluations, and without any room for discussion, the district proposed the exact homebound program that resulted in Austin's admission to KKI. All the while, they allegedly looked for an unnamed, unidentified, residential placement for Austin. 'You can have anywhere in the United States of America, just not here'."

As he moved through his oration, he reviewed the witnesses for the district. They included paid consultants hired as a private child study team by the district and a clinical expert who didn't properly notify the family of his observation. Not one of them recommended a residential placement. Paul pointed out, "There's only one witness, judge, who testified that he recommends a residential placement for Austin: Mr. Asinello, the Director of Special Services. In fact, he testified that Austin should return to a neurobehavioral unit before going to a residential placement. With all due respect to Mr. Asinello, he's not a doctor, he's not an expert in autism, he's not a behaviorist, he's not a BCBA, and he is legally incompetent to make that conclusion."

Regardless of how emotional I was at the moment, Paul's use of the phrase "legally incompetent" roused a silent cheer in my mind.

There was much talk about case studies and how they applied to Austin's situation, and I got lost trying to follow all the information. Codes from Department of Education were discussed. Paul listed the array of mistakes the district had made when they neglected to follow protocols set forth in the New Jersey Administrative Codes.

To sum up his statement, Paul again reminded the court that this decision was about two IEPs: one dated June 5, 2003 and one dated June 23, 2003. Paul read from Ms. Papageorge's testimony recorded on our first day in court.

> Paul: "Ms. Papageorge, I would like to show you a document. Can you tell me what this is?"
> Ms. Papageorge: "This is a proposed IEP plan dated June 5th."
> Paul: "Do you remember developing this IEP with the family and the child study team?"
> Ms. Papageorge: "Yes, I do."
> Paul: "Do you remember in general what the IEP provided for?"
> Ms. Papageorge: "For Austin to stay in district with home services."
> Paul: "And at the conclusion of the IEP meeting, was there an agreement among the parties and the participants that this was an appropriate program?"
> Ms. Papageorge: "At the end of the meeting, we were going to go forward with that plan."
> Paul: "So, all parties were in agreement?"
> Ms. Papageorge: "Yes."
> Paul: "And this was an IEP meeting, right?"
> Ms. Papageorge: "Yes."

Paul concluded his statements to the judge. "All the Gallaghers seek is the enforcement of the June 5, 2003 IEP." He asked the judge to include in any decision that Clarity Behavioral Consulting, Dr. Louis Hagopian, and Dr. Dave Holmes be a part of any team to develop a transition plan. He asked the judge to right the wrong, "so that this district may never again say to this family, 'You can have any place in the United States of America, just not here'."

Paul was fantastic; if I could have clapped I would have. But an uneasy feeling settled in my gut once I realized that those were the final words spoken in our case. While Billy and I drove home, we bounced thoughts back and forth about whether the judge would give any weight to Dr. Roark's testimony, and about how she reacted when Mr. Asinello described why Austin couldn't be in the district. We replayed hours of testimony in our heads, even though we knew we couldn't change anything now. It was in the judge's hands, and we had to wait for her decision.

February 2006 to June 2006

It was near the end of a work day when the phone rang. It was Paul. "You won."

"What? We won?" I was sure I didn't hear him correctly. He said he would send us a copy of the judge's decision, but that we shouldn't get too excited because the district had the right to appeal. From what I knew of this district by now, they would likely wait until the eleventh hour to file any appeal. In this case, they had forty-five days to file.

Paul sent me an email that included the decision. I must have read it five times before it sank in. Judge Gracias' conclusion stated that Austin Gallagher, now a thirteen-year-old boy, had been the subject of a litigation case started on his behalf close to three years earlier by his parents. She reviewed the two IEPs, and detailed all the court dates with a brief synopsis of the outcome of each. I kept looking for the part that said "You won."

Austin's educational history was documented, as well as the events before and after his admission to KKI, including each meeting held to discuss bringing Austin home and what he would need to be successful. She explained the provisions of the June 5, 2003 IEP, and listed the eight reasons from the June 23, 2003 IEP supporting the recommendation of residential placement:

1. Austin is not made to wear his shoes unless he is going on a walk.
2. He cannot participate on class trips.
3. He requires a different schedule than the other students in the class.
4. During the extended school year, Ms. Gonclaves is the only staff member trained in VB/ABA.
5. He cannot participate in group activities.
6. He cannot tolerate loud noises (there is a student in the class who can scream and speak in a high pitched voice).
7. Two additional students were placed in the projected class since the 6/5/03 meeting, making the class size seven including Austin, instead of the original five.
8. There is another student in the class who can become aggressive at times.

The judge summarized Mr. Asinello's responses to all eight points and provided a brief overview of the testimony of each person who took the stand. I was still looking for the "you won" part.

Then I found it, on page nineteen of the twenty-seven page decision. "For reasons set forth below as part of the Findings of Fact, I find the petitioners have met the burden of proof, and further find the June 5, 2003 IEP, based upon the totality of the circumstances, complies substantially with the requirements of NJAC 6A:14-3.7 and is the controlling IEP in this matter which shall be enforced. I further find, for reasons to be discussed further below, the petitioners are entitled to compensatory education for the district's failure to provide Austin with a free and appropriate education."

It was all so technical. I wished it had just said, "You won." But I did find it satisfying that she made it perfectly clear she fully understood that the district's argument was a personal vendetta from Mr. Asinello. She highlighted the flaw in their argument: "Knowing the intensity of structure that Austin required in years past, and in acknowledging KKI's request for a ready program with supports immediately upon discharge, it is incomprehensible how the district could on June 23, 2003 summarily announce it could not comply with the IEP it had been working on since January 2003."

"Incomprehensible" stood out amongst all the other words until I read on, "I find the reasons set forth in the June 23, 2003 IEP to be weak, perhaps reaching the level of being disingenuous, not based upon reliable information, and to be ultimately responsible for the regression Austin suffered from no educational and behavioral program being offered to him until the petitioners sought relief herein. Mr. Asinello testified that the fact that Austin did not wear shoes may be in particular a reason to support a residential placement... No expert opinion was set forth by the district prior to proposing an unnamed residential placement because an eleven-year-old child did not wear his shoes in the classroom."

Incomprehensible and *disingenuous.* Two really big words to describe a really small man, but so fitting.

Judge Gracias ordered that, because Austin was approaching fourteen years of age, Robyn and Clarity Behavioral Consulting, along with Louis and Dr. Dave, were to be retained by the school district to transition Austin into a classroom setting "with the least amount of potential regression possible."

Now that was a dream team for Austin.

We didn't have to wait the forty-five days. The district conceded the loss and scheduled an IEP meeting with us and our dream team to move forward with bringing Austin back to district. When the meeting was held, the room was full. In addition to Billy and me, the attendees included Paul, Louis, Dr. Dave, Robyn, and Jen King, a BCBA from Clarity who would supervise the transition to the new space. From the district side was Mr. Asinello, Mr. Edwards, who was the principal of the high school, a vice principal, and the district's new attorney, Jean Fitzpatrick. After the district's loss, they had to reimburse us $104,000 in legal fees. They fired Mr. Natale's firm.

Mr. Asinello sat at the head of the table on one end, too close to me for comfort. He began to talk about how all who were present had Austin's best interests in mind. I remember thinking, "He's breathing, and I want someone to make it stop." It seemed unlikely that this meeting could be productive. How could we cooperate with someone who just tried to take our child away from us?

Shortly into the meeting, Mr. Asinello brought up a plan to transition Austin into a classroom at the high school, and mentioned the goal was to get him there as quickly as possible. My blood was boiling. "This district has not had Austin's best interests in mind," I snapped, "and based on what the judge has ordered, our treatment team will decide the course of this transition, not you." Paul stepped in and tried to get us back on track, then Dr. Dave took over and brought the focus back to Austin. I tried to remain quiet for the rest of the meeting.

It took several more meetings before Austin was fully transitioned back into the school. Billy and I finally came to an agreement with the district. They asked that their attorney be present at each meeting, a highly unusual request for IEPs and child study team meetings. But due to the previous errors of the district in not following the administrative code, and most importantly for keeping Mr. Asinello's mouth on a tighter leash, the district wanted an extra set of eyes and ears present. If one party's attorney attends, the general rule is the attorney for the other side does so as well. We couldn't afford that, so we compromised. We agreed to allow Ms. Fitzpatrick to attend the discussions if the district would ensure that Mr. Asinello never showed his face at any of our meetings or in our son's classroom. The district agreed.

We Can Fly

June 2006 to September 2007

Austin started in the Brick school district in the summer of 2006 in a classroom made for him from a small office inside the library. Robyn's team continued to work with him in that room as part of the transition, and we looked for opportunities where he could be included in other areas of the school. He walked around the track outside and climbed the bleachers. He went out to ShopRite one day per week to purchase his reinforcers, and he continued to learn inside his room.

I remember visiting one day and seeing our neighbor Brandon with his class in the library working on an assignment. He and Austin were the same age, and on occasion Brandon would come over and jump on the trampoline or just hang out with other neighborhood kids. It brought a smile to my face to know that someone was there who knew Austin, even if just to say "Hi" to him. It was something he had never had.

There were a few episodes of behavioral challenges, but nothing more than he had experienced in other settings in the past. The issues we did have were not always because of Austin; other students played a part as well. For example, Austin always used the same bathroom stall. His staff called in to see if anyone was inside before letting Austin into the bathroom, and on one particular day no one answered. But apparently a young man was in the stall and didn't answer the staff; he was hiding because he was using his phone. He hadn't locked the door to the stall. Austin walked in on him. Immediately the young man became upset and pushed Austin up against the wall. But it didn't take long for him to recognize that Austin was "different" and he didn't continue his attempt to hurt Austin. However, because he "let the kid go," his friends mocked him. This in turn led to the young man destroying the library. We would later learn that he was classified as emotionally disturbed, and this wasn't his first fight.

I was asked to come to the school to speak with Mr. Edwards. I was sure that something awful had happened. He called me into his office to explain the incident in the bathroom. He also informed me the district had decided that the other young man would be moved to the other high school in town. I was shocked at the severity of their decision, but he explained this was the last straw for that boy and didn't have much to do with this particular episode. I thanked him and asked if he needed anything from me. He said no, and as I stood to leave, he added, "I just want you to know, you are nothing like what I've heard." I laughed, and he continued, "and Austin is not as bad as several other children we have in our school." I thanked him again, and there wasn't much more I could say except, "well, consider the source." I knew that everything Mr. Edwards had heard about me and Austin came from Mr. Asinello.

The district hired staff to be trained for Austin's program. Two special education teachers were brought on, but one was quickly asked to leave because of her unorganized nature and hyper mannerisms. She did not pair well with Austin. The other, Nicole Logan, started off in the role of an aide. She was slowly introduced to Austin, his behavior plan, and his programs. Our eventual goal was to have Nicole take over as teacher and gradually fade out Clarity's staff. At this time, a Clarity staff member named Chrisanne Rancati—or, as Austin called her, Christmas—served as Austin's teacher. Nicole soon began to feel she was not respected as a teacher, and she wanted to take on more of the planning and programming. Everyone agreed to give her a chance to design a schedule and a few programs.

I came to the school in November to observe the new programs created by Nicole. Austin was making a hand turkey for a craft. My fourteen-year-old son was being asked to trace his hand and color it to look like a turkey for a Thanksgiving craft. I tried to explain diplomatically that I didn't want my son making hand turkeys—it was a preschool-level task. I felt we should find something more age-appropriate, and Nicole agreed.

I returned to the school a few weeks later to find a string of hand turkeys lining the border of a blackboard. I realized that I was dealing with someone who had her own agenda. Mr. Edwards was also concerned, and he let me know that he was more Nicole's therapist than her boss. She was coming to him on a regular basis to complain that her "expertise" was not respected. I wished I could tell her: "Sit down, shut up, and learn something."

The year was passing quickly, but progress toward training staff for Austin was not moving forward as we had hoped. Nicole was not able to lead the team, yet Mr. Asinello was pressuring our staff to phase out Clarity and transition to a full Brick Township staff.

In addition, Austin was becoming known as the "boy in the room." Rumors were spreading about him. Billy was talking with our neighbor Bob while an electrician was making repairs at Bob's home. The conversation went to the tax rate in our town. The electrician pointed out that our taxes were so high because of a variety of reasons, including school taxes, specifically when they have to provide a room and multiple staff for one child. Bob tried to give the electrician all the non-verbal cues he could to stop the conversation, but he kept on about how there was a kid in the library who had all these people working with him. Billy interrupted him and said, "That's my son." He gave the man a brief synopsis of our story, but nothing could ease that awkward situation.

Billy and I knew that Mr. Asinello would always play some part in destroying Austin, whether by hiring inept staff or insisting that the high school administration move Austin prematurely into another classroom. So we were happy when Ellen Luminas was put back on as Austin's case manager. More good news followed: she learned that the Wilson School had an opening for Austin. We decided to take it.

We attended a meeting at Wilson, and it was confirmed that Austin would start during the summer. We had mixed feelings. Alanna had now been at Wilson for a few years, but Austin was last there when he was nine years old. The staff and administration reassured us that they would do their best and would staff Austin's programs with BCBAs and other trained individuals, but they did inform us that they would be changing Austin's behavior plan a bit. I was scared, panicked actually, but if changes were going to be made this was the place to make them.

In June Austin started at Wilson and traveled to school in the same van as Alanna and our friend's son Kevin. In some ways we had returned to where we had started, but in so many others we had made tremendous gains. This would be a fresh chapter in our lives. We couldn't predict the future, but we could at least ensure that our children were with some of the best people in the field. Billy and I had to learn to trust others to help Austin. It would take us a long time to absorb this lesson, but being at Wilson was a start.

During this time, I had completed my course work and graduated with my master's degree in special education. I opened my own office, the Autism Center for Educational Services, or ACES. ACES services were developed to help children with autism and their families, including educating parents about the IEP process, telling them how to get the services their children needed, and setting up ABA programs in their homes.

I continued school and pursued my BCBA certification through the Florida Institute of Technology. I was adamant about doing my part to help other families with children like Austin. I never wanted another parent to have to drop their child off at an institution or endure dark times of regression at the hands of incompetent people.

I wasn't the only one continuing her education. Chelsea had graduated from high school, and we could not have been more proud of her. She was and still is an exceptional young lady. She had every right to resent her siblings and how their needs often left little energy or attention from Billy and I for her, but she never did.

It was difficult to get Chelsea to fill out college applications. She was a homebody and change was always difficult for her. But once she was thrown into a new situation she thrived due to her drive to be successful. I think a part of her also felt like she needed to be present for Billy and me. She was in so many ways a third parent. Billy and I knew it was time for her to go out into the world and find her place. She needed to become her own person, not just the sister of Alanna and Austin. Chelsea was accepted to Stockton College in the Criminal Justice Program and decided from the outset to complete their four-plus-one master's degree program.

That summer we also decided that our family needed some fun memories. Billy had befriended a local man, Thomas, who owned a parasail company. Billy provided him with seafood throughout the summer, and in August he offered the entire family a parasailing adventure. Billy is the one who pushes us to try new things. If it were up to me, I would live quietly and securely inside the walls of our home and be perfectly happy. Billy is the one with the confidence to get us to venture out and see the world.

All five of us went parasailing for the first time. I was very nervous but tried not to show it, mostly for Chelsea's sake. Billy and Austin went up first. Austin followed the instructions beautifully and got into his life vest and harness. He sat at the end of the boat, and my heart was in my throat. I kept telling myself, "He'll be okay, and if he's not Billy can handle it." The first jolt as they were pulled up into the air was a bit startling for Austin, but then he was up and away. He looked a bit concerned about what was happening, and I just prayed he would enjoy this.

Austin was more than okay. His screeches of joy could be heard by everyone on the boat, even though he was more than three hundred feet in the air. Billy had found a new activity that Austin loved. When they returned to the boat, Austin was laughing. We probably should have guessed he would love it; he always wanted to be at the highest point of any place we were. I remembered how he used to climb on top of the mantel when he was two years old just to sit and watch the world.

It was time for me and Alanna to go up. My heart pounded but I put on a brave face. Alanna was not so sure about all this, and neither was I. After a startling jolt we were high above the ocean, a little too high for comfort for both of us. I immediately starting singing, "We can fly, we can fly, we can fly," from Peter Pan. I tried to keep her calm while being far from calm myself. I wracked my brain for other songs about flying and I launched into a short rendition of "Let's Go Fly a Kite," from Mary Poppins. Good thing no one could hear that back at the boat, because a singer I am not.

Eventually, Alanna calmed and so did I. I began to feel how incredibly peaceful it was that high up in the air, and could understand why Austin loved it. I turned to Alanna and told her that we needed to find Ariel, the Little Mermaid of Disney fame, because she lived in the ocean. Focusing Alanna's attention made both of us calmer, and she looked down and recognized the boardwalk that we visited often. By the time they brought us back in, she was smiling and asking to go on the carousel.

Chelsea loved it when she and Billy had their turn. This was one of our last days with her before she packed her bags for college. A few days later, we loaded the car and trekked her boxes and bags across the campus to her new room. Chelsea was much braver than she even realized. When I was her age, I am sure I would have been too afraid to live away from home. I held my emotions in check until she kissed me goodbye in the parking lot, where I broke down in tears. I was happy about this next adventure in her life, but I was already missing her.

Chelsea was my companion through so much of what our family had suffered. Billy was often out fishing, and maybe I leaned too much on her, but she was always there. She made every effort to make me laugh or feel better when the rest of the world was fighting us. Even at a very young age, she would tell me that she was going to make people do the right thing for her siblings. She loved to watch the cooking channel from the time she was a little girl and she would often bake or make something for us to eat, a huge help in hectic times. Billy and I had done a good job. She was ready for this. I wasn't, but she was. She would excel.

All three children, now fifteen, sixteen, and eighteen, were in good schools and making progress. My business was growing, I was finishing up my schooling, and we had so much stress off of our plates now that we no longer had to deal with Mr. Asinello.

With 2007 behind us, 2008 was going to be our year. Or so I hoped.

Gallagher Normal

January 2008 to January 2010

Chelsea's freshman year passed quickly, full of social interactions with new peers and overreactions to academic challenges she would end up meeting with ease. She joined a sorority. Meanwhile, Alanna and Austin took the bus ride to school each day with only a few protests. Austin didn't like Alanna's singing and vocalizations, and Alanna didn't like when Austin told her to stop. Austin continued to have staff with him after school, including Andrea Bradshaw, a special education teacher. She was the type of person who made you smile when she entered the room, and she rarely became flustered. She was perfect for Austin.

Chelsea came home for the summer and worked as a camp counselor at her old school. She was living the life of a typical nineteen-year-old. She packed her bags in August to return to school, and this second time wasn't nearly as traumatic. After her freshman year, I realized that she came home more often than I had anticipated, and she was great at checking in enough to keep my worries to a minimum.

Alanna and Austin made it through another summer break, or maybe I should say I made it through another summer break. One day Austin escaped from the house, climbed a neighbor's fence, and got into the downstairs apartment of their home. He started watching television while the tenants were there. When I realized he was missing, I called 911 and ran out to the front yard calling him. The neighbor who lived in the upstairs section of the home in question, was also outside on the phone. She was calling 911 because her renter informed her that there was a stranger in her home. As she heard me yelling for Austin, she put two and two together and called to me, "I think I know where he is."

There he was with his headphones on, listening to his MP3 player and watching their television. I apologized profusely. They had just moved in with their young son and didn't know us. I felt awful that Austin had scared them. Later we would read the 911 report; they thought the intruder was on drugs because he wasn't saying anything and was just sitting there.

Around ten o'clock that night Austin came to me in the living room and said, "boo boo," while showing me his hand. It was swollen to three times its size. I realized he must have broken something, so I took him to the emergency room. We got through most of the process with little incident, and after the x-rays were completed we were informed that he broke his finger. Due to the severity of the fracture, pins would be needed to reset it. We had to go see the surgeon the next day. Soon after they scheduled the surgery that would fix Austin's finger. Or so they thought.

When he came out of surgery, I told the doctor that Austin would be able to easily remove the cast they had provided. He assured me, "You have to use a saw to get those off." I insisted that the cast needed to be made larger, but the doctor disregarded my concern. After the procedure Austin was groggy and resistant to getting dressed, he just wanted to sleep. He fought me a bit, but I got him clothed and back home. Once he was settled in his bed, I asked Andrea to stay a bit longer while I ran out to get the medications the surgeon had prescribed and picked up a pizza for everyone.

I was still out when I got a phone call from Andrea. "Bobbie, he got it off." Austin had walked out of his room with the cast in his hands, handed it to Andrea, and said, "No." I rushed home and took him back to the emergency room. After a long wait, they told me there was nothing they could do and that I should go back to the surgeon. I cringed as Austin played with the pins that poked through his skin. Was there really nothing they could do for me?

The next morning we were back at the surgeon's office. He made Austin a new cast, this time with a ninety-degree angle at the wrist to prevent him from pulling it off. But next morning Billy opened the door to Austin's bedroom and saw the cast on the floor. Billy yelled out, "You better call that doctor again." My life always operated on plan B. I made arrangements to get stuff done, and inevitably those plans would be changed by events beyond my control.

Back to the doctor we went. This time the cast started at Austin's bicep, bent at the elbow, and had a ninety-degree angle at the wrist. It took seven days, but that one also made it to the bedroom floor. On our final visit to the surgeon, he pulled the pins out of Austin's finger and told us it would have to heal on its own, there was nothing more he could do. I couldn't wait for the school year to start. I needed the break.

Come September school was back in session and we were all finally back to our routines. Then one night Billy's older brother Patrick called, which was a bit of a surprise. When Patrick and Billy were kids they didn't have much of a relationship. When we were younger Patrick worked in my father's motorcycle shop and was friends with my brothers. He and Billy spent much of their childhood and teenage years at odds with each other. As adults there was no animosity, but also no great bond. We didn't hear from Patrick often. He had called to tell Billy that he had colon cancer, and that Billy should go get checked out too.

Upon hearing the news, I was obviously upset for Patrick. Our family had lost enough young people to cancer, including my brother when he was only twenty and Billy's stepsister at forty-two. I was hopeful that they had caught it soon enough for Patrick to be okay.

Patrick and Billy led very different lives. Billy spent almost his entire life in New Jersey. Patrick traveled the world regularly, visiting places that weren't for the average tourist like Tasmania, Mongolia, and Antarctica. Patrick put hot sauce on everything, he said that it killed bacteria. There was a time when he was very ill in a foreign country, being cared for by people who could not understand him because he didn't speak their language. He described the dirt floor in the makeshift hospital and the chickens that walked freely. I was sure the cancer was probably due to some bacteria or virus he must have been exposed to in one of those places.

The part that Billy left out when giving me the news was that Patrick had a genetic form of cancer, and his doctor had recommended that all of his siblings be tested. All Billy said to me was that Patrick's doctor suggested that his siblings get checked out. Billy scheduled a colonoscopy for October and the day after it he took a flight out to see Patrick in Idaho.

During the colonoscopy they had "removed a few polyps," Billy said, and the doctor wanted to see him to discuss the results. Shortly after his return home from Idaho he went for the follow-up appointment. When I returned home that day I opened the front door to find Billy standing in front of the television. He grabbed me and hugged me. Hugs are not an unusual experience here at the Gallagher home, but I could tell something was up. While holding me, he leaned back a bit and said, "I have cancer."

I collapsed into his chest and sobbed. "I can't lose you," was all I could get out through the tears and sniffling. He told me he had an appointment with a surgeon, and that there were too many polyps to remove. They were going to have to take out his entire colon.

I tried to hold it together, to avoid overreacting until we knew more. But it was impossible not to worry about what this meant. We had been hearing the chronicles of Patrick's cancer, and it was not going well. I made dinner, trying to be strong and keep to our evening routine. But when I sat on the couch I cried. When I looked at Billy I cried. When I looked away I cried. When we went to bed, I slipped away as he dozed so that he wouldn't hear me cry.

I cried because of what Billy would have to go through, but mostly I cried because I feared I would lose the best thing that ever happened to me. Billy was my rock, my support, my biggest fan. He was everything to me. The thought of living without his hugs, without having him near me, was unimaginable. The thought that I would have to raise our children without him was impossible. I was not that strong.

Billy's operation was scheduled just before Christmas. Billy put on a brave face and acted like it was all no big deal. Because I had to get the kids on the bus I couldn't drive him to his surgery, but I promised him that I would be in the waiting room when he got out. I wanted to be with him, I wanted him to know every second of every moment that I loved him.

When I got to the waiting room Billy's uncle Bill was already there, and my mom arrived a little later. The minutes passed slowly while we waited for an update. The nurse kept telling us that the doctor would come speak to us when the surgery was over. Uncle Bill was reading the paper, and it was open to the obituary page. As I glanced over I saw a face I recognized. My first boyfriend had passed away suddenly, leaving a wife and baby behind. My heart sank. I had lost another boyfriend to a horrific car accident just prior to Billy and I dating, and now Freddie's picture was in the Press. I prayed that it wasn't a sign while I wondered what was taking the doctor so long.

Eventually we were told that Billy was in recovery, and that the doctor had already left the building because he had not been informed that we were in the waiting room. The nurse had him call me, and when he did he said all went well. Billy didn't need a colostomy bag because they had been able to attach the small intestine to his rectum, but he would be in the hospital for a few days. He needed to build up his diet until he was passing solid stools, then he could go home.

Billy could be an amazing advocate if you were the one in the hospital, but he was not the best patient. He was in a great deal of pain and was very short with the nurses. Eventually they found a medication that was effective, and his personality returned.

Once he got back home he pushed himself harder than he should have, but all seemed to be going well (or as well as could be expected for a man with no colon). Every trip to the bathroom was a reminder that he was sick.

Patrick had flown to India for medical treatment. His cancer had reached a stage that required treatments he couldn't afford without insurance. He needed chemotherapy, and he could get more treatment for less money in India. I wasn't sure this was a good idea, but I had no say in the matter. What I did know was that travel was always a good thing for Patrick mentally. Billy had contemplated going with him, but I couldn't allow it. I needed him to be here, and I needed to be with him every minute possible.

We celebrated the New Year quietly, with hope that 2009 would bring about positive change. Our children were all doing well. Billy's doctor said he was fine, though I'm not sure anyone touched by cancer can ever feel that they're completely free. Billy was learning what he needed to do to stay healthy now that his body had to adjust to not having a colon.

Billy eventually returned to the fishing boat, working just as hard as he had before his surgery. He needed a few more breaks during the day than he used to, but he was able to do his part, but we weren't sure for how long. I was pushing myself to finish school, get my BCBA certification, and get him off the ocean.

Spring arrived and we were back on track until a phone call from Billy's mom woke us late one night. Billy's stepfather had died suddenly. PopPop Bindrim was a man who Billy adored. They shared many once-in-a-lifetime moments, like going to Daytona and seeing a Holyfield fight. Any adventure Billy was up for, PopPop was in too. They were more like best friends than stepfather and son. His death was so sudden that it was hard to believe. None of us knew how MomMom, Billy's mother, would get through it. I had to believe her faith would see her through.

Losing a loved one makes you reflect on how short life really is. For me, it was a reminder that Billy needed to keep taking care of himself to prevent his cancer from coming back. For Patrick, that was exactly what happened. Soon we had news that there would be no more attempts at treatment, the cancer had metastasized to other areas of Patrick's body. In October, he passed at the age of forty-nine, surrounded by his Idaho friends who read and sang to him, and ensured his last moments were peaceful.

Losing Patrick was so sad, he was taken from us much too soon. After his death, I worried that Billy would be next. I followed his every movement, every grunt and groan. I would ask him five times a day, "Are you alright?" I'm sure he grew sick of me asking. But he had the same genes as Patrick, and I worried he would also have the same fate. The constant lingering fear was tearing me apart.

Billy flew to Idaho for Patrick's memorial, but he never made it there. He was suddenly in such pain that he couldn't move. He was brought to the emergency room in Driggs, Idaho and then driven by ambulance to Idaho Falls hospital. After two days there he flew back to New Jersey and was admitted to Monmouth Medical Center. I was petrified with fear, unable to move. I got the children on the bus the next day and drove to see him. When I entered, he joked about not getting to see much of Idaho. It was typical of Billy to try to make me laugh when I was upset.

He was in the hospital for many days with no results. The doctor said he had a twist in his intestine, and that these things usually worked themselves out. But after more than seven days of vomiting, the doctor opted to take a look. Billy had a strangulated hernia, his intestine had swollen so large that they were unable to do laparoscopic surgery and had to cut him open from chest to belly button. They removed a piece of his small intestine and closed up the hole. The doctor told us that he would be fine, but recovery would take some time. His body had been through quite a bit and he had lost twenty-five pounds. But in true Billy Gallagher fashion, he was up and around faster than he was supposed to be, and soon was back out on the fishing boats.

So, 2009 pretty much sucked. During another quiet New Year's celebration, Chelsea told me not to hope that 2010 would be better, since I had said that for the past two years with little to show for it. Instead, she told me to just wish 2009 away.

I understood her fear, and I agreed.

January 2010 to January 2011

Chelsea was right to not jump for joy about a new year. Austin was not well, and we couldn't figure out what was wrong. He would sleep fourteen to sixteen hours a day, and much of it was while he was at school. We took him for some tests and the doctors found issues with his thyroid, but none of their recommendations helped. Our neurologist sent us to the Children's Hospital of Philadelphia to see a specialist. For months we hopped from one doctor's office to another, unable to find an answer.

When he was awake at school, Austin was less and less cooperative. They informed us that Austin was getting aggressive and was biting others. We talked about different ways to increase his enjoyment at school, perhaps changing the behavior plan back to the KKI version, but no solution could be found. At home he rarely wanted to do anything except be on the computer, and he was biting himself more often. He refused to leave the house even for things he enjoyed, like visiting the boardwalk. He gained forty pounds in three months, and the acne on his face was worsening. We couldn't find any answers.

My family was holding a reunion over Memorial Day weekend in Tennessee. Billy and I decided to go, even though we usually avoided most family gatherings and social situations because of Austin's behaviors. My cousin Stephanie was hosting the event on her farm. She offered her guest house to us so we wouldn't have to stay at a hotel. This was a great help because we probably wouldn't have been able to get Austin out of a hotel, and that would mean one of us would have had to stay with him.

When we arrived Austin immediately searched her home for a computer. Many family members were already there, and most had not met our kids yet. We tried to get Austin out of the crowded kitchen to show him where we were going to stay, but he interpreted that as having to leave and he wasn't ready to get back in the car. He tried to sit on a glass-topped table, and family members tried to explain to him that he couldn't. He became overwhelmed and started biting himself. Billy grabbed him to get him out of there. Austin put up a fight, and during the struggle to get him out Billy felt a pop in his abdomen. We got Austin into the guest house and set up his electronics, a DVD player and a small laptop with an internet hot spot.

Once Austin was settled, Billy and I joined the family for a much-needed glass of wine and a few laughs. Chelsea and Alanna met many of my cousins and their children. It was nice to see how well Alanna adjusted to new people, and how they accepted her. At first some of the younger children were a bit put off by Alanna's oddities, but by the end of the visit several of them were engaging Alanna in her "Disney speak" and filling in the words. Alanna would quote Peter Pan, "Oh Peter!" and one of the girls would finish the line, "you saved my life."

On our way back to New Jersey we stayed one night at the home of Billy's aunt Carol, then made the long haul back home. We drove in separate cars. Billy, Alanna, and Uncle Bill were in one car, and Chelsea, Austin, and I were in another. Somewhere along the way, I missed a turn and got separated from Billy. Austin had been biting himself and pushing his feet into Chelsea, and I lost track of what the GPS was telling me to do. The next thing I knew he had put his feet through the steering wheel and I was unable to control the car. I was driving at seventy-five miles an hour down a highway I didn't know, and I couldn't steer. Chelsea tried pushing his feet out, which made him angrier so he began to bite himself even harder. She finally got his feet out and I got the car pulled over to the side of the road. Austin continued to bite and kick. Chelsea and I were both hysterical, we couldn't figure out how to continue. Chelsea called Billy's cell phone and we decided to find a place to meet up. I had to wait for Austin to calm down before continuing, I couldn't drive knowing he might do this again at any moment.

When we met up, Chelsea got out of our car and into Uncle Bill's with Alanna. Billy drove my car the rest of the way home. Austin refused to get out at any rest stop and stayed in the back seat for the entire eleven-hour ride. We finally made it home and crashed for the night.

Billy had to schedule a doctor's visit to get that "pop" looked at. It turned out that struggling with Austin had caused a hernia, and surgery was needed to repair it. The doctor said he put extra mesh in Billy's abdomen to ensure there would be no repeat surgery needed.

As the school year wound down, Austin's decline continued. His bus driver and aide, a husband and wife team named Wayne and Martha Isner, told me that Austin was spending more time on the floor of the van than in his seat. On one occasion he came to the front of the van and sat in Martha's lap. When she attempted to move him, he bit her. I felt sick. She was such a sweet woman, and she tried to make me feel better by saying she was fine, but I knew he must have really hurt her. I didn't know what we were going to do if he kept this up. They also said that by the time they reached the school Austin was usually asleep, and that the school staff had to physically remove him from the van to get him to into the building.

This was way too much physical handling of Austin. He was being uncooperative in situations in which he typically had no problems. We continued to search for answers. Wayne and Martha had to take some time off to deal with a medical issue of Wayne's. The transportation company replaced them with two new people. On their first day, the new bus staff took a different route than Wayne usually did. The change disturbed Austin, and he got out of his seat and came to the front of the van. He aggressed toward the aide and the driver. They pulled over into a bank parking lot and called the police.

I received a call from the Wall Township police telling me I needed to meet them at the bank on Route 34. I was in a panic. I didn't even get out of my pajamas, I just grabbed my keys and purse. When I arrived, Austin was sitting on the ground outside the van. Alanna was crying, still in her seat. She didn't like commotion and certainly didn't like when her routine was interrupted. Kevin looked fine, he was playing a game on a device.

The police explained what happened. They apologized that when Austin first exited the van and sat on the ground, he found a chewed piece of gum and put it in his mouth. The Wall police had been through a First Responders training given by Gary Weitzen, of POAC Autism Services, so they had some understanding of how to interact with children with autism in these types of situations. They knew it was best to be hands-off as long as Austin was safe, and that was what they did. He was sitting quietly on the ground. Once he got the gum in his mouth, no one was going to get it out. They just stood near him to keep him safe and block him if he headed for the road. I put him in my car and drove him home.

I was afraid we were heading down a road that would lead to KKI again. I needed to figure out what was happening with Austin. We tried one more time to put Austin on the bus and hoped he would make it to school. Our hope was short-lived. The new driver called almost immediately, and I could hear Austin in the background. I jumped into my car and drove to Route 138.

This time I arrived before the police. I pulled up behind the van to see the aide on the outside holding the door, trying to keep Austin from opening it. Austin was in the passenger seat, kicking and grabbing at the driver who was hitting him back. As I got closer to the van I heard her yell, "if you kick me one more time," and I opened the door. "You'll do what?" I asked. She had no answer. I understood that she needed to protect herself, and that this was a challenge she didn't sign up for. But I never understood why transportation staff doesn't receive training in how to deal with our children. I got Austin out of the van and put him in my car just as a police car arrived. It was one of the officers from the week before. He told me that something would have to be done, the drivers couldn't keep calling for help. We needed to find a way for everyone to be safe.

A meeting was called, and the district agreed to put Austin in his own vehicle with two staff people. Alanna and Kevin would go to school separately. At least their routines wouldn't be interrupted. The next day two very intimidating men showed up to take Austin to school. But I didn't want this to become about bullying Austin into compliance. Austin wouldn't have made the determination that these men were strong. He still would have attempted to hurt them, and possibly get hurt in the process. It was the end of the year and there were only a few days left, so I just kept him home.

Although the summer granted us a reprieve, the challenges returned with the new school year. On the first day back in September, a little yellow school bus arrived. Inside was a driver and two aides, one very large man was assigned to Austin. As we watched the bus drive away, I told Billy I knew this was not going to work. I waited for the phone call from the police, but it didn't come. Austin did make it to school, but it hadn't gone well. The bus company informed the school staff that they would not be transporting Austin home, nor back to school again. Billy and I would need to make other arrangements for the future. We had no idea what had happened, but we were told that the large male aide assigned to Austin was bleeding.

I went to the school at the end of the day and drove Alanna and Austin home. Once we got the kids settled, I gave Austin a bath. As he stepped into the tub I saw a bruise that took up the entire left side of his ribcage. I didn't know what happened on that bus, but I knew Austin was hurt. I also knew we would never learn the truth from the bus company staff. Billy was home from work, so he agreed to drive Austin in the next day and talk to the school staff about what we could do to move forward.

Austin did fine on the ride in with Billy until they got close to the school. Just as they were about to make the left turn into the parking lot he began to repeat, "No, no, no." Billy pulled up to the side of the building. He got out of the truck and saw Austin's teacher Beth Goldberg. He explained to her that he was in no rush to leave, that Austin was saying "no" on his way in, and because no one really knew what happened the day before on the van, they should just take it easy. He suggested, "Maybe we could even just get him inside and read his Dr. Seuss books to him."

Then Austin's BCBA Tim Fischbein came out and asked, "Did we give him his two minutes to exit the vehicle?" Beth responded, "Yes." Without time for Billy to intervene and ask to slow things down as he and Beth had just agreed, Tim approached the passenger side of Billy's truck, opened the door, and with little notice placed his arms under Austin's armpits to lift him up from the seat. With this motion Austin knocked a glass ceiling light cover out of Billy's truck and it shattered on the ground. Billy ran to the truck and tried to get the glass out of the way.

Austin struggled, fell, and landed hard on his bottom on the cement. Billy was beside himself. He was just saying how he had all day to make this work. He couldn't understand why everything had gone so wrong. Austin started crying, reaching his hand up toward Billy and pleading, "Daddy." Billy told everyone to just stop for one second. He took Austin's hand and said, "C'mon bud." Austin stood up. Billy took him into the cafeteria, sat him at a table, and read Dr. Seuss books to him.

After reading a few books, Billy walked Austin down to his classroom and headed back to his truck. He called me as soon as he left the building. As he replayed the scene, Billy couldn't hold back his tears. "He's not going back there again," he sobbed, "not after that." If that was how the staff treated Austin when Billy was present—especially after the events of the day before—there was no way he could continue going there. I didn't know what we were going to do, so I called Ellen. She scheduled a meeting with the Wilson School.

Wilson had done wonders for Alanna. She was learning and productive, she completed some internships, and most of all she was happy. She liked to do work and stay busy. Austin was very different from his sister. He needed much encouragement to step away from his electronic devices. Everyone described Alanna as "sweet." She had some behavioral challenges, but they were more subtle than her brother's. His tended to frighten people.

Some of Alanna's challenges came from her desire to be independent. She would try to cook a pizza in the middle of the night only to set off the smoke alarms. Once when Alanna was sent to her room, she decided to take the air conditioning unit out of her window, put it on the floor, and climb out the opening. Once on the roof, she climbed from one end of the house to the other, down some lattice, and onto another window air conditioner. I heard a noise and thought an animal had gotten into the air conditioner, but found Alanna there instead. I still don't know how she managed to cross the entire roof without falling.

Alanna also liked to break glass. Mostly drinking glasses, but also plates, bowls, mugs, light bulbs, anything that would shatter on the ground. We never figured out how this behavior started. We often thought it might have come from watching things break in Disney movies. Cinderella drops a tray with a tea set, and animals break plates over Lucifer the cat's head when he is trying to hide the key to the door that would free Cinderella. In the Little Mermaid, animals shatter plates over Ursula's head when she disguises herself and tries to marry Prince Eric. Regardless of the origin, it was and continues to be a challenge because it is so dangerous. The solution is that we only have plastic dinnerware in our home. No one is happier than me when Target brings out their annual summer barbeque stuff—it means I get new plastic plates.

All children have their challenges. Our girls weren't void of them, but for the most part they brought us great joy and pride. A sorority sister had nominated Chelsea as the first Stockton Hero. This was part of a designated driver awareness campaign from the John R. Elliot Foundation. As the Stockton Hero, she was on a huge billboard on a major highway near the college that stated: "Be Chelsea, be a designated driver" with my beautiful daughter's face twenty feet tall. We all sort of laughed about the phrase, "Be Chelsea," because many of us in the family often wished we could be Chelsea. In fact, I have often said that when I grow up, I want to be Chelsea.

Chelsea had become a resident assistant, which helped reduce her tuition. She got good grades and was on her way to completing her master's degree. Every teacher I ever met raved about her, and she was always the best big sister two siblings could ever have. Whenever Austin faced challenges she would get very upset, and she often approached the situation with a desire to change the system. She also worried about how Austin's inability to go to school would impact me and Billy. She had spent all those years watching Austin at home while we fought the school district. She knew that having him home all day was draining. But she also knew that we would always do what was best for our kids.

We felt it was best for Austin to stay home again. We met with the director and other staff from Wilson. They did not support our decision to bring Austin home, and they would not provide staff to implement a home-based program. They felt that if we could just get Austin to school each day, they could teach him. Despite the fact that he was spending much of the day sleeping, and that when he was awake he often needed to be physically managed, they still felt that the school setting was the appropriate option.

Ellen reviewed Austin's history, and it showed that being home had often been a good option for him. Each home program we implemented showed progress that was not made when he was in school. Because the lawsuit forced us to educate him at home for nearly three years, it was a setting in which he was comfortable. We looked to another agency to provide staff to help us. We needed someone who was ready to take him on for several years. He was now eighteen, and Billy and I decided that whatever move we made would be the last one before he turned twenty-one and entered the adult services world.

I had recently partnered with a local agency on some cases, so I asked them if they would be interested in helping us. Luckily, they were. The turnaround was quick, and Austin once again had staff in our home to teach him. The agency hired Jen, the BCBA from Clarity that Austin had been with in the high school setting. We were ready to start making progress again.

I had completed all my coursework and supervision, and I sat for the BCBA exam in September. In November I got the news that I had passed.

Billy and I started talking about finally moving him off of the fishing boat and letting me take a larger load of our financial needs. Now that Austin was home and more of a man than a boy, I needed Billy around. Billy was a bit hesitant. He had fished nearly all his life. Change was always hard, and not knowing whether I could bring in the necessary funds to support the family made it even harder. Billy wanted keep fishing, but he also wanted to be home more to help and his health was not conducive to being a fisherman. But in the end, Austin made the decision for us. He had other plans.

He's Dying

January 2011 to September 2011

Austin challenged the new staff. He refused to go out into the community; any attempts lead to challenging behaviors. He often bit himself, and on two occasions he broke the window of a staff person's car. At times he attacked the staff.

His world was getting smaller, his desire to stay home under the covers and shut out the world was increasing. This just wasn't Austin, he used to be so active and loved being outside. He started to refuse foods he never would have turned down in the past, like McDonald's fries. He played with gummy bears instead of eating them. We knew something was physically wrong with him, but he couldn't tell us and we couldn't find an answer.

On an early Sunday morning in mid-August, Austin's condition seemed to worsen. Although he appeared fine when he woke, a few hours later Austin called me, and asked me to place my hands on his stomach, and said, "Mommy push." I thought maybe he just had an upset stomach, but then he grabbed my fingers and tried hard to press my fingernails into his stomach.

It was hard to explain pain to Austin, and he certainly didn't understand the concept of being sick. If Austin had a sore throat, he would try to place my hand down his throat as if I could pull out whatever was bothering him. On this day, he was trying to get my nails deep into his abdomen to get to what was hurting. I explained to him, "No push, Mommy will rub it." But he kept insisting that my nails go into his skin. He tried to say "Mommy push," again, but it was just a rush of air as though he was using his last breath to get the words out. I called Billy and told him that I was taking Austin to the emergency room.

I drove to the local hospital in Brick. Billy had been on his way up the parkway, but turned around to meet me at the hospital instead. After a bit of a battle, the nurse drew Austin's blood so some tests could be run. When the doctor returned, he explained that Austin had pancreatitis, a painful inflammation of the pancreas. The protocol for recovery was to go without food for a few days. The doctor gave us a choice: he said we could take Austin home, or he could be admitted to the hospital. Keeping Austin from food at home would be nearly impossible, so we decided that we would be more successful in the hospital.

Austin was admitted to the nearly-empty pediatric floor. He was laying on the bed in a great deal of pain, and little was being done to ease it. Billy took him to a play area in an attempt to keep his mind off of the discomfort. The staff told us they needed to get a hold of Dr. Rakesh Patel—the treating physician—before they could do more for Austin. They had heard that the nurses had a difficult time putting in an IV, and that he had a history of being aggressive. I saw a security officer bring up restraints, and the nurse must have seen my eyes widen. She explained that this was just a precaution to keep Austin safe as much as it was to keep the staff safe. I just wanted them to bring up some pain medications and take care of my son.

I had to leave and get home to Alanna, so Billy stayed with Austin. Dr. Patel finally called. While the nurse was on the phone with him, Billy approached the nurse's station. "Ask for a plan A, and then for a plan B," he told her. "Don't hang up until you have a plan B," he pleaded. Austin had a history of not following the usual path of any medical intervention, and Billy didn't want to wait for the doctor to call again if plan A didn't work.

Dr. Patel ordered two milligrams of Ativan every 6 hours, but the medication had minimal effect. Austin moved restlessly around the room: getting up and down off his bed, into and out of the chair, into the bathroom to lay on the cold floor, and back in the bed. Billy begged the nurses to help, because Austin was clearly in pain. Around 10 pm, he became agitated and pulled out his IV. The nurses wouldn't attempt to put it back in. Around midnight they gave him a second dose of Ativan by melting it in some juice. But the Ativan wasn't helping; it was a sedative, not a pain killer. The pain was so intense that the sedative was having no effect on Austin. He continued to move around the room, crying. He tried to get Billy to open the door so they could leave.

Billy was trying to just keep Austin on the bed. He called to the nurse and asked, "What's plan B?" The nurse told him there was no plan B, she would have to call the doctor again. She mentioned that Dr. Patel was going to be upset if they kept calling. "That's his job, my son needs help," Billy responded. When the doctor called back, the nurses increased the dose of Ativan to three milligrams every four hours, but it still had no effect. Billy was physically exhausted from trying to keep Austin in the room, and emotionally exhausted from trying to advocate for our son while being unable to offer Austin any relief or honor his request to leave. Billy finally hit the call button and yelled, "This is not fair to him or me." Something needed to be done to get Austin comfortable enough to sleep.

Austin was unable to identify his level of pain verbally, and he couldn't use the visual system of smiley faces to communicate it either. The nurses were hesitant to suggest pain medication because Austin couldn't express his pain. Perhaps if they understood autism they would have seen that he was hurting: he could not stay still for any period of time, he laid on the cold bathroom floor, and he tried to escape from the room. Austin was communicating his pain as best he could.

The night shift came in, and they got the IV back in. Billy warned them, "He's trying to rip it out," as he watched Austin wiggle his fingers under the tape. The new nurse on the shift said, "He's okay." But when she tried to start the IV machine, it immediately beeped. She tried to restart it twice, and then acknowledged, "he must have pulled it out." They refused to make a third attempt until Dr. Patel came in at 6:30 am.

I arrived at nine o'clock the next morning and passed Dr. Patel in the parking lot. He explained that Austin had been given enough sedatives to put an elephant down, but they had no effect. He told me that Austin was in a lot of pain and that his amylase and lipase levels were so high they were moving him to the Critical Care Unit (CCU).

Before bringing Austin down to the CCU, Billy, me, and one of Austin's staff members worked together to hold him down while three nurses put in a new IV line. Once he was settled in the CCU, the nurses started IV fluids to rehydrate him. The doctor finally added pain medication, and shortly afterwards Austin was able to rest.

Austin was calm, but soon his breathing became jerky and short. Billy questioned the nurse about the respiratory numbers displayed on the machine Austin was hooked up to, but she told him not to pay attention to the numbers. She said she could see Austin breathing, so she knew he was okay.

The days flew by. Austin had been admitted on a Sunday and it was already Tuesday. After yet another shift change, one of the new nurses asked about the color of Austin's lips. "He looks pale to me, kinda blue," she pointed out. I agreed with her and said, "He's practically purple." She spoke with Dr. Patel, and he ordered a blood gas test. Austin's number was so low they were sure they had made a mistake. They ran the test a second time and Austin's numbers were the same.

When the medical team's first attempt to give Austin extra oxygen didn't bring up his numbers, Dr. Patel ordered a C-PAP mask. Austin quickly began to improve, and the color started to return to his face and lips.

The next morning Austin was taken for a CT scan. Everything seemed fine until I saw the nurse and the rest of the team rushing Austin back to his room. They immediately hooked him back up to the C-PAP machine, but they couldn't get his oxygen numbers to stabilize. Austin needed to be intubated so he could get enough oxygen. Although we always insisted on being present for every procedure, we were asked to step outside because we would not want to see what was about to happen. I was losing my son. He couldn't breathe, and I couldn't help him.

As we waited nervously, a doctor came to give us the results of Austin's CT scan. Austin had pancreatitis necrosis with pseudocysts. Essentially, bile produced by the pancreas was burning the pancreas itself, and it was leaking into his body and damaging other organs. Austin was in renal failure and respiratory distress, and he needed the help of a specialist. We needed to get him to Shore Medical Center, a facility that was better equipped to treat his condition.

The team at Shore Medical Center treated Austin using a three-pronged approach. He was intubated to maintain his oxygen levels, medicated to keep him sedated and pain free, and hydrated with IV fluids. The doctors explained that Austin had an internal burn and his body needed to be flooded with fluids to put out the fire, similar to cooling burnt skin by soaking it in water. Austin was pumped with bags of IV fluids so quickly that his body swelled. After that, all we could do was wait for him to heal.

Billy slept at the hospital every night and acted as advocate, staying on top of Austin's treatment plan. I took a shift when I could, but that wasn't often. Chelsea had to return to college, Alanna wasn't back in school yet, and I needed to work. I took over at the hospital during the day so Billy could get some things done, but he insisted on being there every night, sleeping in a chair beside Austin's bed.

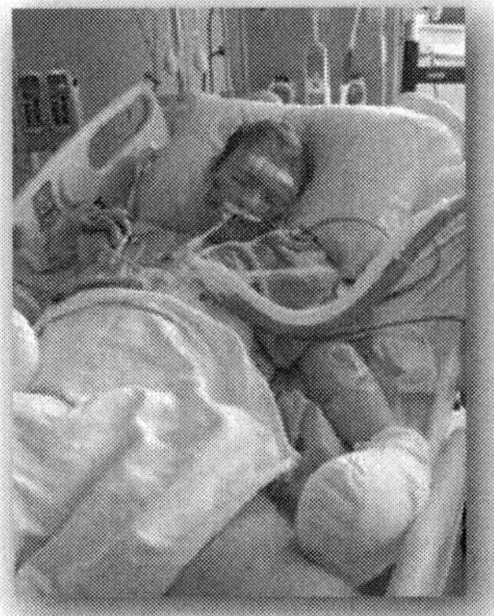

Austin's days in the hospital were mostly quiet aside from regular x-rays and medication adjustments. We played his favorite DVDs to him over and over, holding the headphones up by his ears. I wanted to him to hear comforting sounds he would recognize from home. One day he woke for a moment, which was a bit scary because he had the ventilator tube in his throat. I leaned in to tell him "it's okay" and waited for the nurse to bring more sedatives. He put his hand behind my head, pulled me close, and rubbed my nose with his before he fell back asleep. That tiny moment was greatly needed and gave me so much hope.

Austin's healing slowly progressed, and finally the day came when the doctors wanted to see if he could breathe without the ventilator. We steeled ourselves. Because the sedation needed to be decreased as part of the procedure, Austin would briefly be awake with the tube still in his throat. Billy and I stayed near his face to help keep him calm.

The tube was removed and Austin tried to breathe on his own. But he was breathing too fast, wheezing and unable to get enough air. I tried to stay calm as I rubbed his head and we cheered him on. "Come on Austman, you can do this," Billy chanted, trying to focus on something besides Austin's breath. But the numbers on the machine were plummeting, and Austin was gasping and panicking. The fear in his eyes as he desperately tried to breathe was too much for me. I tried not to cry while he could see me, but I couldn't hold it back. I grabbed both sides of his face and placed my lips on his forehead, repeating "I love you, I love you, I love you," as if I could brand it into his skin. In case he didn't pull through this, I needed him to know that more than anything else.

The CCU doctor, Dr. Walter Murad, said he had to put Austin back on the ventilator, his heart couldn't take the lack of oxygen any longer. It felt like a huge failure: we woke him up and saw his beautiful eyes, only to frighten him half to death and end up putting him back on the machine. The doctor promised me that Austin wouldn't remember this experience. But I would.

They intubated him, and again he was sedated. We were back where we started. All we could do was wait for his body to heal. Every day Billy would wake up to help the staff perform the chest x-ray, and then wait for the doctors to arrive with the results. The staff often told him to go home, but Billy wouldn't leave Austin's side.

Less than a week later the doctor tried to remove the ventilator again. Once again we surrounded Austin with love and tried to keep him calm enough to take deep breaths. We cheered and prayed for him to pull through this time, but again we watched as he struggled and panicked. He looked into our eyes with such fear, and there was nothing we could do to calm him. Again, the doctor ordered him back on the ventilator.

He was nineteen, but at that moment he was just a little boy and we couldn't explain any of this to him in a way that he would understand. I hung onto the doctor's promise that Austin wouldn't remember these moments. I needed to believe he would not remember. It was painful for the medical staff too, even though one might expect these sorts of challenges to be routine for them. Some of the nurses had developed strong attachments to Austin, especially because Billy was there every day to tell them about who Austin was before all this happened. One nurse who had been present at both attempts to remove the ventilator said, "I can't do this again. When they schedule this next time, I don't want it to be on my shift. I just can't watch."

Luckily, none of us had to watch it again. Instead, Dr. Murad ordered a tracheotomy. The procedure would allow Austin to breathe through an incision in his windpipe in place of the ventilator tube in his throat. He would need less sedation and could be awake enough to watch videos and listen to us read books.

As Austin slowly improved, Billy really had his work cut out for him. Austin was moved out of the CCU and onto a regular floor. Now he would just be one of many patients for the nurse to attend to. Billy needed to advocate for Austin more than ever before, because we needed the staff to make Austin a priority.

As Austin began to breathe for longer periods of time without mechanical assistance, other issues came to the forefront. Billy was concerned because Austin had not had a bowel movement in quite some time, and he appeared to be in pain. One of the nurses told Billy she would address it with the doctor. Shortly thereafter she returned and gave Austin a medication through his IV. It was supposed to be administered slowly over a five- to ten-minute period, but instead she injected it into his IV line all at once. Austin's heart stopped. She banged on his chest with her fist and yelled his name until he came through. In shock, Billy asked her "what the hell was that?" She answered that was an anti-diarrhea medication. "Anti-diarrhea? The boy hasn't shit in a week!" Billy shouted. I arrived at the hospital soon after, but Billy didn't tell me what had happened until much later. He tried to spare me details of events that couldn't be changed.

I have heard others describe children with autism as being "locked inside their bodies," as though their skin was just a shell and someone was trying to get out. I never felt that way about my children until that anti-diarrhea medication stopped Austin's heart. He became frozen on the outside; only his eyes would move to follow me around the room. Those eyes were filled with fear.

A neurologist was sent to look at Austin, who was now barely able to lift his hand and having tremors just trying to reach his computer keyboard. The neurologist said, "He has autism, right? Isn't this his baseline?" I don't know what this doctor knew about autism, but if he thought this was Austin's normal state, he was crazy. I pleaded for him to investigate what happened. Austin had been typing on his computer and enjoying videos just one day prior. The neurologist ordered an MRI, and the results didn't show anything abnormal. Austin remained in that frozen state for several days. It eventually passed, but his needs would still prove to be too much for the unit.

Austin was moved back to the CCU and Billy asked the doctors to address the constipation. He specifically asked that they attempt the most intrusive intervention first because Austin had been backed up for so long. He appeared to be in so much pain, kneeling on the bed and unable to get comfortable. A nurse increased his sedatives while also giving him a laxative through a feeding tube. They pumped in nearly a gallon of liquid medication with no results.

Billy was beside himself with exhaustion and frustrated by the blatant lack of urgency on the part of the hospital staff. The doctors asked him to go home and get some rest. He listened, and I took the night shift. Chelsea came to keep me company. That night, Austin had a major blowout from all the laxatives while still in bed. We tried to get him to settle down while we called the nurse. She said she would be with us in a minute, but she didn't come. Together, Chelsea and I found the bed linens and hospital gowns, moved Austin off the bed, cleaned him up, re-made the bed, and got Austin settled again—all before the nurse showed up. "I was coming," she protested when she saw what we had done. I told her he shouldn't have to wait for her while sitting in his own feces.

Even after passing several more bowel movements that day, Austin was still in pain. The nurse's answer to the pain was to increase his sedatives. But she should have taken his temperature and evaluated some other basic vital signs, because they would have indicated that something else was wrong. A night shift nurse discovered that Austin had a fever, and when she investigated further she found that he had a urinary tract infection. No wonder he couldn't get comfortable.

Even after all these issues were resolved, Austin still refused to eat solid food. I thought he would be excited for the opportunity to taste his favorites again, but he didn't want to eat. After thirty-nine days in the hospital the doctors decided to send him home with the feeding tube still in place. I didn't think it was a good idea. The doctor kept telling me, "Once he gets home he'll do better. He needs to get back into his routine." Billy wanted Austin to be home and he wanted to sleep in his own bed. If anyone deserved to sleep in his own bed by now, it was Billy.

The nurse who helped us to the car commented, "I've never released a patient directly from the CCU." There was probably a reason for that.

Within a day of returning home, we had to contact Dr. Murad because Austin was not himself. He was walking around the house and unable to settle down. The doctor adjusted some of Austin's medications, which decreased the behavior. He complained of pain in his abdomen, which he indicated by asking me to push on his belly. That request made me panic; it reminded me of the first day we took him to the hospital.

That evening while we slept, Austin pulled out his feeding tube. This would happen several more times during his recovery. Each time we would learn that the tube had a defect or that something was wrong and causing Austin pain. He always tried to tell us when something was wrong. I just wished it was in less dramatic ways. Every time he pulled it out he would be more active and in less pain. But this was short-lived, it had to be put it back in because he needed nourishment. Austin was getting so thin that it was difficult to look at him when he had no shirt on. Prior to all of this he was getting way too heavy. Now he was skin and bones.

Near the end of September, we took Austin with us to Congressman Smith's office. The congressman was announcing the reauthorization of the Autism CARES Act, and he asked us to be present at the office where it all started. Alanna joined us in the office for the announcement, but Austin remained in the car with a staff member we had brought along. He refused to come in, and nothing could convince him.

After the press conference was over, Congressman Smith came out to the car to see Austin. Austin was lying in the back seat of my car, unable to even acknowledge the congressman. It was obvious he was not well.

That evening Billy was out with his son Shaun while I was home with the kids. I was talking to my mom on the phone and updating her on all that had happened. As I walked into the dining room I looked toward our sunroom where Austin was on the computer. Through the sheer curtain I saw him fall off his chair. I ran into the room to find Austin on the floor having a seizure. His body twitched violently with his head turned so far to the left it looked as if it might twist completely around. He was turning purple and couldn't breathe. I dialed 911.

Operator: "What's your location and what's the emergency?"
Me: "508 Bellevue Street. My son—there is something wrong—I think he's having a seizure."
Operator: "Does he have seizures?"
Me: "No… What do I do? My god, please help me, he's dying."
Operator: "Ma'am you have to calm down."
Me: "Just tell me what to do." (As I dialed Billy on my cell phone.)
Operator: "Is he laying on his side? Be sure he is on his side."

Me: "He's on the floor. I have him on his side. He's purple. He can't breathe. Please! Please help me!"
Operator: "Put something under his head, try to keep him from getting hurt."
Me (to Billy): "Billy, it's Austin. Something's wrong. Get home."
Operator: "Ma'am you NEED to calm down."
Me: "Stop telling me to calm down and tell me what to do. He's dying!" (Billy heard this just before I hung up my cell.)
Operator: "The ambulance is on its way. I will stay on with you until they get there. Just try to keep him on his side and keep him from hurting himself."
Me: "He's gagging, there's phlegm coming out of his mouth, he wet his pants. Please Austin, please! Breathe baby!"

Austin began to come out of the seizure. The operator instructed me to keep him on the ground, but Austin wouldn't stay down. He insisted on standing up. I couldn't fight him, but I got him to the couch.

Operator: "The ambulance is at your door, you have to open it."
Me: "Thank you. I'm sorry."
Operator: "It's okay. They will help you now."

Billy had called a neighbor to come to the house and they arrived at the same time as the ambulance and the police. Billy showed up while Austin was being evaluated. Austin was loaded onto a stretcher and into the ambulance. Billy rode with him. I followed but had Shaun drive my car. I was too shaken up to drive.

The emergency room doctors drew blood for tests. When the results came back, Austin still had pancreatitis. The medical staff ordered a CT scan of Austin's brain and treatment for pancreatitis, including IV fluids and pain medication. Austin was once again admitted. Dealing with the many different personalities and procedures of a hospital can be overwhelming, but feeling as if your voice is not being heard is even worse. The hospital treated Austin's illness as a reoccurring bout of pancreatitis instead of a continuation of the condition he had left with just days before. This meant that no one would look deeper into his pancreas while we were there. They just focused on getting his lipase numbers down using IV fluids and pain medication.

I had assumed that people in the medical field would have some understanding of autism, and I was shocked to learn how little they knew. When we reviewed Austin's history of pancreatitis with the intake nurse and mentioned his recent CCU stay, she asked, "Is that when you found out he had autism?" I snapped. "Seriously? What do you think, he's just been aloof for the last nineteen years?" She quickly apologized, "I'm sorry, I've never met someone with autism." I couldn't believe that. Autism was my world. I had no idea that not knowing someone with autism was even possible in 2011. I apologized to her; my response was uncalled for. I should have been a kinder, more educated advocate. I'm glad she understood the stress we were under.

Austin accidentally pulled out the IV when it got caught on his bed. Six people spent twenty minutes unsuccessfully trying to put in a new one. We repeatedly told the staff that Austin would need a sedative, but each time someone thought they would be the one who could get him to cooperate. It was so unfair.

We finally found a system that worked. Either Billy or I would lay on top of Austin and carefully use our body weight to hold him down. We asked that only two people be in the room with us: one to hold his arm, and one to put the needle in. With my face close to his, I'd begin to sing his favorite Disney songs, "I can show you the world, shining shimmering splendid…" I always prayed that it would take only one song for them to get the needle in. That wasn't always the case, but at least this method left Austin less panicked.

The doctor told us the feeding tube would need to be put back in if Austin didn't start eating by the next morning. We tried our hardest to get him to eat, but he didn't want food. We suspected that his memory of food causing him pain was just too strong. The medical staff believed Austin was ready to eat because his lipase levels were normal, but they were only normal because he had eaten no food for more than a day. No one was really looking at his pancreas to see if it was healed.

When we finally did get Austin to eat, it seemed as if his pancreas was responding well. We stayed in the hospital a few more days to be sure. He was sent home with a new dose of seizure medication. But we wouldn't be home for long.

I jumped at Austin's every move, burp, and fart. I wished that it was easier to tell when he wasn't feeling well, but because he couldn't communicate with us all I could do was watch for the signs. I was worse than any helicopter mom, I was hovering even closer. I waited for him to act a little less happy, or start touching his abdomen, or not be able to sit still for long. I watched him so closely I found every change in every freckle. And I was right to worry. Within a few days he became less active and refused to eat again.

By the end of October Austin would need to be admitted once more. He needed another CT scan, but this time he had to consume a barium drink first; it would help create a more detailed image on the scan. I would have bet money that he wouldn't drink that awful-tasting liquid, so I asked the doctor if I could use Skittles as a reward. I was told it wasn't ideal, but anything that would get Austin to drink even a little bit would help. Barium and Skittles—it sounded like a song in the making. Austin amazed me again. He drank more than one and a half bottles of the barium just to get a few Skittles. After the CT scan was complete, we were told everything was okay and we were sent home. But a little later we got a call that said just the opposite: Austin's blood work had come in, his levels were too high, and we had to go back to the hospital the next day. I couldn't understand why it was so hard to figure out what was wrong with him.

The gastroenterologist, Dr. Mark Cerefice, ordered a feeding tube with a j-tube in an effort to give Austin's pancreas a rest for six weeks. This type of tube went past the stomach and into the jejunum. By placing the tube that far past the stomach, the pancreas wouldn't kick in to do its job. This also meant no food or water by mouth for six weeks—one way to treat this level of damage to the pancreas. All Billy and I could say was, "let's try it." But silently we knew that we'd be lucky if Austin made it even one week with the feeding tube. At a minimum, we needed to cross it off the list of interventions before we could see what would come next.

The first attempt to place the tube was unsuccessful, so Austin was scheduled for a surgery that was performed under x-ray. After the surgery was complete, we learned why the first doctor had such a difficult time placing the feeding tube: Austin had a malrotation of the intestine. What didn't this boy have?

After a few more days in the hospital to ensure his body could handle the tube feedings, we were able to bring Austin home. I was so frightened. In the hospital we could control his access to food, but could we manage to do that at home once he felt well enough to want solid food again? We made sure none of the items he liked were in the house. We filled the refrigerator with only vegetables and yogurt. He would never eat those. We took all of the cereal, pasta, and everything else he liked out of the cabinets and put them on the shelves in the garage or threw them out. We couldn't take any chances.

I truly learned the meaning of "one day at a time." Each day that he tolerated the feeding tube and didn't access any other food was a success. We couldn't have managed without my mother's support. She made most of the meals for Billy, Alanna, and me, cooking everything at her home, storing it in plastic containers, and stocking our refrigerator so we could reheat what we needed in the microwave. We tried not to cook in the house to avoid torturing Austin with the smell of delicious foods.

Austin didn't like being hooked up to the feeding pump for the required fourteen hours a day, and he would fight us each time we had to connect him to the machine. We did most of the feeding at night while he slept, but that wasn't enough. From watching us, Austin learned how to turn off the machine and disconnect the line from his feeding tube. We would often wake in the morning to find that he had shut it down. He never ceased to amaze us, but we needed him to stay hooked to keep him healthy. He was losing even more weight. At 5'10" and 130 lbs, we could see his hip bones.

After five weeks of no solid food by mouth the doctor said we could try clear liquids. I was so excited for Austin to finally have the sense of taste back in his repertoire. I walked into his room and handed him a cup of juice. He took a small sip and then handed it back to me with a "no." I was shocked and disappointed. So I brought him an ice pop and hoped that was the answer. He wouldn't even taste it. I felt defeated. All I could imagine was that food had caused him such pain in the past that he was actually afraid to eat. It took us several days to get him to eat ice pops and then drink juice.

Within a few days of taking fluids Austin was worse. I believe this is why he didn't want to take the juice that first day. He was trying to tell us he wasn't healed. He slept for nearly twenty-two hours a day and refused any fluids or ice pops. We headed back to Dr. Cerefice, who told us he had done all he could. It was time for us to look outside of New Jersey, so he recommended we go to someone he knew at Cornell Hospital in New York City. For the first time, we learned there was more that could be done for Austin, it just wasn't going to happen locally.

We arrived at Cornell and a plan was quickly put into motion for Austin. We were told to return the following day for a CT scan. As we got back into our car Austin said, "No. Mommy I want doctor." By this time he had learned that doctors made him feel better. He didn't want to drive away, and it was impossible to explain to him we would be back the next day. He laid down in the back seat, curled his knees up to his chest, and fell asleep. Our boy was in pain. We could only hope Cornell would have the answer.

The next day Austin gave us no fight to get back into the car for the hour-and-a-half ride to Cornell. He was a champ at drinking the barium again, and cooperated for the CT scan. I had to believe he somehow knew we were trying to make him better. After the doctor read the results of the CT scan we were told Austin needed an endoscopic retrograde cholangiopancreatography, or ERCP. All those big words basically meant that a surgeon would go down his esophagus and past his stomach to look at his pancreas. Once inside, the doctor would clip his biliary tube to allow for drainage of the sludge that was inside his pancreas and preventing him from healing. Then stents would be placed into the tube to allow the drainage to continue over time.

The surgery was conducted on Christmas Eve. It went well, but took longer than expected. Austin's pancreas was more damaged than the doctors had realized. Three stents were placed. One was much smaller than the doctors had hoped, but the duct was so clogged they couldn't use a larger one. Austin would have to return in a few weeks for more surgery. He got pancreatitis again, which we had been told to anticipate after all the surgical manipulation of his pancreas. He was treated at Cornell this time, so Billy stayed with him and slept in a chair (there are no spare beds in New York City hospitals). I had to get home to the girls for the night, and I planned to drive back up to see both of my boys on Christmas morning.

Chelsea decided it wouldn't be Christmas at our home until Austin was there, so the Gallagher family celebrated Christmas on December 27th. We came home to a clean house, wrapped presents, and a wonderful handmade welcome home sign for the big guy that said, "Welcome Home Buckethead." Austin's second surgery was moved to six weeks away instead of the original two. The doctor didn't want him to have another bout of pancreatitis so close to this one. It was understandable, but disappointing. Four weeks feels like forever when you just want your child healthy.

Billy decided to cover a fishing trip for someone over the New Year's Eve weekend because we needed the money. The day after he left, I found blood in Austin's feeding tube. When I called the doctor's office, a nurse told me to suction it out and see what happened. Austin seemed fine for a day, but then more blood appeared. I took him to our local emergency room, but they contacted his doctor at Cornell and it was decided that we would be taken to Cornell's emergency department by ambulance. Arranging that took until the morning. It was strange to drive through Times Square at seven o'clock New Year's Eve morning. I watched the setup for the joyful nighttime festivities while I prayed my son would be okay.

The doctor pulled together a team to complete the procedure on New Year's Eve so we wouldn't have to wait any longer. They found that one of the stents had fallen out, something it was supposed to do, but it must have nicked some tissue along the way and caused the bleeding. Austin would be able to go home in the morning. Billy called me as soon as he got home. He felt awful that he wasn't home when this happened. He wanted to come up and be with us, but I insisted he stay at home until the morning. There was no way he was going to get to us on New Year's Eve in New York City. Besides, there was only one chair to sleep in. We were sent home in the morning as planned, but our relief was short-lived.

Seven hours after arriving home, Austin pulled out his feeding tube and broke the end off of it. His Cornell doctor told us to go to the local hospital. But it was a holiday, and there weren't any outpatient procedures being scheduled there. Dr. Cerefice was appalled as he said, "It's not like we're in retail. This is a hospital." It was two more days before anyone would place the tube. We couldn't wait at home, Austin had to be admitted because there was no way to get fluids into him. Even though he was no longer an "outpatient," still no one would perform the procedure for several days. I bet they would have all thought differently if the only way they could eat was through a tube in their stomachs.

In less than a month we would return for yet another feeding tube placement. Austin pulled it out again. This time we discovered that the tube was defective and the food going in was actually leaking out into his stomach. He was in pain. Every time he pulled out a feeding tube it was because he was in pain. He was always trying to communicate what he needed. We took him back to the local hospital. This time it was the wrong decision.

I acknowledge that a bit of a healthy ego is necessary, especially in the medical field. No one wants a doctor who lacks confidence. However, when the doctor who tried to place Austin's new feeding tube had difficulty, he should have asked for help from his two colleagues at the hospital who were successful in the past. Instead, he discontinued the procedure and left Austin without a way to receive nutrition. He was the head of the department, and I can only guess that he was too proud to ask for help. He was such an egomaniac that he insisted Austin leave the local hospital and return to Cornell. There was no reason for him to send my son with autism away to another hospital and make him wait when there were others at this hospital who were capable of performing the procedure successfully.

We insisted that they contact one of those doctors, but then we were told they couldn't coordinate an anesthesiologist. Really? They couldn't find one of those at a hospital? Billy lost it, yelling, "I'm not at a fucking hardware store, I'm at the damn hospital." I calmed him and said, "Let's just go to Cornell, we can't keep fighting them here." Austin went a week receiving only IV fluids before the tube was finally placed.

At Cornell, the doctor ordered placement of another j-tube, as well as a second ERCP procedure to put in larger stents. It was Superbowl weekend, and I offered to take the hospital shift to allow Billy to enjoy the game. Billy rarely took me up on my offers, but I think because we were at Cornell he felt that we were in good hands.

During my watch, Austin got a new roommate at one o'clock in the morning. This man would prove to be too much for Austin to tolerate. He constantly coughed and cried, "help me." Although the nursing staff insisted he was fine, he kept pushing the call button. They started refusing to come in. After being kept awake all night by the commotion, Austin had enough. He pulled back the curtain that separated the two beds, stared the man in the face, and told him firmly, "No huhhh (cough). S-T-O-P." I couldn't help but laugh a little, though I was embarrassed too. In so many ways, Austin was his father's son.

We went home after all the procedures were completed, and had an appointment to return again in March. As usual, Austin had other plans. Twenty-two days later he was back in the hospital. The latest CT scan showed he had more fluid on his pancreas than before. The stents hadn't been enough, so a pseudocyst drainage procedure was performed to help remove the fluid. After few days of recovery, we were sent home again.

We held onto hope that Austin's feeding tube might be removed in time for a vacation we scheduled in June. Over the next few months we returned to the hospital emergency room a few times, but all ended up being minor events and Austin slowly continued to heal.

Alanna celebrated her twenty-first birthday, a scary one for a family with a disabled child. It was time for her to move from the education system to the world of adult disabled services. Then Billy ended up in the hospital one more time with an intestinal issue. It took several days to find a solution, but eventually it resolved. Our family desperately needed this vacation to happen.

We were blessed with a happy event in May: Chelsea graduated from college with a master's degree in criminal justice. Billy and I could not have been more proud of her. She completed all her courses in record time and, at the age of twenty-two, walked across the stage to receive her diploma. Despite all our family endured during her last year of school, the guilt she felt for not being able to be with us, and her fears about her brother's health, she was able to succeed. Chelsea has always brought us such moments of joy and pride. I nicknamed her "my sanity," and I'll admit I often missed my sanity when she was not near.

Finally, Austin's feeding tube was removed, the cysts on his pancreas had drained, and he was permitted to eat foods again. We planned breakfast at my dad's house, a place that Austin loved to visit before he got sick, but somewhere we couldn't go while he was sick because of all the temptations. My dad was famous for his southern-style breakfast, and Austin had earned a piece of real bacon. It felt as though things were getting back to normal. At least Gallagher normal.

June arrived, and we were off to Disney. We had planned the trip to fall after Alanna's graduation from her school program but before her adult services started to keep any educational gap to a minimum.

We probably should have planned for more than a two-week trip.

Here We Go Again

June 2012 to October 2013

More than anything I needed this vacation to go smoothly. I wanted to put all the hospital visits for both my boys in the past, enjoy some time with my children, and not think about the future for just a little while. I intended to focus only on princesses and one special mouse.

Austin did better than expected. He enjoyed the pool and tolerated not having his usual snacks. We used a wheelchair because he didn't yet have the strength to walk the entire day. In the chair, he could make it until ten o'clock for the fireworks. I took the girls out to a few more places throughout the two weeks, and we let Austin dictate to us if he felt like going anywhere. We didn't want to push it.

Once we were back home it felt as if we were thrown off a cliff when we entered the world of adult services for families of children with autism. I was naïve to believe services would start shortly after Alanna's graduation. We endured a long process of questionnaires, interviews, and meetings. It was only after all this that we finally learned the budget intended for Alanna would only cover either three days per week of full-time coverage or five half days.

I didn't understand. What would she do for the rest of the time? For the last seven years, she had been in school five days a week, plus an after-school program three days a week. Before she left Wilson, she had an internship at a local hotel as the house attendant and was showing incredible progress. The Division of Developmental Disabilities told us that this budget was what everyone got, but I was fully aware that others in the community were getting more.

I stressed that Alanna would regress if she didn't receive appropriate services. The staff at her old school helped us with our plea and wrote a letter of response. We had to hire an attorney again. I called Paul and explained our situation. He was now a partner at the firm. He passed our case on to his associate Maria Fischer. We trusted his decision and knew he would be there to help us if needed.

The Division of Developmental Disabilities took the stance that we should give their plan a chance and see what happened. I was terrified that once again I would need to let my daughter regress to prove that she needed services. I was not confident that she would bounce back this time, she was much older now. I didn't have the energy for this fight, and I certainly didn't have the stamina to withstand another regression. Why was regression always the only answer? Why didn't they understand that regression was inevitable if Alanna didn't get the supports and services she needed?

My dad's wife Gayle offered to help us as much as she could. She took Alanna for walks around the local reservoir nearly every morning, and sometimes she kept her for the whole day. But this arrangement couldn't last forever, Gayle needed to work and have a life. She and Alanna had a special bond, but this wasn't fair. Gayle was a grandmother to Alanna, not a staff person. She shouldn't have needed to step in and jeopardize her relationship with Alanna. We appreciated all that Gayle did for us, but we needed to have something in place that would support Alanna for the years ahead.

At the beginning of that summer Chelsea was around to help, but this was also temporary. Now that Chelsea had graduated she was interviewing for jobs and hoping to land one of the positions. None of what we had in place was sufficient, and none of it would last over time.

The minimal services offered to Alanna didn't start until September, three months after graduation. We were told that was fast in comparison to other cases, so we were lucky we had family support. When her services did start, Alanna's staff came from the same agency as Austin's. Some of them had worked with Austin in the past, so Alanna knew them already. But having them there just a few days a week was not going to be enough. Regression was inevitable.

Alanna began to hurt other people, grabbing some of the clients in her building. Her vocal stereotypy, the constant talking in Disney scripts, returned. She was at a loss when we didn't have a daily schedule for her and constantly asked to know the time. If we told her, "You're staying home with daddy today," it would set off a series of high-pitched noises, slamming doors, and broken items.

The more she stayed at home, the more she despised being near her brother. Austin had a habit of saying "no" to many questions asked of him. Alanna disliked the word "no," and could only hear it so many before she became seriously upset. First she would put her hand in front of her eyes to block her view when he said the word "no" or "know." If he continued, she would grab and squeeze his arm or smack his back. We called it "sharking," because once she was in this mindset she would circle him and wait for an opportunity. She was adamant about a successful attack.

We worked together with the staff to protect Austin, but it was impossible to always watch everything that happened. For example, at two-thirty in the morning. When everyone else was asleep, Alanna went into Austin's bedroom and bit him on the leg. We were woken by the slam of his bedroom door, followed by his cry.

As in the past, her regression led to her becoming more and more withdrawn. She had longer bouts of crying alone in her room. Once again, I had to sit and watch while others made decisions for my daughter. I couldn't afford to quit work, and Billy couldn't be there all day for both Alanna and Austin. It felt like the Division of Developmental Disabilities was forcing us to decide to institutionalize our daughter. Alanna's regression was making our lives miserable, and the need to be on high alert at all times was exhausting.

Maria gave us the legal support we needed to appeal the Division's decision. First, we met with a man from the Division who was supposed to interview us. Maria and I explained Alanna's needs and provided him with documentation. He took the paperwork from us without looking up from his laptop. As we talked, he typed. We told him how successful Alanna was before leaving her school program, and that she now needed the same level of support that she had there. He looked up over the computer screen for the first time as he laughed, "You're never going to get that." I was floored. On February 23 she had been eligible for it, but when she turned twenty-one one day later she suddenly wasn't? Did her autism just fall out of her ass? Was she cured?

The Division took its time reviewing our appeal. Months later they sent a letter saying that we had not given their offer enough of a chance before deciding that the funding wasn't enough. Did they think they could penalize me because I knew immediately that it wasn't going to be enough to support my daughter? I had been right to start my plea early; because of all the time they took to make their decision, Alanna had regressed. She was extremely difficult to live with. We were all miserable.

For eighteen years she had a place to go, a schedule to follow, and things to do. She had been successful because of it. How could her father, who was also caring for her sick brother and his own ailments, maintain a schedule at the level that Alanna needed while I worked to support the family?

Alanna was capable of so much, but she needed someone to supervise her. At school she baked and sold cookies every week in the cafeteria. She would announce over the intercom when the bake sale was open, then she would man her station. Everyone loved Alanna, her smile and laugh were infectious. When one staff person approached the bake sale table and told Alanna, "I'm so sorry, I forgot my money," she responded, "No money, no cookies." Everyone was hysterical with laughter.

It took more than a year to finally settle our case and agree on a budget that could support Alanna. She went through a few staff members before we finally settled on Amanda Heulitt. Amanda and Alanna were born just one month apart, and they were as close as best friends could be. Alanna was finally paired with someone who could help us not only get our daughter back, but also move her forward.

During that year of fighting for Alanna, Austin also turned twenty-one. Once again we were thrown off that adult services cliff. Austin ranked extremely high on a scale used at the Division to determine need for level of care, yet his budget was similar to what was initially offered for Alanna. "Here we go again," I thought, "another fight."

Austin's needs were even more clearly documented than Alanna's. He had gone to KKI. His behaviors resulted in police being called on multiple occasions. His recent medical issues were not far enough in our past to be considered over, and had left him with a seizure disorder. The first agency assigned to Austin as his support coordinator informed the Division that his needs far exceeded any other client they had served. Again we were told we needed to "give this budget a chance."

I wrote the Division asking them to review our case. The Division's response was that Austin didn't need a higher budget because they had already provided Alanna with more support. I was completely confused. Their argument was that they had eliminated the source of the problem.

Somehow they decided that the only problem Austin really had was the possibility of being hurt by his sister. Now that his sister was out of the home most of the day, he should be fine. It would be a dream if Alanna was the only problem Austin had.

It had been ten years since Austin left KKI, and it was true that his behavioral challenges were under control, but this was only because of the supports in place for him. Without maintaining his current level of support, he would certainly regress. Although we were forced to wait and watch Alanna's regression, that was not an option for Austin. I would not allow him to regress. My panic at the thought of it was unbearable.

Why did they essentially encourage families like ours to abandon their children? If we had dropped Austin off at a hospital and refused to pick him up, they would have had to provide him with twenty-four-hour care and find him a home and a day program. We were asking to keep our children with their family, but to do so without either being in danger of regression. And hopefully without burning out their parents in the process.

All of the rulings from the Division came without anyone ever actually seeing Austin. We asked that they come to meet him before making a decision. This time I went through the appeals process alone. I had learned quite a bit from Maria and was trying to do this without the financial drain this time. We still owed Paul's office for the work Maria had done for Alanna. We couldn't afford to bring an attorney in, at least not until we were closer to the end of the case. I had to manage this one on my own. Fortunately, Hillary Freeman, also a special needs attorney, guided me and proofread all my letters before I sent them to the Division. Our family always had all the best people on our side when we needed them.

I went to another mediation meeting to provide my side of the story. The new mediator was a bit more engaged; at least she looked up and asked questions. But inevitably her report would fall short for Austin, and instead of ordering services she ordered that the division conduct an evaluation. So they had decided to come and see him with their own eyes... exactly what we had been asking for in the first place.

Two women came out to do the evaluation, but after more than a month we heard nothing back. We contacted Congressman Smith, and he helped us get a meeting with some higher-ups in the Division. He came to the meeting with us and we were hopeful we would get some resolution, but on that day they refused to speak about our case because it was still in their legal department. *Sigh!! You have got to be kidding me. They take months to review paperwork, finally schedule this meeting, but they won't talk about our case.*

When we finally did meet I presented as much information as I could, but it was pointless. The Division wouldn't give me any answers. I could knock on doors and write letters until I was purple—and I would—but there was always some way they could wiggle around telling me why they were refusing to provide appropriate services to Austin. We left the meeting disappointed.

More letter writing followed, including requests for their legal department to review the case again. More than a year after we started this process, I received a very simple email explaining that Austin's file had been reviewed and the Division was placing him on the community care waiver. We would be able to move forward with the services Austin needed. The tone of the email led me to believe that the person writing it realized that the Division had treated us unfairly and felt that it was time to put an end to the madness. I wrote back a simple, "Thank you," and hoped that he would understand the sincerity in those few words.

This chapter in our lives was finally over. We could once again focus on our family and our children. And for once, Billy and I could focus on ourselves.

Renewal

October 2013 to October 2014

THE NEXT 12 months brought joyful memories and difficulties that we've since learned we will face for years to come. Austin's seizures came and went, so visits to the doctor happened frequently. Alanna had nearly returned to her former self, though the residuals of her regression still lingered. Austin and Alanna needed such high level of support that we constantly worried what the future would hold for them.

While overseeing the care of Austin and Alanna, Billy also worked to maintain his bond with Shaun and remind him that he loves and supports him too. Chelsea got a job and moved an hour away. We missed her greatly, but we were so proud of her. She decided to use her background to support individuals with developmental disabilities, and I could think of no one better for the job. I continued to work on behalf of families of children with autism with a goal of making a difference in their lives. Billy grew accustomed to being the partner who had to adjust to plan B each day.

There were events that brought pain we hope to never experience again. We lost loved ones, some too young, and still feel the inexplicable hole they left in our hearts. Superstorm Sandy tore into our Jersey shore town, and the damage left behind was massive. Luckily, our family suffered little in comparison to our neighbors. We went twelve days without power, and some minor repairs were needed on our home. But Billy's rental properties just north of us were not so lucky, and a year later he was still constantly either fixing something, dealing with an insurance company, or managing mortgage issues. He finally got them all rented again, and we hoped to eventually catch up on the financial ramifications.

The last twelve years had brought us so much pain and so many blessings, and Billy and I made it through all of them together. We were stronger and closer than we could have ever imagined. We removed old ghosts that lingered from our past and found a new love for each other. We decided that for our 25th wedding anniversary we would renew our vows in early October in our backyard, with a small celebration of family and friends.

The weather report for our special day was dreary. The rain was expected to continue until about an hour before our ceremony. But we kept moving forward as though all was going to happen as planned. One hour before our guests were expected to arrive, the sun came out and the sky was blue. But the rain delay had kept us from getting all the decorations up in the yard. We spent most of the morning doing what we could, but we needed for the rain to stop before we could finish. I went inside for a bit to help Chelsea prepare all the homemade autumn-themed desserts she had made for the event. When I returned to the backyard, there was my friend Trish and her wife Gwynn hanging decorations. Soon MomMom, my sister-in-law Donna, and her entire family had arrived. Everyone was pitching in and helping, insisting they could handle it, and telling me to just go inside and get ready.

Everyone present knew that this day was more than just a renewal, it was a celebration of survival. They had all stayed in touch with each and every update about our family over the years. They were here to celebrate with us, and if they could offer to hang one decoration it was their way of letting us know that they too needed this day to be special for Billy and me.

Prior to our ceremony I asked my mother to paint a picture for me. Billy and I each provided her with three items that we felt represented the other to be included in the painting, but we did not tell each other what we shared with my mom. On the day of our renewal the painting was revealed during a very special moment in the ceremony.

I chose musical notes, a compass, and an anchor to represent Billy. Musical notes because Billy writes songs and sings, of course, but also because music is how Billy expresses his emotions. When he is sad, he writes. When he is happy, he writes. I am hopeful he will have more happy times to write about from now on. The compass was chosen because without him I would be lost, and because I would follow him wherever he may lead. The anchor signifies both strength and hope. To me Billy embodies the strength needed to keep our family grounded through the difficult moments, and the hope we look for when weathering the storms.

Billy asked my mother to incorporate into the painting an oak tree, a pedestal with a puzzle piece, and two scrolls representing two pieces of legislation that I had contributed to, the Autism ASSURE Act and the Autism CARES Act. He explained that the oak tree held steadfast and weathered storms, which I had certainly done through our years together. He believed that I belonged on a pedestal and that my contribution to the world of autism had only just begun. The scrolls signified my contributions to those pieces of legislation, and represented hope that my efforts would eventually be recognized by larger autism organizations.

A friend presided over the ceremony. He touchingly expressed his admiration for our union and our commitment. He told everyone present that our dedication to our children was unsurpassed. By the time the ceremony came to a close there wasn't a dry eye to be found, including Billy's. If I was I able to go back and relive my first wedding, I would rather it be just like this day.

The celebration continued, and so did the miracles. At one point Austin left his computer and came out into the backyard. I immediately asked my stepson Shaun to request that the DJ play "A Whole New World," from Disney's *Aladdin*. It took a moment, but the DJ found it. Austin and I took the floor—well, the grass, but we were the only ones on it—and he danced with me for the entire song. He took both my hands and we swayed back and forth as the song played. The song symbolized all I hoped for Austin in this moment, and always—a whole new world. A world of peace and health.

Uncle Eddie, who sang our wedding song the day we were married, brought his mandolin to play it for us again. It was such an unexpected gift. Billy and I held each other as we listened to the words of the old George Jones song, "Take My Hand, and Walk Through This World With Me." We had indeed walked through this world together, and would continue to do so. We had no idea what the future would hold for us or our children, but we had a strong history of weathering the storms and enjoying the meaningful moments.

When we booked the DJ we also asked for a karaoke machine. This was mostly so Billy could sing, but also to have a little corny fun with our guests. Billy sang several songs, and during one Alanna had come out of the house in a bit of a mood. We got her to grab a microphone and the next thing we knew she was singing an Allman Brothers tune, a song she had never heard. She had figured out that you sang the words when they changed to green on the karaoke screen. We asked the DJ to find a few

Disney princess songs. Suddenly everyone was standing in front of the DJ station, hands in the air, swaying to the songs while cheering on Alanna. Everyone was beaming with joy, and my eyes filled with tears. We were loved, and our children were loved, and that really was all that mattered.

We had no idea what the rest of our lives would hold. Just two days before this celebration, Austin was diagnosed with type two diabetes. We didn't tell our family and friends at the time because we wanted this to be a day to celebrate, not to focus on the "what ifs" of the future or be angry about how unbelievably unfair the diagnosis was to him. The day was about saying goodbye to the past, celebrating the love of those with us and those we had lost, and looking to the future with a promise that we would stick together no matter what it brought.

The night came and so did the chilly October weather. Our guests started to leave, and Billy and I went inside. We had specifically told our guests not to bring gifts, but my dad, Gayle, and two of my cousins didn't listen. There on my dining room table were several beautifully wrapped boxes. Inside was matching melamine dinnerware for eight, with plastic glasses, a pitcher, new silverware, serving bowls, and a tablecloth. Gallagher-quality fancy dishes that could withstand Alanna to use on the holidays. After a joyful day surrounded by family and friends and a loving confirmation of my marital commitment, I got fancy plastic!

No one could have been happier than me at that moment.

Epilogue

Much has happened in the two short years since renewing my vows. Today I am standing in the parking lot of a local hospital with my dear friend Jimena Fuerza. We just finished a visit with her son, Diego, who was admitted to a crisis unit two weeks ago. Diego lives in a group home with three other young men with autism. He had recently become violent toward staff and this time 911 was called. Here at the hospital, he is in a room as small as a jail cell and equally as inviting. The twin-sized bed, with restraints dangling from its sides, looked so tiny as Diego's body filled it. One chair and a television behind safety glass completed the inventory for the space.

As I walked into the room I was overwhelmed by the smell of urine. Jimena went to sit on the edge of the bed, and as she steadied herself on the mattress she put her hand into wet bedsheets. Her son, toilet trained for nearly twenty years, had wet the bed and was lying in it. As she lifted him upright, I put my hand on his shoulder and found that his hospital gown was wet all the way up to his neck.

Tyrell, the caretaker assigned to Diego, acknowledged that he too had smelled the urine when he first arrived for his shift an hour and half earlier, but was unaware of the source. No one bothered to look, not Tyrell or the hospital staff. Jimena convinced Diego to leave his bed and get into the shower. Tyrell took him down the hallway while Jimena found cleansing wipes and bed linens. This has become a common scenario for Jimena during the last two weeks. For unknown reasons Diego has opted to not leave the bed to use the bathroom. Although Diego cries to go home, during his stay in this place he has lost all desire to participate in life.

In the parking lot, Jimena struggled to hold back tears as she tried to explain to me all the conflicting advice she was being given while having to watch her son deteriorate. "This is why people do crazy shit," she said. How do I tell Jimena to hang in there for one more day? That each day, she just needs to tell herself, "One more day"? How can I help her find the strength I already know she has?

But no one will tell her how many more days her son will have to live this way, and no one seems to care. Her phone call to the support agency was just another phone call, there was no sense of urgency on the part of the person answering the call. She was lucky to get an answer at all.

Families are being asked to endure an unfair amount of pain while they become spectators in their children's lives. I don't have an answer for how someone gets through their darkest moments. I don't know why one mother may choose to end their child's life, and another does not. I do know that Jimena will get to the other side of this, because like me she has the love of a husband and children who adore her, and support from her biological and her autism family. We will do whatever we need to do for her. But not everyone has such a strong support system.

Without Billy, I am positive that things would not have turned out the way they did for me, for our family, and most importantly for Austin. It is impossible to explain the strength that he brings. It is a huge responsibility for my husband to have to be so strong for so many. I have often told others, teasingly, that back when Billy was a fisherman and I was overwhelmed by raising three children I divorced him in my mind a thousand times. I would fantasize about a life that was easier, with weekends off, or even just a holiday or vacation. But then he would walk through the front door and instantly my day got better. Any thoughts of being without him vanished. As corny as it may sound, all I need is to be near him and to touch his hand, and life is good.

Each day can bring tests of our strength. Some tests are easier than others. Billy and I now deal with Austin's diabetes and seizures, and the resulting need for him to be constantly monitored. It makes for challenging decisions. He wants foods he can't have, and his world is so small that denying him those pleasures seems unfair. He is unable to understand the benefits of kale chips over potato chips. We try our best to balance what is good for him and occasionally allowing him some small pleasures. The seizures happen out of nowhere and all we can do is watch him and keep him safe.

Bigger questions linger. How long can we keep Alanna and Austin home with us? Who will care for them when we are gone? Is it fair to think Chelsea may be the one to step in? No matter what lies ahead, I know that Billy and I will do this in the same way we have done everything: as a team. Others will try to steer us in the direction they believe is best for Alanna and Austin, and even more will offer their unsolicited opinions. For now, I continue to take things one day at a time, no matter how naïve that may sound to others.

We will not make decisions for our children's future based on the fear that there won't be options when the time comes, instead we will make those options happen when they are needed.

As for Jimena and Diego, I will do all I can to help them get through many more "one more days." I hope that this book will be complete in time for the next family who feels there is no end in sight for the pain they are experiencing, or are forced to become a spectator in their child's life. I hope that this book will bring them some strength to get past any thoughts of the unthinkable. And I hope that they too find they can hang on for one more day.

Acknowledgements

Much of this book focuses on just one of our four children, Austin. I was driven to write it due to the challenges that raising a child like Austin brings. However, without all of our children, we would not have had the same story.

Chelsea, you have and always will be our sparkle, bringing so much joy to us through your caring and creativity. Your accomplishments have been astounding, and your love for Alanna and Austin unmatched by any other. You truly are my sanity and you continue to make us so proud. We never could have done this without you.

Alanna, you are simply sweet. You have been described this way since you were a toddler. Your laugh is infectious and people are unable to help but smile in your presence. You don't even know how perfect you are. But like Daddy says, you are like Mary Poppins, Practically Perfect in Every way.

Shaun, my step-son, we are challenged by not living geographically closer, but hope that you know how much your dad and I love you, and are so impressed with your adventures and accomplishments. I am so happy that you share your love of music with your Dad.

I would like to thank all the people that made this book possible. To all of the people in it, and those that aren't but have worked with our children, please know how much we have appreciated your contribution to our children's successes.

Kimberlee McCafferty without you I would not have written this book, your words of encouragement made me want to get to the next chapter and the next chapter. I was a little sad when the writing ended.

Judy Matthews, Virginia Matthews, Jill Porcelli, Suzanne Buchanan, and Gary Weitzen thank you for your candor and feedback during the initial edits. I listened, I made some changes, and I left some things as they were, and please know my gratitude to you for taking on this project.

Nicole Klemas, ELS, The Brainy Lady, thank you for helping me to make my words come to life. You Rock!!

Jen Sansevere you did an *amazing* job on the cover, using P.A's original photo, thank you.

Congressman Chris Smith, I thank you for your contribution to this book, all you have done for us, and your dedication to the autism community. I know the fight isn't over and that you will continue it with us.

Thank you all from the bottom of our hearts. And always remember to find time to laugh and enjoy your loved ones.

Made in the USA
Middletown, DE
02 August 2016